Controversial Concordats

Controversial Concordats

*The Vatican's Relations with Napoleon,
Mussolini, and Hitler*

edited by

FRANK J. COPPA

The Catholic University of America Press
Washington, D.C.

The paper used in this publication meets the minimum requirements
of American National Standards for Information Science—
Permanence of Paper for Printed Library Materials, ANSI Z39.48-1984.

∞

Library of Congress Cataloging-in-Publication Data
Controversial concordats : the Vatican's relations with Napoleon,
Mussolini, and Hitler / edited by Frank J. Coppa.
    p. cm.
Expanded versions of papers presented at the Twenty-seventh
Annual Meeting of the Duquesne University Forum, held in Oct.
1993, in Pittsburgh.
Includes bibliographical references and index.
    1. Concordats—History—Congresses. 2. Catholic Church.
Treaties, etc. France, 1801 July 15—Congresses. 3. Catholic
Church. Treaties, etc. Italy, 1929 Feb. 11—Congresses 4. Catholic
Church. Treaties, etc. Germany, 1933 July 20—Congresses.
    5. Catholic Church—Foreign relations—France—History—19th
century—Congresses. 6. Catholic Church and fascism—
congresses. I. Coppa, Frank J. II. Catholic Church. Treaties, etc.
France, 1801 July 15. III. Catholic Church. Treaties, etc. Italy, 1929
Feb. 11 IV. Catholic Church. Treaties, etc. Germany, 1933 July 20.
v. Duquesne History Forum (27th : 1993 : Pittsburgh, Pa.)
BX1791.C65   1998
261.8'7—dc21
98-23276
    ISBN 0-8132-0920-X (alk. paper).—ISBN 0-8132-0908-0 (cl : alk.
paper)

Contents

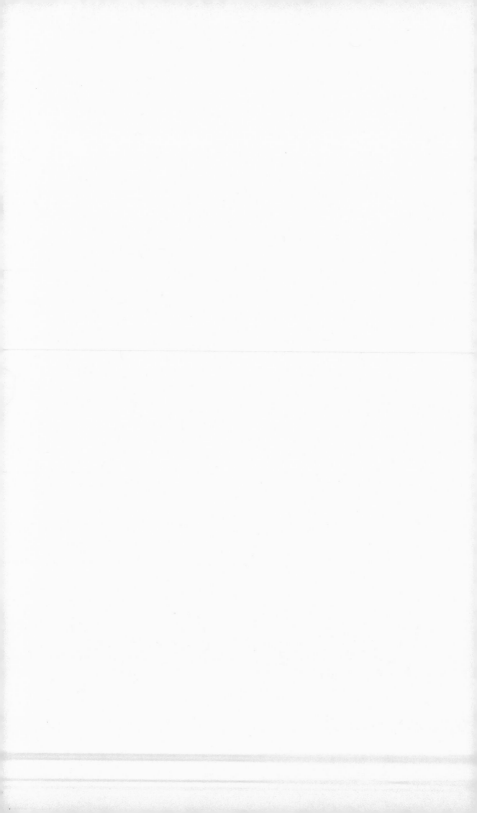

Preface

The origin of this short volume was a panel the authors presented for the twenty-seventh annual meeting of the Duquesne University Forum in Pittsburgh, in October 1993. Entitled "Controversial Concordats: The Vatican and the Dictators," the panel attracted one of the largest audiences of the conference, and the papers were very well received. Indeed, the audience continued to pose questions and make comments long after the close of the session, until we had to evacuate the hall for the next scheduled presentation. The feedback we received afterward, and the numerous requests for papers that followed, encouraged us to present our papers in book form.

The three essays and the commentary included in the present volume represent expanded versions of the original papers, which we subsequently modified for presentation before such forums as the American Catholic Historical Association and St. John's University Vatican Symposium. As revised they examine the factors that led to the concordats, the agreements themselves, and finally the long-range consequences. In all, five individuals have contributed to this collaborative project: John K. Zeender, Professor Emeritus of The Catholic University of America, provides an Introduction that places the three concordats in historical perspective; William Roberts of Fairleigh Dickinson University writes on Napoleon and the Concordat of 1801; Frank J. Coppa of St. John's University focuses on Mussolini and the Concordat of 1929, while Joseph Biesinger of Eastern Kentucky University, discusses Hitler and the Concordat of 1933. A Commentary and Conclusion by Stewart Stehlin of New York University rounds out the presentation. We have included a bibliography, divided into three sections, which examines the origins, negotiation, and impact of each concordat. At the suggestion of the editor of The Catholic University of America Press we have added English translations of the three agreements, which are not collected in any other single volume.

Frank J. Coppa

Introduction

JOHN K. ZEENDER, *The Catholic University of America*

The enormous power of the state over the church [after the Protestant Reformation] of the sixteenth century was suddenly there in reality. It is the greatest step toward omnipotence which the state has taken in past times. Then there followed on the Catholic side Louis XIV. The subsequent completion of state omnipotence through the theories of the Revolution could not have taken place so easily without this preceding Caesaro-papalism.[1]

—*Jacob Burckhardt, 1860*

Your Majesty lays claim to be Emperor of Rome. To this we answer with Papal frankness that the Supreme Head of the Church can boast, as no other ruler for centuries has been able to do, that he has never now or in the past recognized in his States the existence of another power than his own, and that no Emperor possesses the smallest jurisdiction over Rome.[2]

—*Pope Pius VII to Napoleon, March 1806*

1. Jacob Burckhardt, *Judgments on History and Historians*, trans. Harry Zahn. (Boston, 1952), 111.
2. F.M. Kircheisen, *Napoleon*, trans. Henry St. Lawrence (New York, 1932), 416–417.

> *The conclusion of such a work of peace with a self-conscious and difficult treaty partner like the Fascist State was a model of such importance its psychological effect on other states was not to be under-estimated.*[3]

—*Ludwig Kaas, 1932*

THE THREE STUDIES that constitute the core of this volume deal with the concordats that the papacy concluded with Napoleon, Mussolini, and Hitler. Each of these pacts was the subject of criticism, sometimes quite severe, from persons or groups on the side of the church or the state. The agreements even caused distress to many Catholics, and the pact between the Vatican and the Nazi government has been for years the cause of a bitter controversy between the critics and the defenders of Pope Pius XII. The Vatican had hoped to negotiate a similar agreement with Joseph Stalin's Soviet regime, but those talks collapsed by 1928.[4] The papacy's fear of Communism and the Soviet Union explains in part why it did not boldly confront the Hitler regime after it began to consistently violate its concordat obligations.

The concordat has been a favorite instrument in papal diplomacy since its inception in the early twelfth century. Prior to that time most monarchs had harnessed the Church to their service when they undertook the difficult task of establishing order in their domains. Even devout rulers like the German Holy Roman Emperor Henry III (d. 1056) and William the Conqueror of England (d. 1082) thought of themselves as the heads of the Church in their lands. But to Pope Gregory VII, the noted leader of the eleventh-century ecclesiastical reform movement, the appointment of bishops and even lesser church officials by rulers, pious or not, bordered on sacrilege. That pontiff and his immediate successors engaged in a bitter and prolonged conflict with the Holy Roman Emperors Henry IV (d. 1106) and his son Henry V (d.

3. Professor Ludwig Kaas, "Der Konkordatstyp der faschischten Italien," in the *Zeitschrift fur auslandische offentliches Recht und Volkerrecht* (Berlin, 1933), 494.

4. Hans-Jacob Stehle, *Eastern Politics of the Vatican, 1917–1979*, trans. Sandra Smith (Athens, Ohio, 1981).

1125), and Pope Paschal II (d. 1118) waged a similar struggle with King Henry I of England (d. 1135) over the same issue.[5]

These investiture conflicts proved costly to both sides and finally ended in compromise agreements, the Concordat of London or Westminster of 1107 and the German Concordat of Worms in 1122. They stipulated that only the Pope could invest the episcopal nominee with the symbols of his spiritual office but only the ruler could bestow those of the bishop's temporal power.[6]

A later Holy Roman Emperor and subsequent Popes would find, however, that they could not agree on just what powers the emperor might legitimately exercise in Italy. Frederick II of Hohenstaufen (1194–1250), a brilliant monarch, thought it not worthwhile to try to build a strong centralized government in a Germany that was still populated by a people with firm tribal loyalties. He preferred to focus his ambitions and energies on making Italy the seat of his imperial rule. But Frederick II ran into opposition from the papacy, an urban league, and the French monarchy. Following Frederick II's demise in 1250, the French army seized his heirs and put them to death.

After Frederick II's death, first Italy and then, more slowly, Germany became power vacuums. The papacy tended to fall into the hands of the old Italian nobility and occasionally into those of the newer urban elite. Some of the later medieval and Renaissance Popes were

---

5. Most textbooks in medieval history treat in some detail the conflict between the Popes and the emperors in this period and then in the thirteenth century. On the less widely treated subject of differences between the heads of the Church and the English monarchs, see: David L. Douglas, *William the Conqueror, the Norman Impact on England* (Berkeley, 1964), 343–344, and William L. Warren, *Henry II* (Berkeley, 1973), 403–407.

6. The Concordat of Worms did not become the norm with respect to the agreed-upon mode of appointing bishops in the High Middle Ages because it permitted the emperor to preside when a cathedral chapter in Germany held an episcopal election. He could thus decide who the successful candidate would be. Calixtus II apparently made this concession to Henry V so that episcopal elections could be carried out in Italy in accordance with canonical norms. However, the Worms concordat became void in the later thirteenth century after the emperors lost all real power, not only in Italy but in Germany itself. Their weakness in Germany was primarily due to the strength of tribal particularism rather than to their more highly publicized struggles with the papacy. See Burckhardt, *Judgments on History and Historians*, 84–85.

churchmen of real piety, but others considered their offices as another form of power to be enjoyed by themselves and their families, for whose younger members they found places in the papal administration, inclusive of the College of Cardinals.[7] In Germany, despite the monarchy's increasing weakness, a concordat in 1448 limited the papal power in the selection of bishops to their confirmation after election. The cathedral chapters in which those elections took place were dominated by aristocratic canons, often younger sons who had entered clerical orders without wealth or a vocation. They were often noblemen first and clerics second, if they were clergymen at heart at all.[8]

In contrast to the German Holy Roman Emperors, the kings of France, Spain, and England had established themselves as strong rulers and as the administrative heads of their Catholic churches before the papacy was first confronted with the new Protestant Movement in 1517.[9] Like their predecessors of the pre-concordat era, they knew that the Church had great influence over the middle and lower classes, and they wanted those subjects to think that the higher and lower clergy were engaged with them in the exalted work of government. During the Hundred Years' War (1336–1453) Joan of Arc (d. 1431), an uneducated but highly intelligent girl, wisely advised the dauphin to have himself crowned king in the religious coronation service at Rheims Cathedral before he tried to expel the English army from French soil. Most rulers recognized that the Church, because of its long history and extensive administrative reach, was a school for the training of administrators. Thus in the period from the 1490s to 1530 three high churchmen served as the first ministers of France, Spain, and England: Car-

7. See Philip Hughes, *A History of the Church* (London, 1952), vol. 2, ch. 5.

8. *Ibid*, 339. On the nobility of the Church in late medieval Germany, see the important study by Aloys Schulte, "Der Adel und die deutsche Kirche im Mittelalter" in *Kirchenrechtlichte Abhandlungen*, ed. Ulrich Stultz, 62–64 (Stuttgart, 1922): 62.

9. The Popes may have had more influence in dealing with the English kings than in negotiating with the French and English monarchs, possibly for reasons of diplomacy. F.M. Powicke described their relationships in matters of episcopal appointments as an "uneasy cooperation." See his *Medieval England, 1066–1485* (London, 1942), 144. It is probably meaningful that among the high clergy only Bishop John Fisher and a few Carthusian abbots went to the executioner's block rather than recognize Henry VIII as the head of the English Church.

dinals George d'Amboise (d. 1510), Ximenes de Cisneros (d. 1517), and Thomas Wolsey (d. 1530), respectively. High churchmen would continue to serve French monarchs as chief ministers until the Enlightenment. Cardinals Richelieu (d. 1642), Mazarin (d. 1662), and Dubois (d. 1723) were the most prominent of those French ecclesiastical head ministers. Of these important church dignitaries in monarchial service, d'Amboise and Wolsey later recognized that they had served their monarch too well and their church not well enough.[10]

The European monarchs envied the Church's wealth. In the earlier Middle Ages, rulers and major noble families often donated land to bishops and abbots for pious reasons. Unlike the properties of lay owners, those of the Church rarely, if ever, came onto the open market for sale. In fact, there was a common saying in the Middle Ages that when the Church came into possession of a parcel of land, it laid a "dead hand" on it. Jacob Burckhardt, the distinguished Swiss historian, wrote that the German princes who converted to Protestantism did so out of a desire to seize the Church's lands in their states.[11]

The French kings of the later Middle Ages were eager to tap the Church's wealth in France and, like the episcopate of their country, to significantly reduce the flow of currency from the French Church to the papacy. The Papal Curia had increased the taxes and fees which it exacted from the various national and territorial churches and also the number of benefices to which the Popes could appoint holders. It was hardly surprising then that the Gallican and Conciliar Movements sought to impose severe limits on the popes' governmental powers.[12] In 1438 King Charles VII presided over a French national church council at Bourges that was attended by the episcopate, learned theologians,

10. On Wolsey's rise to power and his later fall, see Garrett Mattingly, *Katerina von Aragon* (Berlin, 1962), 158–160. Historians, like Shakespeare in his *Henry VIII*, relied on Wolsey's head servant for his famous last words. On the similar dying words of Cardinal d'Amboise, see *Le Petit Larousse Illustre* (Paris, 1912), 1121.

11. Burckhardt, *Judgments*, 197–198. He spoke of "the most enormous spoilation of a . . . millennium."

12. For an authoritative and succinct treatment of the Conciliar Movement, consult the textbook by Brian Tierney and Sidney Painter, *Western Europe in the Middle Ages, 300–1475*, 5th ed. (New York, 1992), ch. 16. For more detail, see Professor Tierney's *Church and the Conciliar Movement in the Middle Ages* (London, 1975).

royal counselors and high judges. The council issued the Pragmatic Sanction of Bourges, which decreed that a general council of the Church was superior to the Pope, that the French Church should no longer pay the annate tax (the income of a diocese in the first year after the death of its bishop), and that bishops and pastors should be popularly elected.[13]

Like other European monarchs, the French rulers were not interested in vesting supreme Church authority in an international body or in letting the lower clergy and people elect bishops, who were so important in their government systems. For internal political and diplomatic reasons they sought to avoid a serious breach with the papacy. Nevertheless, they were determined to make the Popes accept their direct administrative control over the French Church. After the armies of King Francis I (1494–1547) smashed those of an Italian coalition at Pavia in 1515, Pope Leo X and his court found themselves in a helpless position. The King threatened that his government would put the Bourges decrees into effect if the pope did not accept the French monarch's terms. Leo X then suggested they open concordat negotiations.

Philip Hughes, a well-known church historian, described the Concordat of Bologna of 1516 as "a great Papal surrender" and Albert Guerard, a French scholar, portrayed it as "a magnificent prize for the French Crown." It was also the foundation of the Gallican Church, since the French kings received thereby the right to appoint the ten archbishops, eighty-three bishops, five hundred and twenty-seven abbots, and many holders of lesser benefices. In return, the French ruler, much to the discontent of many theologians and judges, agreed to abrogate the Pragmatic Sanction of Bourges, to approve the continuation of the annate taxes, and to acknowledge the Pope's right to appoint a certain number of clerics to benefices in the French church. One might conclude that this royal form of Gallicanism was a death blow to the basic objectives of the Conciliar Movement.[14]

13. For the text of the decrees, see *Church and State through the Centuries*, ed. and trans. Sidney Z. Ehler and John B. Morrall (Westminster, Md., 1954), 118–121.

14. Hughes, *History of the Church*, vol. 3, 446; also, Albert Guerard, *France: A Modern History* (Ann Arbor, 1959), 144–147. For the French opposition to the Concordats, see the still worthwhile account in the work of the French statesman François Guizot,

The successors of Leo X were frustrated during the course of the sixteenth and early seventeenth centuries by the refusal of the French crown to join Catholic coalitions against the German Protestant states and by its participation in the Thirty Years' War of 1618–1648 on the Protestant side. It also made treaties with the Turkish state that threatened the Austrian Empire until the decisive battle of Vienna in 1683.

The justification for these policies in the minds of French rulers and their chief ministers was that their country's security required a balance of power in Europe against the powerful Catholic Hapsburg dynasty, whose extensive Austrian, German, and Spanish possessions surrounded France on three sides. Both Cardinal Richelieu (d. 1642) and his successor Cardinal Mazarin (d. 1661) sought to humble the Hapsburgs. Richelieu subsidized the participation of Protestant Sweden in the Thirty Years War and later, when the Protestant forces seemed on the edge of defeat, he brought the French army into the conflict. Mazarin later kept the war going till the Hapsburg coalition agreed to a compromise peace. The Treaty of Westphalia of 1648 provided for the sovereignty of the German Protestant states and their right to determine the religion of their subjects.

It would be a mistake to conclude, however, that the papacy had ceased to be an important factor in the lives of the various European Catholic nations. The Popes who led the Church after the reforming Council of Trent were of high moral character. They also had a new, elitist, and militant religious order at their service. Its founder, Ignatius Loyola (d. 1556), a Spanish nobleman and ex-officer, had recognized that if the Catholic Church were to be saved, it would need a united and strong leadership. The Jesuits, his followers, in addition to the usual three monastic vows of poverty, chastity and obedience, swore strict obedience to the Pope. The Council of Trent also understood that the Catholic Church required effective religious leadership.

Catholic churchmen who wanted to become their monarchs' first ministers were eager to acquire the title of cardinal and wear the distinctive red hat and robes of its holder. Only a Pope could confer that title. Richelieu, who thought that his first loyalty was to the state, obviously believed that he needed to be a cardinal in order to become the first minister of King Louis XIII (d. 1643). Cardinal Mazarin undoubtedly held the same view. Paul de Retz (d. 1679), a young nobleman without a vocation, sought to become archbishop of Paris and a cardinal, with the aim of replacing Mazarin as first minister. He managed to reach the first two objectives but not his main goal.[15] Not long before the French Revolution, the leading French bishops recommended their talented young colleague Charles de Talleyrand (d. 1838) to Rome for the cardinalate. At Marie Antoinette's insistence, however, Pope Pius VI rejected the nomination, and Talleyrand felt that his political career had suffered a serious setback.[16]

In the eighteenth century, the French Church's episcopate was a closely guarded preserve of the French nobility. That class had often in the past produced worthy churchmen and churchwomen, but it had also often showed an eagerness to find positions in the Church with lucrative incomes for their landless sons and unwed daughters. That their son did not want to be a priest did not keep Talleyrand's parents from forcing him to take holy orders. Lord John Acton (d. 1902), the noted English Catholic historian, has claimed that in another instance their colleagues nominated for the cardinal's rank five bishops who led irregular lives.[17] An archbishop of Rheims who died in 1777 kept a mistress and daily set a sumptuous dinner table for his aristocratic friends. His successor was a Talleyrand uncle who had a reputation for piety but who also tried to promote his nephew's career in the Church.[18] These aristocratic prelates who lived worldly lives were drawn to the Church because of its wealth.[19]

---

15. See Gustav Lanson and Paul Tuffrau, *Manuel d'Histoire de la Litterature Française* (Paris, 1935), 234–238.

16. Louis S. Greenbaum, *Talleyrand: Statesman and Priest* (Washington, 1970), 10–11. Also J.F. Bernard, *Talleyrand: A Biography* (New York, 1973), 54–57.

17. Lord Acton, *Lectures on the French Revolution* (London, 1910), 169.

18. Bernard, *Talleyrand,* 30–31, 45.

19. C. Langlois and Timothy Tackett have pointed out that the Church was wealthier in the north of France than in the south. In some of its northern dioceses it owned from ten to forty percent of the land: "A L'Epreuve de la Revolution (1770–1830)," in *Histoire des Catholiques en France,* Editions Privat (Paris, 1980), 220.

It is doubtful that the French Church, even if its leadership had been more spiritual and closer to Rome, could have avoided a collision with the revolutionary National Constitutional Assembly and the Republican governments prior to Napoleon's First Consulate in 1799. The men who led the Revolution from its beginnings were mainly from the educated middle class and were influenced by the hostility of the Enlightenment's major writers toward religion and the Catholic Church. They were also keenly aware that the monarchy and the aristocracy had long controlled the Church and thought it in the nation's interest to reform the Church. However, they proved insensitive, arbitrary, and politically inept in dealing with the sensitive and complex Church question.[20]

The pre-1789 absolute monarchy had been most concerned with screening out episcopal candidates critical of its policies and limiting the money that its laity and clergy sent to Rome. The Revolutionary National Assembly of 1789-91 introduced a broad reorganization of the Church's administrative structure. It confiscated the Church's property, placing all the clergy, higher and lower, on salary.[21] The Civil Constitution of the Clergy provided that the office of archbishop should be abolished, the number of bishops reduced to fifty, and that they would be elected by the lower clergy and the people. In addition, the new bishops would merely report to Rome that they had been elected to their office and not travel there to receive papal approval. Finally, all clergymen were required to swear an oath pledging to uphold the whole Constitution.

The National Assembly's legislation reorganizing the Gallican Church's structure confronted the episcopate with a crisis which it could not resolve and from which it would not recover. The leading bishops soon found themselves in a dilemma: they desperately wished

20. It should be recalled that the Revolution began with very broad support among the lower clergy and the lower classes. See Albert Mathiez, *The French Revolution*, trans. Catherine A. Phillips (New York, 1964), 33-39.

21. Some results of the confiscations were socially costly. They ruined the religious teaching orders, whose schools had given free education to thousands of boys before 1791. See R.R. Palmer and Joel Colton, *A History of the Modern World*, 5th ed. (New York, 1978), 355.

to avoid a breach with the Revolutionary parliament but at the same time worried that some of the legislation might be in conflict with canon law.[22] They decided to seek guidance from Rome. After a long delay, Pope Pius VI (d. 1799) responded with a flat condemnation of the Civil Constitution of the Clergy and the Clerical Oath. Faced with a papal threat to excommunicate any bishop or priest who took the oath, only 12 of the nearly 140 members of the Church's hierarchy dared to do so. A larger minority of the lower clergy also did so, but the numbers of the non-jurors were appreciably larger.[23]

Nevertheless, whatever satisfaction Pius VI and his advisors might have taken from their victory must have been short-lived. In the autumn of 1792, the Jacobins under Maximillian Robespierre (d. 1794) seized power and established a radical republic. They charged that the clergy, like kings and noblemen, were enemies of the people, exposed them to physical danger, and suppressed religious practice.[24] There was a reaction against this extremism in 1794, and the Directory government of 1795–1799 tended to be less aggressively hostile toward the Catholic Church and its religious practice, but, as William Roberts points out in his essay, the Church had to function in a climate of uncertainty and insecurity. When another Republican government, the Consulate, under the leadership of the war hero General Napoleon Bonaparte, came into being in November 1799, the papacy had no reason to expect a marked improvement in the relations between the French state and the Church.

Some of the leading thinkers of Napoleon's time thought that he

22. *Ibid.*, 110–118. On the profound effects that the Civil Constitution of the Clergy and the Oath had on relations between the Church and the Revolutionary State, see Timothy Tackett: *Religion, Revolution and Regional Culture in Eighteen Century France* (Princeton, 1986), 11–13. Robert Gildea says that the Civil Constitution of the Clergy "made the attitude of every village to its priest a part of national politics," *The Past in French History* (New Haven, 1994), 7.

23. See Albert Mathiez, *The French Revolution*, ch. 9. Also, Lord Acton, *Lectures on the French Revolution*, 168–173; and Guerard, *France*, 246–247.

24. Before his own death in 1794, Robespierre proudly wrote that the monarchy had been annihilated and that the nobility and the clergy had disappeared. Mathiez, *The French Revolution*, 246–247.

was a man of truly remarkable greatness. Goethe, the distinguished German poet, said of him: "Napoleon was the man . . . his destiny was more brilliant than any the world had seen before him, or perhaps will ever see after him."[25] Hegel, the noted German philosopher, spoke of him as "that soul of world-wide significance."[26] Napoleon had a remarkable intellect, unusual clarity of vision and demonic energy. Like his civilian colleagues and subordinates he was a product of the Enlightenment and therefore a skeptic. Associates and subordinates did not want him to conclude a concordat with the papacy.

Nevertheless, Napoleon, like Mussolini and Hitler a century later, wanted the papacy's aid in keeping him in power and in keeping his government on an even keel. The saying attributed to him, "You can do everything with a bayonet except sit on it,"[27] is probably apocryphal but it certainly reflected his thought around 1800.

Napoleon's immediate interest in a concordat in some respects anticipated the prime reason why Mussolini and Hitler would seek a similar pact with the papacy. Like those more modern dictators, Napoleon had been facing a Catholic movement or party opposed to him. He claimed that there were "fifty bishops who were subsidized by the English government"[28] who led the opposition against his regime.

Therefore, Pope Pius VII's two major contributions to Napoleon were his recognition of the French Consulate as a legitimate government and his acquiescence to Napoleon's demand that he make the bishops appointed by the old monarchy resign from their posts. Aristocratic and upper-middle-class royalists would bitterly complain that

25. J.W. Goethe, *Conversations with Eckermann (1823–1832)*, John Oxenford (San Francisco, 1981), 199.

26. Karl Löwith, *From Hegel to Nietzsche: The Revolution in Nineteenth Century Thought*, David E. Green, tr. (Garden, New York, 1967), 214. G.B. Shaw would refer much later to Napoleon's "terrifying ability" in *Nine Plays* (New York, 1930), 955.

27. I have gone through several books of quotations, including two editions of Bartlett's *Familiar Quotations* and Cte. Ate. G. De. Liancourt's *Political Aphorisms: Moral and Philosophical Thoughts of the Emperor Napoleon* (London, 1848), and have not found this quotation in them.

28. See Georges Lefebvre, *Napoleon: From 18 Brumaire to Tilsit 1799–1807* (New York, 1969), 248.

the papacy had abandoned the monarchy, which had long protected the Church, and had recognized in its place "a usurper."[29]

One might assume that Napoleon showed no significant judgement in choosing to achieve an agreement with the Holy See. However, another French dictator, already aware of the anticlericalism in his own ranks, might also have reasoned that the papacy could not be of much help to him. Pius VI had died in captivity in that country in 1799. The papacy had then long been in dire financial straits, having been cut off since the early 1790s from the French Church, which had long supplied it with annates and fees. It had also been separated from the German Catholic Rhineland after its annexation to France by French armies in 1797. That region had possessed some affluent dioceses and abbeys. Nevertheless, it must be said that Napoleon had shown keen political insight in thinking that the lower clergy in parishes and the members of the numerous religious orders still felt a sense of loyalty to the Pope in distant Rome. Unless one concludes that this was the case, it would be difficult to understand how the new French bishops, the papacy and the French ministry of religious affairs, collaborating with each other, could have restored the French institutional Church as readily as they did.

Napoleon had an unusually high regard for efficient and strong administration. He saw that the state could benefit much from the use of the Church's own extensive administrative system, using the clergy, who were paid by the state, as civil servants. This was not new, of course, because the traditional monarchical regimes had relied heavily on the Church's services. Their rulers had valued the union of Church and state because the clergy taught its congregations and students to revere, pray for, and obey the monarch. In addition, monarchical governments had also relied on the local clergy to read their decrees in their churches. In his administrative system Napoleon probably did not go as far as the Emperor Joseph II of Austria (d. 1790) had gone in his regulation of the Austrian Catholic clergy. That ruler even prescribed what the footwear of the priesthood should be.[30] Nevertheless, Napoleon re-

29. Louis Bergeron, *France under Napoleon*, trans. R.R. Palmer (Princeton, 1982), 17, and Bernard, *Talleyrand*, 236.

30. See my review of Alan Bunnell's *Before Infallibility: Liberal Catholicism in Biedermeier Vienna* (London and Toronto, 1989) in *Histoire Sociale/Social History* (Nov. 1991): 373.

vived and fortified the tradition that priests should exhort their congregations to appreciate the Christian virtues of the ruler and that tradition would continue down through the reign of his nephew Napoleon III (1852–1870). Alexis de Tocqueville (1805–1859), the noted French writer and parliamentarian, later attested to the spirituality of the ordinary French parish priest but thought that he would have demonstrated more civic virtue if he were still a property owner.[31]

After several years of strained relations with the Holy See, the French emperor would imprison Pius VII in France in 1809 and keep him there till 1814. There is no evidence that Pius VII and Cardinal Ercole Consalvi, his very able secretary of state, ever thought of denouncing the Concordat with France. The treaty had made possible the restoration and revival of what had been the largest and most affluent branch of the international Catholic Church and reestablished the papacy's bonds with it. In addition, the French Consulate and its head, by entering into a formal treaty with the Pope, had recognized his position as the leader of the international Catholic Church.

In exile on St. Helena island, the deposed emperor would claim that he and Pius VII had fallen out as "rulers," meaning that they had differed over grave temporal policy matters.[32] That Napoleon planned to govern all of Europe was evident to Pius VII and Cardinal Consalvi when they learned that the French First Consul planned to make himself the French emperor in 1804. In the winter of 1805–1806, when Napoleon urged the Pope to bring his temporal possessions into a new Italian confederation, Pius VII balked at doing so. There was then a written exchange between them in which the French ruler asserted that while the Pope was "the sovereign of Rome," he himself was its "emperor," to which Pius VII responded proudly that "no Emperor possesses the smallest jurisdiction over Rome."[33] But Napoleon's immediate desire to rule over Italy was undoubtedly due to the exigencies of his struggle with his worst enemy, England. That country's loans and supplies enabled her allies to fight the continental wars against France. The

31. Alexis de Tocqueville, "The European Revolution" in *Correspondence with Gobineau*, John Lukacs. ed. and tr. (Garden City, New York, 1959), 293.
32. Lefebvre, *Napoleon*, 248. Also, Kircheisen, *Napoleon*, 503–4.
33. See the second quotation on the first page of this introduction.

French emperor could only hope to bring this industrial and commercial power to her knees if he could deny her exports access to European markets. On Cardinal Consalvi's advice, Pius VII chose to follow as a temporal ruler a policy of neutrality and to keep the papal states open to English shipping.[34] In an obvious effort to break the Pope's will in this matter, Napoleon in 1808 took military possession of the papal territories, inclusive of Rome, and later made Pius VII a prisoner in France. Six years later, militarily weakened by his disastrous Russian campaign of 1812–1813, he would be himself a prisoner.

In the first decades following its emancipation from French rule, the papacy and also the wider Catholic Church came to enjoy a respect that neither had known in the eighteenth century, when the French *Philosophes* and other rationalist writers had scorned the Church. But around 1800 the Romantic poets and novelists began to attract the reading public. Lovers of intuition and tradition, they either treated the Church with warm sympathy or with gracious respect. In the long run, however, the Church profited more from the research, writing and teaching of the new university historians. From them the educated adult reading public and students on both sides of the Atlantic would learn much about the earlier civilizing work of the Church, its great saints and thinkers, its impressive theological and philosophical systems, and its magnificent cathedrals — and also its defects and mistakes.

The new university historians and other scholars were especially impressed by the remarkable age of the Church. Leopold von Ranke (1796–1886), a Protestant whom many scholars in the nineteenth century thought was the greatest historian of the age, wrote a monumental history of the Popes in the early modern era. One of his best students, Jacob Burckhardt (1818–1897), was profoundly moved by it and much later judged it to be one of the two most impressive of Ranke's extensive publications.[35] And then Lord Thomas Macaulay, the noted

34. Lefebvre, *Napoleon*, 248–249. And also with profit, consult John Tracy Ellis, *Cardinal Consalvi and Anglo-Papal Relations* (Washington, 1942), pp. 15–17. For the later course of papal diplomacy, see the important work by Alan J. Reinermann, *Austria and the Papacy in the Age of Metternich. I: Between Conflict and Cooperation, 1809–1830* (The Catholic University of America Press, 1979).

35. *Letters of Jacob Burckhardt*, trans. and ed. by Alexander Dru (New York, 1937), 162.

English liberal historian, made this eulogy of the Catholic Church and the papacy in a review of the von Ranke history of the papacy:

There is not and there will never be on earth a work of human policy so well deserving of examination as the Roman Catholic Church. The proudest royal houses are but of yesterday when compared with the line of the Supreme Pontiffs. The Papacy remains, not in decay, not a mere antique but full of life and vigour.[36]

Around the time that Macaulay wrote his review, a brilliant young Anglican scholar, John Henry Newman (d. 1890), decided to become a Catholic because he was impressed by the continuity in the Church's long history and because he feared that philosophical liberalism was leading to Protestantism's disintegration.[37] He had difficulties in trying to win acceptance in his new church, but Pope Leo XIII (d. 1903) would raise him to the cardinalate soon after he himself became pope in 1878.

However, when Leo XIII took over his papal office in 1878 he found that the papacy was in desperate diplomatic straits, being, as Carlton J. H. Hayes, a prominent American Catholic historian, once wrote, in a feud with nearly every European government.[38] Pius IX (1846–1878), Leo XIII's predecessor, had not been effective in negotiating with secular governments with whom the Church came into conflict. But to do him justice, Pius IX was Pope in rapidly changing times.

Pius IX is often remembered as a foe of liberalism but in fact some of the worst blows to the papacy itself or the wider Church had been delivered by monarchical governments. It was the monarchical state of Piedmont-Sardinia which united Italy by force between 1859 and 1870, taking Rome in that latter year as its capital. Otto von Bismarck (1815–1898), the new minister-president of Protestant Prussia after 1863, profited from the study of the Piedmont-Sardinia achievement and, using Prussia's military strength and astute diplomacy, he brought about Germany's union in approximately six years. In 1866 Prussia defeated Catholic Austria on the battlefield and then excluded her from

---

36. Karl Adam, *The Spirit of Catholicism*, trans. by Dom Justin McCann, O.S.B. (New York, 1935), 7–8.

37. Wilfrid Ward, *The Life of John Henry Newman* (New York, 1912), 2: 170–175.

38. *A Political and Cultural History of Modern Europe* (New York, 1936), 2: 424.

any future participation in Germany's affairs. In 1870 Prussia and her German allies won such a quick victory over Napoleon III's French army that the emperor's government was overthrown and replaced by a right-wing liberal republic.

This sudden reorganization of German political life was soon costly to the Prussian Catholic Church and deeply painful to Pius IX. Bismarck was proud of his new German Reich, erected in 1870, but he was nervous about its stability. He believed, wrongly it should be said, that German Catholic leaders wanted to undermine the new national state in which their co-religionists were in a minority. With the support of the liberal parties he soon unleashed a legislative campaign against the Prussian Catholic Church that led to the imprisoning or exile of its bishops, the closing of over a thousand churches or chapels and the dissolution of the major religious orders. It was an abuse of governmental power on a large scale and after four years or so Bismarck wanted to find a way to a peace with the papacy in which he would not lose face. It would be well over a decade before he and a representative of Leo XIII could work out a settlement in 1886–1887.[39]

Liberals were, nevertheless, very important in the European parliaments of the era from the late 1850s down to, and in some states through, the First World War. Except for brief periods, the economies of Europe were in a boom phase in that long stretch of time. This condition worked to the benefit of the middle classes in industry, commerce and the free professions, who supplied most of the votes which sent liberals into office. Some liberals chiefly represented the interests of the upper middle classes, and were sometimes willing to pair themselves with conservative parties, while the so-called "radical liberals" were more ideological and closer to the lower middle class of small property owners and small taxpayers.

Nevertheless, the members of the different liberal parties did share

39. For a substantial and highly readable account of the Prussian *Kulturkampf*, consult Margaret L. Anderson's biography of Ludwig Windthorst, the brilliant Catholic Center party leader in that conflict: *Windthorst, A Political Biography* (Oxford, 1987). For Windthorst's successful coalition strategy, which forced Bismarck to accept a thinly disguised defeat in 1886, see my article "Ludwig Windthorst, 1812–1891," *History*, June 1992. The Catholic University of America Press will soon publish Ronald J. Ross's book-length study on the Prussian *Kulturkampf*.

some important views on important issues. They were the real spiritual fathers of the emancipation and union of peoples. In a sense, then, one could say that the ministers of the king of Piedmont-Sardinia and Bismarck had stolen their clothes. Both the right- and left-wing liberals would have liked to see the secular state principle triumph in Europe, but the right-wing liberals often made a compromise with conservatives on this issue, accepting the ties between the state and churches. Both types of liberals much disliked concordats because they limited the sovereignty of the parliaments in legislation and reinforced the churches' control of the state's unitary primary school system.[40] When the Austrian liberals took the leading positions in the new Austrian Reichsrat in 1866, they immediately demanded that the monarch, Emperor Francis-Joseph (d. 1916) should declare the Concordat of 1855 to be out of force, which he did after a polite delay of four years.[41] In 1905 a coalition of left-wing liberals and social democrats in the French parliament would break with the Catholic Church and secularize the national school system, completely ignoring the papacy in the meanwhile. The loss of these two major concordats was extremely painful to the Popes reigning when they occurred. However, the deepest deprivation was when the Vatican was forced to relinquish the governance of Rome.

After the completion of the Prussian-Papal accord of 1886–1887, Leo XIII began a determined diplomatic effort to regain Rome for the central government of the Church. He was apparently convinced that foreign governments would not consider the Popes to be sovereign rulers without its possession because sovereignty presupposes the ownership of territory. But it is also very probable that he assumed that the papacy would lose prestige if it were permanently separated from the rule of this most historic of Europe's cities. Around 1860 Nathaniel Hawthorne, the American novelist, had described it in these words: "Rome, the city of all time, and of all the world."[42]

40. On European liberal movements, see the still-useful work by Guido de Ruggiero, *The History of European Liberalism* (Boston, 1959).

41. Arthur J. May, *The Hapsburg Monarchy, 1867–1914* (Cambridge, 1951), 43–47. Also William Jenks, *Under the Iron Ring, 1879–1893* (Charlottesville, 1965), 122–123.

42. The Shorter Bartlett's *Familiar Quotations*, Christopher Morley, ed. (New York, 1964), 159.

While usually wise and realistic in his political judgments, Leo XIII failed to understand the workings of European balance-of-power diplomacy. In the late 1880s and early 1890s, the European great powers were forming diplomatic and military alliances. The pope was shaken by the discovery that Germany and Austria-Hungary had secretly invited Italy to rejoin their secret alliance in the fall of 1887. He and his very capable secretary of state, Cardinal Mariano Rampolla (d. 1913), then turned their attention to nurturing close relations with republican France. That country's government entered into an entente with Russia in 1891 and three years later those two powers would conclude an alliance with each other. But Rampolla and Leo XIII gradually realized that they were not interested in trying to force the Italian state to relinquish Rome to the papacy.[43] Because of the failure of his Roman diplomacy and the deterioration of the French Catholic Church's relations with increasingly anti-clerical French cabinets, Leo XIII's last years must have been sad.

It is interesting to note, however, that while the papacy's stock in European diplomatic affairs was low in the pre-1914 era, its authority and prestige in the Catholic Church world were steadily growing. The causes of this favorable development were complex, but the prime reason for it was most likely the resentments that many bishops and priests felt over the controls which monarchical bureaucrats imposed on them. Pius IX, who had been unfortunate in his foreign relations, had been able to convince the First Vatican Council that it should proclaim the doctrine of papal infallibility in 1870. In later years the German emperor William II (1888–1918) and the American president Theodore Roosevelt (1901–1909) would pay visits to Popes. In doing so, those heads of two major powers were in effect acknowledging that German and American Catholics regarded the head of their church as being much more than a symbol of church unity.

Pope Benedict XV (1914–1922), who would be head of the Catholic Church throughout World War I except for the first weeks of that ca-

43. I treat Leo XIII's diplomacy on the Roman question in some detail in my book *The German Center Party, 1890–1906* in the Transactions of the American Philosophical Society, New Series, 66, part 1 (1976). See in particular pp. 24–26, 72–73.

tastrophic conflict, was well qualified to hold that office in a very difficult time. By training a diplomat, he had considerable acumen, marked
tact, and firm goals. At an early date he, like Woodrow Wilson, hoped
to bring the two groups of belligerents to a common table and lead
them to a compromise peace. Benedict XV finally issued his appeal to
the belligerents on August 1, 1917, when there seemed to be no prospect
of any victory by either side. Except for an advocacy of disarmament
and the use of arbitration measures in international disputes, it did not,
like Woodrow Wilson's plan of January 1918, make ideal proposals like
those for the emancipation of subject peoples. Benedict XV's ideal objective was to end the slaughter of soldiers and so he called for a return
to the *status quo* as being the only peace plan that both sides might accept.[44] However, the French government was unwilling to agree to a
peace that did not require Germany to return Alsace-Lorraine to
France and President Wilson had no confidence in the German monarchy's interest in a just peace.[45] The Pope would suffer a further disappointment when the Allies at the insistence of Italy did not invite the
Pope to send a representative to the Paris peace conference.

It is not completely clear just what Benedict XV's attitude was toward the new postwar Fascist movement because the Pope died rather
suddenly in January 1922, nine months before Benito Mussolini became
the head of an Italian coalition cabinet. Before the national elections of
1919, the pope had approved of the foundation of a Catholic party, the
Popolari. The new party's leader was Don Sturzo, a priest skilled in organization. His two deputies were Alcide de Gasperi, who would serve
successfully as Italian premier after World War II, and Georgio Montini, the father of the later Pope Paul VI (1963–1978). The leaders of the
new Catholic party took as their model the German Catholic Center
Party because it had cooperated with the somewhat larger German Social Democratic party in laying the foundations of the new democratic

44. "Benedict XV," *The New Catholic Encyclopedia* (New York, 1967), 2: 279–280.
45. It is still unclear whether the German military high command would have
permitted the monarchy to return territory occupied by the German armies to their
former governments. See Hajo Holborn, *A History of Modern Germany, 1840–1945*
(New York, 1980), p. 476. Also Gordon A. Craig, *Germany, 1866–1945* (Oxford, 1980),
380.

Weimar republic and had social policies. Don Sturzo and his colleagues distrusted the new Italian Fascist party because it was unprincipled and often used violence against the Marxist parties.[46]

Nevertheless, it is highly likely that Benedict XV and then his successor, Pius XI (1922–1939), wanted to know in advance what Mussolini's thought might be on resolving the differences between the State and the Church, if he came into power. Frank J. Coppa has told us in his essay on the later Italian Concordat that at some point before his death, Benedict XV had sent his secretary of state, Cardinal Pietro Gasparri (d. 1934), to meet secretly with Mussolini. And it is certainly also meaningful that the cardinal electors of Pius XI made it a condition of their electoral support for him that he should bring about a settlement of the Roman question with the Italian state[47] and that Pius XI retained Cardinal Gasparri as his secretary of state.

Like Napoleon over a century earlier, Benito Mussolini felt a pressing need to win the papacy's approval and support. He was more realistic than his associates and followers, who were not always very intelligent, or the old Liberals, the former leaders of the country. The real problems in effecting a rapprochement with the Vatican lay not only in securing a settlement of the Roman Question but in working out a concordat that dealt with sensitive educational and other cultural issues. Pius XI did not expect any large territory from the Italian government[48] and after all, foreign governments had treated the papacy as a sovereign entity even after it had lost Rome in 1870. The Liberals had allowed themselves to get mired in the question of the Vatican's absolute state sovereignty, though, as Coppa illustrates, they would have had a hard time accepting the kinds of influence that the papacy sought in cultural and social matters which Mussolini finally accepted.

The extent to which the Fascist dictator went in acknowledging that Italy was very much a Catholic country was far-reaching. Mussolini was a master at currying favor with the Catholic Church. In the nine-

---

46. On the new Popolari party, see Elisa Carrillo, *Alcide de Gasperi* (Notre Dame, 1965), 45–73. For its views on the Center consult Alcide de Gasperi, *Studi Ed Appelli Della Luna Vigilia* (Rocca San Casciani 1953), pt. 1.

47. Peter Hebblethwaite, *Paul VI: The First Modern Pope* (New York, 1993), 61.

48. See Ludwig Kaas, "Der Konkordatstyp," 492–493.

teenth century, Austrian and German Catholic conservatives and integralists who detested the new liberal system of parliamentary representation had advocated the corporative type of representation based on vocational and professional groups.[49] Mussolini introduced this type of parliamentary organization of the economy with characteristic grandiose fanfare in the later 1920s. With its prohibition of divorce, strict moral codes and stress on family values, Fascist Italy appeared to be as Catholic as Ireland. The intelligent but puzzled young John F. Kennedy inquired of Cardinal Pacelli in 1937 how he would define Fascism and the Cardinal replied that it was like a secular form of Catholic authoritarianism.[50]

Benito Mussolini was no second Napoleon but he was indubitably a far abler politician than Anglo-Saxon reporters gave him credit for being. Accustomed to more conventional prime ministers and presidents, they were alternatively amused and put off by his projecting his prognathous jaw, strutting, and bombastic speeches. The most widely read book in the United States on Mussolini was the study by Gilbert Seldes, an American journalist, entitled *The Sawdust Caesar* (1934), which suggested that the Italian dictator was a sham. But a politician who had outwitted highly experienced upper-middle-class politicians to become the sole ruler of Italy was obviously no fraud. He was of course the leader, like Hitler, of a party that contained thuggish elements and he had apparently approved of political murders. There was, however, a fairly widespread assumption among other governments that he had become moderate with the responsibility of personal rule in the later 1920s. Winston Churchill and Heinrich Bruning, the Catholic German chancellor of the years 1930–1932 believed that Mussolini had become a statesman and were respectful of him.[51] The Italian dictator had ambivalent feelings about Adolf Hitler after Hitler became Ger-

---

49. Zeender, *The German Center Party, 1890–1906*, 13, 42.

50. Nigel Hamilton, *JFK: The Reckless Years* (N.Y., 1993), 190.

51. The efforts of conservative British leaders, in and out of government, to cultivate Mussolini's good will are well-known. On Bruning and the Fascist head of state, see Bruning's *Memoiren, 1918–1934* (Stuttgart, 1970). The ex-German Chancellor says that he told Pius XI soon after meeting with Mussolini that Nazism and Fascism were different from each other, 360.

many's chancellor in January 1933. He was touched by Hitler's open admiration of his person but feared that the German dictator had ambitions in European affairs, which, if realized, would diminish Italy's influence. In July 1934 after Austrian Nazis had murdered his friend,
Chancellor Dollfuss of Austria, Mussolini kept Hitler from interfering
in the affairs of that country by sending Italian troops to the Austrian
border. However, differences with the British and French governments
over his aggression against Ethiopia from 1935 to 1936, and Hitler's
skillful diplomacy, brought Mussolini into a German alliance and later
into a European war. The young John F. Kennedy's prophecy of 1937
would prove to be correct: "Wouldn't Mussolini go if there was a war—
as in all likelihood Italy would be defeated in a major war?"[52]

Mussolini, on becoming premier in October 1922, immediately
began to send conciliatory signals to the Papal Curia. This was an indication that he wanted to win its political assistance in dealing with a
serious political rival. Like Napoleon over a century before, he was
faced with a political party that had the backing of the episcopate and
the lower clergy plus the apparent blessing of a previous pope, Benedict
XV. Because of the Popolari's success in the early postwar elections, he
had to assume that in Catholic Italy this party would in the normal
course of events be a strong factor in the Italian Parliament. He must
have assured the Vatican that he would take eventual steps to recognize
the papacy as a sovereign entity and to give adequate governmental
support to the Catholic schools because in 1924, two years after the
Fascist "March on Rome," the Vatican sent the Popolari's leader, Don
Sturzo, into exile. In 1926 Mussolini, who had just come through a severe political crisis because some of his henchmen had murdered the
popular Socialist leader, Guiseppe Matteotti, dismantled the liberal
parliamentary system. The Vatican and its press made no protest even
though the Popolari lost its existence in the process.

Mussolini was not satisfied with the fact that he had already disposed of a Catholic party a few years before he concluded the Treaty of
Rome and a concordat with the papacy. He successfully insisted that
the Concordat contain articles stipulating that clergymen could not en-

52. Hamilton, *JFK*, 199.

gage in political activity within Catholic associations or in a political party.[53] How important this issue was to Mussolini would be evident in the case of Msgr. Giovanni Montini, the future Pope Paul VI, and the national chaplain of the Catholic students' federation. To the wrath of Pope Pius XI, Fascist squads in 1931 began in a systematic manner to wreck federation offices and to beat up student members. After the Papal Curia suddenly removed Montini from his office, the Fascists left the Catholic student federation in peace.[54]

There was considerable evidence that Adolf Hitler was deeply impressed by the Fascist government's rapprochement with the papacy. In late 1929 he publicly praised the pacts they had recently concluded. In the September elections of 1930, the Nazi Party, benefitting from the deepening depression, increased its Reichstag members from twelve to one hundred and seven; later local and regional elections revealed that the party was on a roll. Then in April 1931 Hitler sent his chief deputy, Herman Goering, to the Vatican and, while we do not know what he said to a member of the Papal Secretariat of State, he apparently left a reassuring impression behind him. The reason why the Nazi leader was interested in improving his party's image at the Vatican was evident in public remarks made in 1930 by Johannes Stark, a Catholic Nazi and a Nobel laureate in physics. Stark said that if a Nazi government reached an agreement with the papacy, then the Vatican would abandon the two German Catholic parties, the Center and Bavarian Peoples parties. Hitler would make a similar remark in a cabinet session on 7 March 1933, approximately six weeks after he had been appointed Chancellor in a coalition government.[55]

No European Foreign Office official could have watched the post-1929 German political scene more closely than Cardinal Eugenio Pacelli, who became the Vatican Secretary of State in December of that year. Cardinal Pietro Gasparri, who held that position since 1914, had

53. Kaas, *Der Konkordatstyp*, 510–511.
54. Hebblethwaite, *Paul VI*, 109–111.
55. See my article: "The Genesis of the German Concordat of 1933," in *Studies in Catholic History*, ed. N.H. Minnich, Robert B. Eno, S.S., and Robert F. Trisco (Wilmington, Del., 1985), 636–638.

successfully completed the negotiations with the Mussolini government over the Roman Question, a concordat and a treaty of compensations for the material losses the papacy had suffered during the *Risorgimento*. Nevertheless, he was suddenly removed from his office to make place for Pacelli.[56] The brilliant Pacelli[57] had served for eleven years in Germany, first as Papal Nuncio to Bavaria and later to Berlin as well.

Shortly after the end of World War II Pope Pius XII, the former Cardinal Pacelli, partially justified the Concordat of 1933 in these terms:

. . . neither the special concordats (already concluded with certain Lander [states]) nor the Weimar Constitution seemed to them [Catholics] to offer adequate protection and guarantees of respect for their convictions, their beliefs, their rights and liberty of action.[58]

If Pius XII had been addressing a group of German Catholic pilgrims of sixty or seventy years of age instead of his actual audience of cardinals, they would have wondered if he had known much about the lives of German Catholics before he arrived in their country in June 1917, or learned much about the new conditions of their lives in the fifteen years or so that followed. Still, as Nuncio in Germany and then as the Vatican Secretary of State, he had labored tirelessly to secure a concordat with Germany to secure the position of German Catholics in the Weimar Republic.

Somewhat over half of the German Catholic population lived in Prussia before and after World War I.[59] Many of its middle-class mem-

56. Peter Hebblethwaite says that Gasparri was shaken by his sudden removal from his high office. *Paul VI*, 105.

57. I remember reading while in graduate school a letter which the noted German-English writer Friedrich von Hugel wrote to a friend in the later 1890s from Rome, in which he said that people in the city were talking about the brilliance of the young Eugenio Pacelli, then in his early twenties. I no longer have a record of the book in which I found this letter. That he was the top diplomat in the Vatican's service was evident from the fact that Cardinal Gasparri chose him to be his representative in talks with Chicheren, the noted Soviet Foreign Secretary, in Berlin in June 1927; Stehle, *Eastern Politics of the Vatican*, 112–113.

58. Frederick Spotts, *The Churches and Politics in Germany* (Middletown, 1973), 29.

59. See Zeender, "Germany, the Catholic Church and the Nazi Regime," in *Catholics, the State and the Radical Right*, ed. Richard J. Wolff and Jorg Hoensch (Highland Lakes, New York, 1987), 92–118.

bers would have agreed before 1914 that they had come forward under the efficient Prussian administrative system and the quality of its schools and universities.[60] The Catholic hierarchy had become increasingly pleased around 1900 by the efforts that the Prussian-Imperial monarchy was making to satisfy the Church in their relationship. The Emperor William II and his ministers needed the support of the Center party, for their Reichstag legislation but also because they feared the growing Social Democratic party, which was Marxist in its ideology. The bishops felt completely reconciled to the Hohenzollern State after the Prussian monarchy and the Landtag put through legislation in 1906 that seemed to guarantee the future of the dominant confessional school systems.

Nevertheless, under the pre-1918 monarchy some German Catholics, along with Social Democrats and Jews, felt like second-class citizens, often denied the right to participate in government at its higher levels. Felix Porsch, the leader of the Prussian Center, said shortly after the establishment of the Weimar Republic, "now we are free."[61] For more than half of the time between 1918 and 1933 the German chancellorship was in the hands of a Catholic and the governing party in predominantly Catholic Bavaria was of the same faith. In Prussia the Minister-President was usually a Social Democrat but he made sure that the Center party got enough ministries and other high governmental positions and that the Ministry of Cults and Education did not make the major political blunder of merging a small Catholic school with a nearby Protestant school for reasons of economy.

The Weimar constitution had not given church schools legal equality with those of an interdenominational character, leaving their future uncertain. That constitutional settlement upset the German bishops, who did not want the Catholic schools' security dependent on the con-

60. At some point before World War II, I was surprised to hear a Catholic German-American man, who had been born into a Rhineland business family in the early 1880s, say proudly, "I was a Prussian." In the early part of 1955 I gave a talk in Bonn to a German Catholic group on Catholicism under the old Hohenzollern monarchy, in which I referred to their second-class situation. Then a young man stood up and with some heat said, "My father never told me that!"

61. Zeender, "The German Catholics and the Presidential Election of 1925," in *Journal of Modern History* (December 1963): 368, note 15.

tinued friendship between the Social Democrats and the Center. Therefore in 1921 they initiated a national petition drive, supported by over four million Catholic voters, calling for the passage of a national law putting the church schools on a legal basis. However, the efforts of the Center and the Protestant German National People's Party to secure its approval in the national parliament were clearly hopeless by 1927.[62] The Catholic Bavarian government had been happy to conclude a concordat with the Vatican in 1924, putting its own church schools system on a treaty foundation, but Pacelli got nowhere in his efforts to convince the Prussian and Baden state governments to do the same when they respectively entered into concordat ties with the Holy See in 1929 and 1932. Still, 83 percent of all the schools in Germany when Hitler came to power in January 1933 were of the denominational kind.[63]

Shortly before Archbishop Pacelli's return to Rome in late 1929 to become Papal Secretary of State, Vatican-Soviet talks virtually broke down. A very active group of religious at the Vatican had had high hopes that the Catholic Church, if given even a modest foothold in the Soviet Union, could, along with the Russian Orthodox church, reconvert the Russian people to Christianity. Hence Pius XI had been willing to make major concessions to the Moscow regime for a treaty securing the right to be heard on episcopal appointments. Consequently, the Pope was profoundly disappointed by the failure of the earlier talks and his old fears of Communism returned to the top of his thought. Those views would be deepened by the growth of the Communist movement during the Depression years of the early 1930s.[64] That the threat of Communism to Catholicism and religion in general was total made it more of an enemy to the Vatican and the Catholic Church than Nazism, whose opposition to them seemed only partial.

Left-wing parliamentary parties had frustrated Pacelli's efforts to se-

62. On the general nature of the relations between the German Catholic episcopate and the Center party, see *ibid*, 368–370; also my "The Genesis of the German Concordat of 1933," 622–623.

63. Spotts, *Churches and Politics*, 207.

64. Hans-Jacob Stehle aptly entitles the fourth chapter in his *Eastern Politics of the Vatican* "From the End of the Dialogue to the 'Crusade,' 1927–1932."

cure concordats with the national German government, Prussia, and Baden, which would provide a better legal position for Catholic schools. By 1931, however, as Papal Secretary of State, he began to take the Nazi Party into his calculations as a parliamentary supporter of a national concordat. That the Nazis were vigorous enemies of the German Communist movement was undoubtedly pleasing and reassuring to Pacelli and Pius XI since they regarded Communism as the worst threat to the Church. But for Pacelli the primary consideration was where its leaders stood on the issue of a German concordat.[65] The visit that Herman Goering paid to the Vatican in April 1931 apparently convinced the Papal Secretary of State that Hitler and his party could open the way for him to engage in meaningful concordat negotiations with the German state. He was all the more optimistic concerning success in that respect because the then German chancellor, Heinrich Brüning, a devout Catholic, was governing on the basis of President Paul von Hindenburg's emergency decree powers and was not immediately dependent on the Reichstag's support. To Pacelli's profound disappointment, Brüning flatly refused either to undertake concordat negotiations with the Vatican or to appoint Nazis to his cabinet. Brüning argued that an attempt by his government to conclude such a pact with the papacy would outrage German Protestants.[66]

There was a curious contrast in the roles the priest leaders of the Popolari and Center parties played in the crisis of democracy in their countries. Don Sturzo could return in honor to his native land in 1945, but Ludwig Kaas, also a priest and a man of considerable sensitivity, had to live out his life in exile, the target for the resentments of many German Catholics who disliked the German Concordat of 1933.

Ludwig Kaas had been forced into a difficult situation by 1930, being required to wear two hats. One was as the leader of the Center party, which had pivotal positions in both the Reichstag and the Prussian Landtag. The other was as the confidential adviser on German affairs to Cardinal Pacelli, the Papal Secretary of State. He had served in that role in Pacelli's service as Papal Nuncio to Germany prior to 1929, and

65. See Zeender, "The Genesis of the German Concordat of 1933," 634, note 30.
66. Ibid., 629–644.

they became close friends before Pacelli returned to Rome for good. Despite Kaas's heavy responsibilities as a party leader in Berlin in a hectic political period, Pacelli frequently called him to Rome for extended periods of time to discuss German political developments. In late 1932 Kaas wrote an extended analysis of the Italian-Papal treaties of 1929, which was clearly intended for the eyes of the Nazi leadership. In it the author eulogized Pope Pius XI and Mussolini as statesmen. However he did not imply that some of the political concessions which the papacy had made to the Fascist regime in the Concordat between them— and catalogued by Coppa—might be possible in a German treaty. Kaas was undoubtedly thinking here of the differences between the situations of Catholics in Italy and those in Germany; in Italy they were a majority whereas in Germany they were a minority.

There is still an element of mystery about the relations between Ludwig Kaas and the Hitler regime after the Reichstag elections of 5 March 1933, which the Nazis and their elitist allies of the German National Peoples Party won by a slender margin. To secure his immediate goal of an enabling act from the Reichstag, he needed the votes of the Center Party in that parliament. On the day after the elections, Ludwig Kaas met with Hitler's vice-chancellor Franz von Papen. Joseph A. Biesinger says in his essay that Kaas acted like a papal nuncio at that meeting. In fact, he did not inform his party's executive council that he had met with the vice-chancellor.

On 23 March, despite the earlier opposing arguments of Heinrich Brüning and Joseph Wirth, the two ex-chancellors in the Center's Reichstag delegation, the delegation voted unanimously for the enabling act bill. Ludwig Kaas would leave Germany on 6 April to participate in concordat negotiations without telling his colleagues that he would be doing so.

Monsignor Kaas left his party headless when he departed for Rome on that day. His old Center friends, other associates, and followers, many priests included, were grieved and then increasingly angry over some articles in the Concordat but also over those omitted from it. They were upset that the negotiations had ensured the demise of the Center party, which had served the Church so well over its sixty-odd years of existence, and that the new pact did not contain specific protection for many Catholic associations. It was probably Ludwig Kaas who tried to persuade the German negotiators that the German bishops should be permitted to appoint a select few priests to serve in the German Catholic parties, but Hitler's representatives were adamant in refusing to compromise on the issue of Catholic clergymen in party politics. They knew that Hitler wanted to separate the Church from the Center and Bavarian Catholic parties. Heinrich Brüning, on learning that the Vatican had capitulated to the German government on this issue, waited a few days and then, acting with his party council, dissolved his old party. The gift that the Church's negotiators received from the German side in return was a pledge to maintain Catholic school systems and to introduce them in those parts of Germany where Catholic education had not existed since the nineteenth century.[67]

The Vatican's abandonment of the Catholic parties, but especially the Center, caused deep resentment and bitterness in German Catholic lay and lower clerical circles. That feeling became even deeper in the next years as the Nazi regime, sometimes by direct action, other times by indirect methods, destroyed the bulk of the Catholic associations. The bishops and the papacy hoped that if they did not seriously protest these acts the Hitler regime would respect the Concordat's provisions about the Catholic schools. The Nazi dictator would destroy that illusion in 1937–1938 when he, now highly popular, fused the Catholic and Protestant school systems so that racism could be preached in them.

The papacy had rarely found it easy to negotiate with monarchical governments but the problems of dealing with modern dictators brought new difficulties. Nonetheless, the papacy relied on its traditional modes of diplomacy. Its representatives had always assumed that its secular partners would violate the terms of a concordat but that the best way to bring them around to respecting its basic elements was to use quiet, patient and persistent diplomacy with them. What was to be avoided at all costs was any public confrontation that might damage their prestige and hence anger them. This policy worked fairly well with Mussolini, who had the Pope and a Catholic king as neighbors in his capital city, but Napoleon had violated his concordat whenever he felt like it. And

67. *Ibid.*, 632–633, 653.

Hitler had already begun to violate the spirit if not the letter of his pact before that treaty was ratified, and did much worse in succeeding years.

The happiest times of Pius XII's life were the years he spent in Germany as Papal Nuncio, where this reserved churchman was popular with Catholics. Therefore he keenly felt the criticisms which came out of that country regarding the Concordat even before World War II. Immediately after the war's end he convoked a solemn consistory of cardinals at which he defended that pact. He had virtually ignored the cardinals in his policymaking in diplomatic affairs over the years.[68] After his death in 1958 his critics focused their attention not on the Concordat but rather on his silence in the face of the Nazi regime's violations of human rights before 1939 and its monstrous wartime crimes against humanity. Their study of his diplomacy vis-à-vis Nazi Germany soon led to an examination of the relations between the German Catholic episcopate and the Nazi government in the same period. The bishops had essentially followed the lead of their strong-willed chairman, Cardinal Adolf Bertram (1859–1945), who insisted throughout that the German Catholic Church should avoid a confrontation with the regime.[69]

Pius XII and Cardinal Bertram had never been close to each other, most likely because of differences over rights of jurisdiction in German Catholic Church affairs.[70] Still they had similar personalities and similar approaches in matters of serious concern in Church matters. Each was intense, ascetic, highly intelligent and sensitive about others but also supremely self-confident about his own judgment and competence in dealing with secular governments. Pacelli showed impressive ease and flexibility in negotiating with Chicherin, the Soviet Foreign Minister, with Otto Braun, the Social Democratic Minister-President of Prussia, and then with the representatives of Hitler.

68. Paul Johnson, *A History of Christianity* (New York, 1976), 502. Johnson claims that Pius XII was a "Louis XIV" in the Vatican.

69. On Cardinal Bertram, see my "Germany: The Catholic Church and the Nazi Regime," 94, 104.

70. I cannot prove this, but I have the distinct feeling, based on extensive research in the published German episcopal documents, that the German bishops, and especially Cardinal Bertram, would have liked to manage their own relations with the German national and federal states after 1918. Cardinal Pacelli did not involve them in

The German episcopate, having seen examples of Nazi ugly conduct at first hand, was less optimistic about the future than Cardinal Pacelli. However, its members welcomed the Concordat because it offered them the prize they had long sought, a legal guarantee of the existence of the Catholic schools. It was not easy for them to abandon the Center and Bavarian People's parties, especially the Center, which had served the Church and laity so faithfully for over sixty years, but they thought that the existence of the Catholic schools was more important than that of the two parties. That the Catholic laity as citizens and voters had rights to be considered in the matter had not occurred to them.

Epilogue

For over eight hundred years, the papacy had made concordats the centerpieces of its outreach to the wider world. But after the death of Pope Pius XII in 1958, his successors, while not moving to revoke them, ceased to stress their importance to the Church.

Pius XII had not been in his grave very long when there emerged a crescendo of criticism of the concordats that the papacy had concluded with Mussolini, Hitler and General Franco, the Spanish dictator.[71] The critics claimed that the papacy's partners in these treaties had been dictators with records of serious violations of human and civil rights, and that the Popes had used concordats to tighten their oppressive grips on their nations. The force of these arguments was not lost on many Catholics, lay or clerical, since Catholics were often prominently represented in the new democratic governments that came into being in Europe after World War II. The commitment of Catholic leaders like Alcide de Gasperi, Konrad Adenauer, Charles de Gaulle and, later, King Juan of Spain, to human rights and democratic government was firm.

---

the concordat negotiations until they were in full swing. In early November 1954, I talked at some length with Papal Nuncio Alois Muench in Bonn about my research on the old German Center Party. He told me that after his arrival in West Germany some years earlier, the German bishops had treated him with considerable reserve and that it had taken him a long time to win their confidence.

71. But Elie Wiesel says Franco protected Spanish Jews and gave government aid to other Jews as well in his *All Rivers Run to the Sea: Memoirs* (New York, 1995), 334–335.

But another factor of signal importance in the papacy's deemphasis on concordat diplomacy was the change taking place within the Church at all levels. Pius XII often demonstrated his brilliance and wide knowledge by confidently addressing varied groups, like artists, midwives, and physicists, on their work. But his mind had been formed before 1914, and he was uncomfortable with democracy.[72] His successor, John XXIII (d. 1963), achieved a remarkable popularity among non-Catholics because of his open and warm personality and strong humanitarian sentiments.[73] He convoked a general church council, but it was his successor, Paul VI (d. 1978), who as a young Catholic student chaplain had incurred Mussolini's disfavor, who brought it to a successful conclusion. In the past the papacy, confident of its own intentions and eager to avoid offending the secular governments with whom it was negotiating, had usually ignored public opinion. The Council's leaders were eager, however, to demonstrate to both Catholics and non-Catholics alike that the bishops would discuss matters of far-reaching Church reform in an open forum. Therefore, they invited non-Catholic churchmen to attend the plenary Council sessions, and recognizing the extensive amount of public interest in the Council, they provided regular press conferences at which officials reported on the Council's progress. The Council itself took positive stands on issues of basic importance to non-

72. Some scholars have written that Pius XII committed himself to democratic principles after World War II, but shortly before his death, speaking of the Italian Christian Democratic Party to Field Marshall Sir Bernard Montgomery, Pius said that he liked the first part of the name but not the second. See Nigel Hamilton, *Monty: The Final Years of the Field Marshall, 1944–1976* (New York, 1987), 875.

73. It is difficult for persons who were not adults at the time to appreciate what a profoundly enthusiastic impression John XXIII made on non-Catholics. Walter Lippmann, writing soon after the Pope's death, stated, "so as he lies dead he is revered and blessed by all sorts of conditions of men all around the globe." And referring to John XXIII's convocation of a general church council, Lippmann added, "For what Pope John began will have very big consequences and the history of our world will be different because he lived." (*Washington Post*, June 6, 1963) And somewhat over three years later, Chief Justice Earl Warren said in part to a Catholic University of America audience: "I believe that no person has made a more impressive contribution in the pursuit of this quest for peace than your great spiritual leader, the late John XXIII. He was able as perhaps no one else within our memory to appraise intuitively the hopes and the needs of mankind." *The Catholic University Bulletin*, no. 1 (January 1967).

Catholics, like the right to freedom of conscience and the acceptability of the separation of church and state.

However, the prime aim of the Second Vatican Council was to update the Catholic Church itself. This meant moving away from a preoccupation with the Church's relations with secular governments and placing a priority on its spiritual relationships with Catholic people worldwide.

Napoleon, the Concordat of 1801, and Its Consequences

WILLIAM ROBERTS, *Fairleigh Dickinson University*

THE CONCORDAT OF 1801, signed by Napoleon Bonaparte and Pope Pius VII and destined to regulate for more than a century church and state relations in France, clearly had its origins in the policies of the various revolutionary French governments that emerged after 1789. For example, the decision of the French National Assembly on 2 November of that year placing Church property "at the disposal of the nation," the decree of 1 February 1790 by the same Assembly that effectively ended monasticism in France, or finally the later decree of 27 November 1799 that imposed the oath of the Civil Constitution on the clergy,[1] all can be considered to be the beginning steps in a process of dechristianization that would continue until at least the end of 1794, and would only end with the Concordat of 1801.

By the onset of the Terror, in the summer of 1793, the Catholic Church in France was already considered by the regime to be in league with the forces of counterrevolution and reaction. The fact that so many of the non-juring clergy, as clerics who had refused to take the oath to the Civil Constitution were known, had gone into exile while

---

1. Adrien Dansette, *Histoire religieuse de la France contemporaine*, vol. 1 (Paris, 1948–51), 69.

remaining in touch with factions hostile to the revolution, reinforced that view. Moreover, during that radical period, even ordinary religious practices and observances had come to be seen as hostile to the nation's new revolutionary ideals and objectives. By late 1794, however, after the excesses of the Terror, in which hundreds, if not thousands, of priests, monks, and nuns were killed, the tide began to turn against extreme religious persecution. A decree of 21 February 1795 stating that "the Republic neither recognizes nor finances any religion" and guaranteeing the free exercise of all religions, even led to the return of a large number of émigré priests and the widespread reinstitution of Catholic services.[2] This mild statement of toleration seemed to be generally welcome by the majority of the population. In reality, what was desired by most Frenchmen was not primarily a return of Tridentine Catholicism, with its hierarchy, doctrines, catechism, and confessional, but a religion concerned with parish life, centered on church services and the familiar rituals of baptism, marriage, and burial. A demand existed for such things and both clergies, juring and non-juring, responded to it.

Yet the Church in France was still not fully secure. On 6 September 1797, a reaction against anti-republican factions, known as the *coup d'état de 18 Fructidor*, brought renewed persecution. Much of the old anti-religious legislation was revived with a new oath demanding "hatred of royalty," which was required of all who performed religious services. Those who did not swear to this oath, and they were mostly nonjuring clergy—the *refractaires*—were subject to deportation to New Guinea. More than three hundred such priests were sent there and many never returned. Thus, while this Fructidorian persecution was less intense and less organized than that of the Jacobin Terror, it still served to dampen the spirit of toleration that had just begun to emerge in France. But all this, too, would change with Bonaparte's coming to power in 1799 in his coup of 18 Brumaire.

Napoleon Bonaparte did not have any strong personal religious beliefs; thus, upon taking office as First Consul, his policies towards religion were governed by only two significant considerations, neither relating directly to spiritual matters. First, he sought to avoid, if at all

2. Ibid., 129.

possible, any troubles over religious issues. Instead, he would concede to popular sentiment and uphold the religion of the people. His policy, he later told his Council of State, was "to govern men as the majority of them want to be governed. That, I believe, is the best way to recognize popular sovereignty. It was by becoming a Catholic that I put an end to the war in the Vendée, by becoming an ultramontane that I won over opinion in Italy. If I governed a people of Jews, I would rebuild the temple of Solomon."[3]

Bonaparte's second and more important motive in this regard was based on the fact that he saw religion, especially in the form of an established Church, as one of the chief means of social control. In his view, this was necessary because, as he stated, society "cannot exist without inequality of wealth, and inequality of wealth cannot exist without religion. When a man is dying of hunger next to another who has plenty, it is impossible for him to accept this difference unless there is an authority that tells him: 'God wills it so.'"[4]

Yet even before he actually took power in 1799, Bonaparte, like the members of the Directory government before him, understood the immediate benefits in effecting a rapprochement or at least some form of agreement with the papacy. In fact, the campaign in Italy that he led in 1796, at the orders of the Directory, was carried out partly to bring pressure upon the Pope and encourage him to come to terms with the Constitutional Church. Bonaparte, however, did not fully carry out these orders, which also involved taking Rome and despoiling the Pope of all his remaining possessions.

Of course, as a result of this campaign, the papacy suffered substantial territorial losses, especially the cities of Ferrara, Bologna, and Ravenna, which the French annexed as they had previously done with the papal territories of Avignon and Venaissin in France. But Bonaparte, who could have taken more, had already privately decided to make the Pope his future ally. He realized that back in France Catholicism was gaining ground. Thus, at some point, perhaps soon, the

3. *Revue de l'histoire de l'Église de France*; see also Andre Latreille, *L'Église catholique et la Revolution française*, vol. 2 (Paris, 1946), 225.
4. Ibid.; see also Latreille, 226.

Church could prove to be of invaluable assistance, and so he set down his own policy regarding Rome. Naturally, his intention was also to deceive the Pope. In October 1796, he wrote to an aide about "gaining time so as to trick the old fox," while a few days later he notified his contacts in Rome that they could "assure the Pope . . . that I covet more the title of savior than destroyer of the Holy See."[5]

Meanwhile, as he ostensibly carried out the orders of the Directory government to march on Rome, Bonaparte also kept open communications with various Italian prelates, making sure that neither French Catholic émigrés in Italy were harmed nor that his troops showed any overt disrespect of religion.

In December 1797, a French official was murdered in the ambassador's residence in Rome, and, in response, the Directory government ordered its armies to quickly advance. General Louis Berthier was sent forward and took the city in a few weeks. Then the Pope, Pius VI, was taken to France, where he died in August 1799. By this time, however, Bonaparte was in Egypt. There he could afford to wait and leave the Directory to suffer the consequences of its blunders. Once his own military losses in the Middle East were covered by the defeats of other generals in Europe, he returned to France in October and was welcomed as a deliverer. A month later he effectively seized power. A short time after that, in March 1800, after a stormy conclave in Venice, Gregorio Barnaba Chiaramonti, the Cardinal Archbishop of Imola, was elected pope, taking the name Pius VII. Chiaramonti was a relatively young choice, being age fifty-nine at the time of his election. He had in fact been chosen partly because he was considered to be a conciliatory individual who would remain neutral should any conflict arise among the major powers.

Earlier, as bishop, Chiaramonti had presided over a diocese whose boundaries fell within the area of the Cisalpine Republic, a satellite state established in Italy by the French. At that time he favored some form of reconciliation of the Church with the Revolution. Later on, as a cardinal, he continued to believe that the Church should try to find some accommodation with the new political and social ideas then

5. Ibid.

emerging in Europe. For example, when the revolutionary government of the Cisalpine Republic had decided that the time had come for its leading prelates to show their loyalty to the new regime by declaring that the laws of the Republic were founded on the gospels, the future Pope preached that the Gospel could be reconciled with a democratic form of government, adding, however, that democracies were also in the greatest need of the Church because the liberty and personal responsibility they accorded to the citizen required more divine grace than that needed by an obedient subject of an absolute monarch.[6]

Because these words have sometimes been taken out of context, Chiaramonti has been misjudged as a liberal. The reality was that he did not completely sympathize with the ideas of the Revolution but had learned the lesson then being applied in France: that Christianity must be able to live with a *de facto* government, whatever its form. It was in this spirit, unlike other more conservative prelates of the Cisalpine state, that he agreed to style himself "citizen-cardinal" and, also in the interest of the principle of equality, had had the baldichino over his episcopal throne removed, clearly pointing out to the authorities, however, that the superiority it implied referred to a spiritual office, not a person. Later, he would refuse to accept one of the more revolutionary innovations of the new government, a policy that required the selection of the clergy by the laity.[7] Shortly after his election as pontiff, Pius VII was to negotiate the decisive Concordat of 1801 with Bonaparte. It was to be one of the definitive events of his pontificate.

When Bonaparte came to power in 1800, he further revealed his intentions to effect a reconciliation with the Church. Earlier, on the eve of the Battle of Marengo, he openly addressed the Catholic clergy of Milan. In that address Bonaparte took the opportunity to criticize the *philosophes* and their atheistic ideas and, while deploring the earlier persecutions in France, asserted his view that the experience of the revolution had caused the French people to reconsider their government's policy towards the Church. He stated that no society could exist with-

6. Ibid.; see also Latreille, 231.
7. E. E. Y. Hales, *Revolution and Papacy: 1796–1846* (London, 1969).

out morals, which could only be ensured by religion, and also told the clerics that he shared their faith. "I assure you," he declared,

that we are re-opening the churches in France, where the Catholic religion assumes its ancient splendor, and the people are full of respect for the holy pastors who return zealously to their abandoned flocks. When I speak face to face with the new Pope, I trust I may have the good fortune to remove the obstacles which hinder a complete reconciliation between France and the head of the Church.[8]

As Bonaparte had said, it was true that there had already been a religious revival in France, although in later years he denied this point, claiming that he himself, through the Concordat, had brought it about—a claim that later also suited the interests of both his followers and the Ultramontanes. But in fact, some efforts to effect a treaty with the Church had earlier been attempted between the Directory and an agent of the previous Pope, Pius VI, on the basis of the Civil Constitution. A draft of such an agreement had even been composed, but afterwards nothing further was done. Various statistics seem to indicate, too, that before Bonaparte came to power, a religious revival had already begun in France. For instance, by 1796, more than thirty-two thousand French churches were already in clerical hands and several thousand more were about to be reopened. Later, in 1797 at the council of Paris, the bishop Émile Lecoz stated that forty thousand parishes had at that point been provided with ministers. These figures were increased in a report issued on the eve of the Concordat.[9] Allowing for the inflation of these numbers, it is apparent that there was a significant return to religious practice during the Directory period. Moreover, as the majority of the parishes represented in these statistics were served by the constitutional clergy, it also can be claimed that the maintenance, and therefore the restoration, of public worship was due at least in part to the Constitutional Church.

On the other hand, under both the Directory and the First Consulate there were factions who wanted no formal reconciliation between

---

8. *Documents Diplomatiques Français* (Ministère des Affaires Étrangères); see also Latreille, *Histoire du catholicisme en France*, vol. 2 (Paris, 1955–62), 156.

9. Dansette, vol. 1, 78.

church and state. Neither the left-wing revolutionaries nor the deists or skeptics wished to reopen official communications between the free and lay society of the Revolution and the papacy. Likewise, the constitutional clergy saw no need for such a policy. Even the non-juring clergy and their supporters, many of whom had largely forgotten their bishops (who earlier, during the periods of persecution, had prudently emigrated), saw no pressing reason for an official rapprochement. All they really wanted was to be free from further persecution and to be able to reenter their churches and minister to their congregations without impediment, something that could certainly have been achieved without a concordat. In fact, before the Concordat of 1801 was actually ratified, thousands of émigré clergy had already returned and willingly took an amended oath to the constitution and the new government, and at the same time gladly acknowledged the First Consul's restoration of religious liberty.

But Bonaparte, in his plan for the Church, wanted something more. He sought to reestablish a Church that was disciplined and regimented, submitting nominally to the Pope, but only on the condition that the Pope submit to him. He also wanted a Pope with enough territory to be considered a monarch, but not enough to be strong, a Pope who required his protection. It was therefore for these and other reasons that Bonaparte initiated the treaty, advanced it personally and autocratically, caused it to be accepted by the Pope, and imposed it on his ministers, government, and military, none of whom actually wanted it. Significantly, on the French copy of the Concordat's ratification, Bonaparte's signature fills the page, dominating all the others. Similarly, even during the negotiations, the representatives often privately recorded that "Bonaparte is the only one who wants the meeting with Rome."[10]

But, while in a political sense Bonaparte's motives can be considered fairly straightforward, those of Pius VII were more complicated. The Church's long history of schisms (Bonaparte more than once during the Concordat's negotiations reminded the Pope of the precedent of England's Henry VIII), as well as the real possibility of regaining lost papal territory, coupled with a concern for the future of the Church in France

10. Ibid.

and perhaps throughout the rest of Europe, all played a part in the reasoning of Pius VII as he entered into discussions with the First Consul. Thus, in analyzing the Concordat, there are several additional issues that should be raised concerning the motivations of the two parties as well as factors related to the negotiations and the treaty's contents, application, and final effect.

As stated, in arranging this agreement, Bonaparte was moved essentially by political considerations, Pius VII basically by religious ones. Naturally, however, both individuals were accused of having other motives. For his part, Bonaparte was seen as acting out of a sense of personal vanity or mere expediency. At the *Te Deum* that was celebrated in Paris in honor of the treaty's ratification, a republican general is said to have grumbled with disapproval, "all that is missing are those hundreds of thousands of Frenchmen who died to be rid of this."[11] Meanwhile, regarding Pius VII, later in his reign, Roman wits were to coin the pasquinade: "Pio VI per conservar la fede perde la sede/ Pio VII per conservar la sede perde la fede" (Pius VI to save his faith lost his throne/Pius VII to save his throne lost his faith.)[12] It was an unfair assessment.

In reality, of course, the actual negotiations started with a wide distance between the two sides. When Bonaparte in 1799 had, in his words, "brought the Revolution to an end," he had also intended to uphold most of its ideas, which had been enunciated ten years earlier. For his part, Pius sought foremost to safeguard the Church's principles as well as regain what the papacy had lost in terms of its temporal power. Any progress, therefore, towards a final accord required strong determination on both sides.

Ever since the earlier pacification of the French Catholic stronghold of the Vendée by General Berthier, Bonaparte had secretly formed a plan of reaching some type of understanding with Rome, but prudently waited until his authority was firmly established before initiating any negotiations. It was his victory at Marengo in 1800 that gave his regime the necessary strength to go forth. The French historian Albert Vandal

11. Hales, 138.
12. Ibid.

has even gone as far as to say that "the Concordat was a consequence of Marengo"—the victory having given Bonaparte the popularity he needed to carry out his plan of reconciliation.[13] After Marengo and before returning to France, Bonaparte stopped at Vercelli, in northern Italy, to present his plan to the local prelate, Cardinal Giacomo Martiniana, whom he then delegated to bring it to the Pope. "Go to Rome," he told the Cardinal, "and tell the Holy Father that the First Consul wished to make him a gift of thirty million Frenchmen."[14] Bonaparte proposed three main points: that the Church in France would be restored with a new episcopate, that the state would pay clerical salaries, and that for their part churchmen would renounce all claim to their former properties. Pius immediately welcomed these preliminary offers but harbored no illusions about the obstacles ahead. He then ordered Martiniana, in whom he really had little confidence, to notify the First Consul of his acceptance and to seek further details. Meanwhile, the Pope also sent a trusted representative, Archbishop Giuseppe Spina, accompanied by a theologian, Father Antonio Caselli, to Vercelli. Their mission was to determine French intentions.

At this point Bonaparte insisted that the negotiations be conducted in Paris where, in his view, the papal representatives would be more isolated and accommodating. To this end he furnished the envoys with passports for France without previously informing Rome. It was the first of several questionable actions on his part. Spina arrived in Paris in late October 1800, accompanied by Caselli who now had replaced Martiniana. But both delegates were actually supplied with instructions from Pius that limited their powers and were only authorized to discuss the French government's proposals, not to pass final judgment on them. The French negotiator in this matter was not to be Bonaparte's Foreign Minister, Charles Talleyrand, who like all the other ministers had been opposed to a concordat, but the Abbé Étienne Bernier, an old Vendéen who was now an ardent supporter of the First Consul. In discussions with Bernier, Spina was circumspect and patient, and four successive

13. Pieter Geyl, *Napoleon, For and Against* (London, 1949), 210.

14. *Documents Diplomatiques Français*; see also John McManners, *The French Revolution and the Church* (New York, 1969), 143.

schemes were studied, modified, and then rejected. Initial negotiations dragged on for six months, but, thanks to Spina, definitive agreements were reached on some points, although not on the crucial ones in which conflicts existed between the principles of the civil and religious powers.

At the end of February 1801, Spina sent Rome a fifth draft which Bonaparte, in his impatience, had personally drawn up. Bernier, now ambitious to become a bishop or perhaps even a cardinal, sought to please everyone and secretly arranged for a paper to be sent to the Roman Curia setting out the issues on which it would be possible to resist the French government's demands. Bonaparte, wanting to further pressure the Pope, sent his representative Louis Cacault as Minister Plenipotentiary. Asked by Cacault how Pius should be handled, Bonaparte replied caustically, "As though he had 200,000 men, no more."[15] When Rome delayed its response, Bonaparte sent an ultimatum ordering Cacault to leave and then ordered General Joachim Murat to march on the city. Cacault, however, saved the situation by advising the Papal Secretary of State, Cardinal Ercole Consalvi, to go to Paris and reopen the negotiations. The Pope's delays and hesitations were not all caused by the different objectives of the two opposing parties. At this point, those objectives were mainly tactical. As the Austrians were still in Italy, Pius had judged Bonaparte's victory at Marengo to be indecisive. It was not yet clear to the pontiff whether the French or the Coalition would ultimately be victorious and he did not want to be on the wrong side. Only after the French had won further military victories and signed treaties with Austria and Naples, leaving Bonaparte master of Italy, were Pius's doubts as to who was the dominant power settled. From that point on negotiations commenced in earnest.

Cardinal Consalvi, the new papal representative, arrived in Paris in June 1801 and immediately rejected a sixth plan that had been drawn up by Bernier, accepting a seventh only after some revisions. But, on 14 July, when Consalvi came to the Tuileries to sign the document, he realized that many alterations had been made in the agreed-upon text. A stipulation about a profession of faith by the Consuls had been re-

---

15. *Documents Diplomatiques Français*; see also Dansette, vol. 1, 124.

moved and a clause relating to married priests inserted. Previously it had been agreed that such issues should be settled separately in a papal brief. This latter change had been instigated by Talleyrand who, because he was an unfrocked and married bishop, was unacceptable to the pope as one of the Concordat's signatories. At this point Bonaparte, in a rage, threw the eighth draft into the fire and then produced a ninth which the Cardinal rejected. Finally, on 15 July, after many hours of negotiations led by Bonaparte's brother Joseph, one of the members of the Council of State, a tenth draft was accepted and signed by representatives of both sides—Consalvi, Spina, and Caselli for the Pope, and Joseph Bonaparte, Bernier, and another councillor, Jean Cretet, for the French government.

In this final document Bonaparte's plan for the French church was revealed. It was straightforward and simple. The Consular government would protect the Catholic religion in France, but would also retain the right to police or regulate it as the First Consul might see fit. All of France was to be divided into fifty dioceses and ten archdioceses and all existing bishops, juring and non-juring, were required to resign and await reappointment. If they refused, the First Consul would appoint others whom the Pope would then institute. Bishops were to nominate priests, but the nominees must be approved by the government. Married or retired priests were to be admitted to lay communion and all clergy had to swear loyalty to the constitution and the Consuls. The alienation of Church property that had occurred during the Revolution was recognized and the rights of the new owners secured. In compensation, all ministers of worship of all faiths would be paid by the state. Finally, the First Consul was to have and exercise all the rights of his predecessors, the kings.

Included in these proposals were many from which, of course, the Pope had at first dissented. Even the Concordat's title and its preamble had, during the negotiations, presented difficulties. The term "concordat" had always been despised by the clergy because it reminded them of the agreement King Francis I had made in 1516, giving the French monarchy effective control over the Church. The French republicans also rejected the phrase because it was a leftover from the monarchist past. In deference to both, therefore, the treaty was officially entitled the "Convention between the French Government and His Holiness Pius VII." Moreoever, in the preamble to the original draft the Catholic religion had been described as "the state religion." But, as this threatened the principles of the Revolution and the spirit of toleration, it had to be withdrawn. The papal representative Spina tried to have the term "dominant religion" accepted, but that too was refused, and so a compromise was achieved by describing Catholicism as "the religion of the majority of French citizens." Finally on 15 August the Concordat was ratified by Pius in Rome and later, in September, by Bonaparte. Then, in April 1802, along with a controversial addendum known as the "Organic Articles," it was approved by the French legislature and publicly promulgated with a solemn *Te Deum* in Notre Dame.

This controversial and unilaterally imposed addendum, the Organic Articles, actually consisting of 77 clauses gathered under four titles, was designed by Bonaparte to reorganize and police the French Church in greater detail. The reasoning was that the Concordat's actual provisions were couched in broad terms and had to be clarified in an additional document. But the Articles in fact went beyond the original text and represented an attempt to reintroduce elements of Gallicanism into the administration and organization of the Church in France. They were in large part also Bonaparte's reaction to the papal representative Consalvi's attempts to gain the Church's complete freedom from governmental regulation.

Here it should be noted that the term *Articles Organiques* means merely "administrative regulations," not fundamental principles. The common English rendering, "Organic Articles," may be linguistically precise but it is inaccurate. Be that as it may, it was through these administrative articles that Bonaparte hoped to regulate and confine public ceremonial within the churches. When, during the final negotiations for the Concordat, Consalvi argued that there should not be any mention at that point of state control, and that later on the Pope could settle any such matters in a papal brief, Bonaparte angrily replied that the Pope should not be allowed to exercise his jurisdiction in France in that way. For this reason the text of the Concordat did not include the details that were later to be found in these added articles.

Briefly, the four main sections of the Articles dealt with: governmental authorization for national and diocesan synods and for the need for government permission for nuncios to exercise their authority; bishops' establishment of cathedral chapters and seminaries (in the same provision the bishops were also forbidden to leave their dioceses even to go to Rome, without the permission of the First Consul); a national catechism and liturgy and governmental permission for religious feasts and nuptial blessings; and regulation of the number and size of dioceses and parishes. Although Pius immediately protested against these unilaterally imposed regulations and reiterated his position during his visit to Paris for Bonaparte's coronation, they remained in place.

The coronation ceremonies themselves, which finally took place on 2 December 1804, were specifically designed to give the pontiff a symbolically limited role in that event. Pius was, first of all, brought to Paris just to anoint, but not crown, the new emperor and empress. Moreover Bonaparte, at the ceremony, read his coronation oath alone, from a throne on a platform that obscured the Pope and clergy surrounding the high altar. The only concession Bonaparte granted was his agreement to a Catholic marriage ceremony, which took place the night before at the instigation of the future empress. And, although many in France after the coronation rejoiced at this new "union of throne and altar," the thought of many others, still loyal to the old regime, was summed up by the diplomat and political thinker Joseph de Maistre when he wrote that "the crimes of an Alexander Borgia are less revolting than this hideous apostasy by his weak-kneed successor."[16]

As mentioned, there also had been disagreement over certain sections of the Concordat itself, but most of these issues were resolved in the final draft. In the brief preamble to the final version the French government acknowledged Roman Catholicism as the religion of the majority of the French people. For his part, the Pope in the same introductory passage expressed the expectation that the greatest good would follow the reestablishment of the Church in France and the particular professions of faith that were to be made by the Consuls. Then came the seventeen articles that comprised the document's major sections.

16. Xavier De Maistre, ed. *Les Carnets du comte Joseph De Maistre*, vol. IX (Lyon, 1923), 124.

Article 1 guaranteed the right to freedom of worship, stressing, however, that public worship had to be conducted in conformity with such police regulations as the government might judge necessary for public tranquility.

Article 2 established new boundaries for dioceses and parishes (Article 9) in collaboration with the government.

Article 3 stated that all titulars were to resign, and if they refused their replacements were to be chosen by the Pope.

Article 4 provided that bishops were to be nominated by the First Consul and then (Article 5) canonically installed by the Pope.

Articles 6 and 7 required bishops and priests to take oaths of obedience and loyalty to the government.

Article 8 required that the prayer "Lord, save the Republic and our Consul" be recited in all churches at the end of the Divine Office.

Article 10 mandated that pastors be named by their bishops in agreement with the government.

Article 11 required each diocese to have a seminary and chapter, not, however, to be endowed by the government.

Article 12 placed all church property not confiscated during the Revolution at the disposal of the bishops.

In Article 13 the Pope promised not to disturb those who had acquired confiscated ecclesiastical goods.

In Articles 14 and 15 the government assured an adequate income to bishops and pastors.

Article 16 permitted Catholics to endow ecclesiastical foundations, but only in the form of government bonds.

Article 17 gave the First Consul and the Republic the same rights and privileges as former governments, and made provision for a new agreement in the event Bonaparte had a non-Catholic successor.

Of these seventeen articles, those most hotly debated during the negotiations dealt with the status of the existing French bishops. Bonaparte had wanted them all to be deposed and replaced, because he considered the émigrés and non-jurors royalists, while the Constitutional bishops were suspected of being republicans and liberals. But there were serious objections to doing this by a papal decree. From the point of view of Rome it was uncanonical and unprecedented, and also unacceptable to anyone who upheld the Gallican Liberties. Moreover, to many, the only fault of the émigrés was that they had been faithful to the old regime and the Gallican Church. The Revolution had pushed them into Ultramontanism. Pius himself had said he could not sacrifice them without violating his personal honor. Nonetheless, he eventually did so. At first, as a compromise, he suggested that he might withdraw their faculties and appoint administrators to act while the existing bishops lived. But Bonaparte rejected this because it would leave them free to agitate as royalists and likely to oppose the Consulate and the Concordat just as they had opposed the Directory and the Civil Constitution. The Pope, in response, declared that he would urge the bishops to resign, "for the good of the Church." Refusal would be considered an act of disobedience and he could justifiably depose them.

It is important to note that, while this action on the part of the Pope was viewed as a capitulation to the French state, it in fact set a significant precedent that ultimately led to the triumph of the papacy and Ultramontanism over the Gallican Church. For the first time an entire hierarchy had been deposed and reestablished in France by a Pope, making the Roman pontiff the ruling ecclesiastical authority in that nation. Bonaparte had eliminated a relatively autonomous Church which later might have proven to be an inconvenience for his imperial administration, but he had inadvertently strengthened the hand of Rome.

The ultimate test of the Concordat rested in its actual application. Bonaparte had requested that a permanent papal legate, a *latere* endowed with broad powers, be sent to Paris. He chose a member of the Curia, Cardinal Giambattista Caprara, a prelate known to be conciliatory to the point of weakness. Bonaparte also created a ministry of cults and gave the post to Jean Portalis, who had Gallican sympathies but was well disposed toward the Church. Bernier, now a bishop, was appointed to act as the unofficial liaison between Caprara and Portalis.

One of the first issues that had to be settled dealt with the boundaries of the dioceses, the total number of which the Concordat had reduced to sixty. As Bonaparte's motives were essentially political, more dioceses would finally be given to the Vendée and the territories along the eastern and northern borders, regions where more popular support for his regime was needed. In terms of the hierarchy, while all the constitutional bishops had followed the Pope's advice and agreed to resign, a number of the non-juring bishops of the *ancien regime* had refused to do so. Their opposition led to the formation of the schismatic "Petite Église," comprised of the small group of clerics who held out against the treaty. Meanwhile, Bonaparte had already selected his new hierarchy in accordance with his principles of amalgamation to avoid the appearance of favoring any party. He renominated as bishops sixteen who had been members of the hierarchy during the *ancien regime* and twelve who had been constitutional bishops and nominated thirty-two more priests—all chosen because they were considered to be moderate, morally irreproachable, and good administrators.

With considerable difficulty Rome accepted the twelve former constitutional bishops. Before these prelates could receive canonical institution, they had to subscribe to an act of submission to any papal decisions concerning French religious affairs, in effect condemning the Civil Constitution of the Clergy of 1790 and retracting the revolutionary oath. As matters turned out, the majority of the constitutional bishops refused to make the retractions that Bonaparte's agent Bernier claimed to have obtained, and it was only in 1805 that they received their confirmation from Rome. Even then Pius was unable to obtain from the most tenacious a formal disavowal. For his part, Bonaparte, anxious for appeasement, made no demands on the bishops besides the acceptance of the Concordat, arguing that acceptance implied renunciation of the Civil Constitution. Meanwhile his government, motivated by the same principles of appeasement and amalgamation, insisted that the bishops reserve for constitutional priests some of the positions of canons, vicar-generals, pastors, and curates in their dioceses. The government also forbade the juring priests to make retractions. To Rome's great disappointment Caprara gave way on this last issue.

Moreover, at Bonaparte's urging, the Holy See was forced to regularize the condition of the hundreds of secular priests who had contracted marriages during the Revolution, many of whom had done so to escape persecution. In a brief, *Etsi apsostolici principatus*, issued to his representative Spina on 15 August 1801, Pius conferred the powers necessary to remove the censures incurred by these clerics and permitted Spina to delegate these powers to bishops and pastors. All priests who had been married before that date were laicized and made eligible to have their marital unions validated. In a later brief, *Inter plura illa mala*, the Pope also regulated the status of any religious, of either sex, who had married before 15 August 1801. Talleyrand, who since before the Revolution had been the bishop of Autun, originally had been responsible for the introduction into the draft of the Concordat this latter clause, known as "the clause of Madame Grand" from the name of the divorced Englishwoman whom he had married. But in that rather outstanding case, Pius granted only Talleyrand's request to be laicized, refusing to relieve him of his vow of chastity or authorize him to marry.

To Rome's displeasure, implementation of the articles dealing with seminaries was carried out so slowly that recruitment of priests in France was seriously impeded. This led to a shortage of priests, and existing clergy were initially in great need of resources. These conditions only changed after 1804, when Bonaparte provided for an annual remuneration of five hundred francs to twenty-three thousand priests, later extended to seven thousand more clerics in 1807. Meanwhile, the laws prohibiting religious orders, except those engaged in teaching, hospital work, and some missionary activity, remained.

Notably, there was no real mention in the Concordat itself of the religious orders. Since the Revolution they had been considered vestiges of the past that would expire naturally. Their return was never contemplated, so they were not forbidden. When, for instance, the Concordat was being written, the Jesuits were still suppressed, and no civil government expected or desired their restoration. Moreover, since the Revolution, the civil power had clearly intended that no form of monasticism should be restored in France. Accordingly, convents too had been dissolved, not only because they were considered decadent and useless and their revenues misused, but because the conventual state was considered a violation of rights enunciated in the *Declaration of the Rights of Man* and the principles of the Revolution.

But, after 1800, some argued that the first article of the Concordat, which grants liberty to the Catholic religion, carried with it of necessity a permission to take monastic vows. Although that may have been one of Consalvi's mental reservations during the negotiations, it was never stated in the final document. At any rate, Bonaparte did not want the orders back. He provided in the Concordat for bishops, curés, and vicars, but not for monks, and in the agreement he referred only to the secular and parochial clergy. There were, however, some exceptions. For various reasons he eventually authorized a few religious orders for men, one of them being the *Missions Étrangères*, which he favored for imperialistic purposes. The Christian Brothers and the Sulpician order were also admitted, but only as bodies of individual teachers under the Ministry of Education.

However, while these were the only male orders authorized by Bonaparte, he authorized more than two hundred "congregations," or communities of women, after he became Emperor. This was because he believed that religious orders for females also served useful social functions, especially in nursing, social work, and teaching. He even subsidized them, placing them under the protection of his mother, Madame Mere. Later, additional congregations were formed, but without legal recognition. In 1809, however, some of the orders for men had to have their recognition withdrawn because Bonaparte believed that they had come too much under the control of Rome.

But the religious orders were not the only example in which provisions of the Concordat were either deliberately misapplied or misinterpreted. Other minor instances arose because neither party really was fully satisfied with all the terms of the agreement, and it was for this reason that Bonaparte often found himself in direct conflict with Rome. At first, Bonaparte believed that he had broken clerical resistance when he replaced the First Estate of the old regime with a department of state with salaried officials, whose leaders he himself chose and who all swore personal allegiance to him. At that time, however, he failed to realize that by making the higher clergy dependent on the State he had not only weakened their position in relation to the papacy, but had impelled them inevitably towards Ultramontanism. Likewise, the lower clergy now became completely subject to and dependent on their bishops, with only a few having the security of tenure. Consequently, they came to regard their leaders to be members of the hierar-

chy, instead of officials of the government. Even the process of nominating bishops did not develop as Bonaparte had expected. The Pope,
not the emperor, became the real head of the episcopate and the real
administrator was not the Minister of Public Worship but the Papal
Nuncio. This all became quite clear when Pius VII refused to immediately institute the Emperor's episcopal nominees. As Article 5 of the
Concordat imposed no fixed time limit, and provided for no alternative
action, the Pope in this case did not actually violate the letter of the
treaty.

When Bonaparte realized that he had not gained complete control
over the papacy he resorted to force. In 1809 he occupied the Papal
States and had Pius taken prisoner, bringing him first to Savona in
northern Italy, and then to Paris. There, the pontiff and his staff were
installed in the palace of Fontainebleau and presented with new terms
by the Emperor who, at the same time, ordered an episcopal council to
be convened in conjunction with these negotiations. But when this
council proved to be too supportive of the papacy it was dissolved and
those bishops who had opposed the state's position were imprisoned.
The remaining bishops then reassembled and, citing ancient canons at
the Emperor's recommendation, soon proposed that no sees should be
left vacant for more than a year. Additionally, they proposed that the
Pope must institute a bishop within six months of nomination. If he refused, the metropolitan or the senior bishop of the province should act.
The council also agreed, however, not to promulgate these acts without
the current Pope's authority.

The proposal was submitted to Pius, who, under pressure from
Bonaparte, accepted it in a brief. The terms were then adopted as the
fourth article of what would come to be known as the "Concordat of
Fontainebleau." This short-lived treaty was signed by Pius and Bonaparte on 25 January 1813 but was repudiated by the pontiff a few weeks
later. The chief interest of this document, aside from Article 4, is that
it covered both France and the Kingdom of Italy. The only other article of importance was Article 9, which stated that the offices of the
Propaganda and the Penitentiary, as well as the papal archives, should
be established wherever the Pope might reside—which might not always be Rome. Bonaparte, of course, hoped to maintain the papacy

permanently in France where it would have been under his complete control. At any rate, this concordat came to an effective end with Bonaparte's final defeat, after which relations between France and the papacy again were regulated by the Concordat of 1801.

As mentioned, Bonaparte in that original treaty had, instead of reestablishing a Gallican Church under his direct control, inadvertently set up an organization that soon became dependent upon the Roman Curia. The Concordat gave the Pope a right of entry into France which he had never enjoyed before and gained for him a secure position from which he could dominate the French clergy and, to an extent, even influence other aspects of French affairs. It is not surprising that Bonaparte soon was to admit that "the greatest error" of his reign had been the Concordat.[17]

Rome, of course, did not see things in the same light, and from the onset had openly shown its displeasure with the document. In 1801, for instance, at a consistory in Rome, a report was presented that described the bishops who had been deposed by the terms of the Concordat as "true shepherds, exiled from their country . . . and separated from their flocks by the very sword of Peter." It went on to argue that the religious orders had been expelled and that chapters and seminaries were left without support while only "the phantom of religion" had been reestablished in France.[18] Clearly, to many in the Curia and the hierarchy, the Concordat initially offered very few actual advantages to the Church.

How can the immediate consequences of the Concordat be accurately assessed? For the Church, the treaty represented a mixed blessing. It demanded great financial sacrifices in terms of the Church's renunciation of all claims for the restitution of alienated ecclesiastical goods. Additionally, the Pope had made another temporal sacrifice when he did not seek to obtain the restoration of the legations—the areas of the Papal States that had been ceded by the Treaty of Tolentino. Avignon and Venaissin also remained in French possession. Great personal sacrifices had been demanded by the clause requiring

17. *Revue de l'histoire de l'Église de France*; see also Dansette, 125.
18. Ibid.

the resignation of the entire hierarchy, and it was certainly a concession for the Church to cede to Bonaparte the right to make episcopal nominations. Moreover, the Concordat did not recognize Catholicism as the state religion of France *de jure*, but only as the *de facto* religion of the majority of the French. And the Organic Articles, which Bonaparte had unilaterally added to the agreement, limited the Church even further.

To the Church's advantage, the Concordat did achieve the disavowal of the Civil Constitution of the Clergy, in effect since the Revolution, thereby ending a dangerous schism. In addition, the papal right to institute and depose bishops was officially recognized. And, of course, a government with its origins in the Revolution had finally agreed to recognize the authority of the Pope. It was a great advantage too for the Church in France to regain legal status, thus enabling it to undertake the religious regeneration of the country.

To Bonaparte the Concordat was the conspicuous achievement of his own policy. He often had stated, "the people need a religion; this religion must be in the hands of the government."[19] Moreover, he believed an agreement with the Pope would drive a wedge between the royalists and Catholicism, and would finally pacify the Vendée as well as reassuring the purchasers of the Church lands confiscated during the Revolution. Had a settlement been reached instead with the schismatic Constitutional Church, it would have brought none of these advantages. Only a comprehensive treaty with the Pope could have achieved all that Bonaparte wanted. As he pointed out, "fifty émigré bishops in English pay are the present leaders of the French clergy. Their influence must be destroyed and to do this I must have the authority of the Pope."[20] This objective in particular was achieved. As the reports of his prefects and police confirmed his view that the French peasantry was still obstinately attached to their churches and priests, there clearly were other tactical advantages in reaching a religious settlement.[21]

In defending his policies Bonaparte maintained his view that society

19. *Documents Diplomatiques Français*; see also Latreille, *Histoire du catholicisme en France*, 45.
20. Ibid.　　　　　　　　　　　　　　21. Ibid.

was basically "a code of morality" and that "a code of morality is unacceptable without religion."[22] He wanted a clergy that would preach resignation and serve as a moral police force on behalf of the state. To this end he planned the Concordat and, because he negotiated from a strong position, eventually got much of what he wanted. His aim, for example, regarding the bishops was to create a corps of "prefects in purple" who would aid in his purpose of social and political control. He had also forced the Pope to accept the inviolability of the rights of the new owners of ecclesiastical property that had been sold off during the Revolution. Yet at the same time he did not even have to agree that the state had any consequent obligation to pay the clergy, that arrangement being decided separately. These issues were crucial, as Bonaparte had to avoid any dispute over the ownership of what had been Church's vast holdings in France in order to maintain the support of an economically significant part of the French population. And in adding the Organic Articles he further increased his advantages. With these articles no papal or conciliar documents could be published in France without the prior permission of the state, nor could any assemblies of clergy be held without government permission. In fact, as a result of this clause no national French episcopal council was held for more than a century. The state gained further control over the institution of marriage through an article that made it illegal to have a religious wedding ceremony before the civil one, a statute still in effect today.

But, for all that was conceded by the Pope, and it was a great deal, considering especially the forced resignation of the French hierarchy and the lack of compensation for alienated properties, the Church did gain in particular areas which ultimately proved very significant. First, a dangerous schism was ended, and French Catholics now were free to practice their religion. Perhaps more important, however, because the status of the religious orders and congregations was not mentioned in the Concordat, they were able to return and even flourish. This eventually had tremendous consequences in terms of the revival of French Catholicism and the strengthening of the Church's position in that nation during the nineteenth century. In this sense, although it seemed

22. Ibid.

that the immediate advantages had been gained by Bonaparte, in the long run the Papacy gained more from the treaty.

Among those who immediately lost out as a result of the Concordat were those faithful and clergy who had been sympathetic to the Revolution. Because of the terms of the Concordat, the refractory clergy soon came to dominate the French Church, especially after the Bourbon Restoration in 1815. And even earlier, in 1801, a number of the newly appointed bishops could have been considered to be in that category as well as the large numbers of the lower clergy who were also *refractaires*. At the same time, members of the higher and lower clergy who had supported the Revolution were discredited. Led since 1790 by the Constitutional Bishop Henri Gregoire, they had always sought to be independent of Rome and favored various reforms, such as lay participation in synods, a vernacular liturgy, and a more tolerant attitude towards Protestants. Now, however, they were replaced by a clergy that sought to impose a Tridentine model of Catholicism, with greater allegiance to the papacy—in short, an incipiently ultramontane clergy. Gregoire, who earlier had been an active revolutionary as well as head of the Constitutional Church, preaching a synthesis of Christianity and the Revolution's ideals, was a staunch opponent of the Concordat. On one occasion he openly told Bonaparte that "all the reasons for acceptance, all the proofs you bring in favor of the Concordat, are precisely the same which we used to justify the acceptance of the Civil Constitution . . . You set Europe on fire, stirred up foreign and civil war, caused massacres and persecutions, only to do ten years later that which we did ten years earlier."[23]

Of course, a greater number of changes within the French Church took place after the Bourbon Restoration. This can readily be seen in the composition of the French episcopate. The bishops, who were the centerpieces of the concordatory Church, had to receive canonical institution from the Pope, but only, according to the treaty, after being nominated by the government. Bonaparte had personally chosen them all, to correspond to the dioceses he planned to reestablish, and their numbers included former bishops who had refused any oath to revolu-

23. Dansette, 145.

tionary regimes, former bishops of the constitutional Church who were included especially at the First Consul's insistence, and members of the lower clergy, only four of whom were former constitutionals.

In 1821, the restored Bourbon government added thirty extra dioceses, giving the new regime the opportunity to nominate a large number of clerics to the hierarchy. Every one of the new nominees came from the clergy of the pre-revolutionary regime. Most were quite elderly; all were counterrevolutionaries, with the majority coming from the nobility. In this sense the French episcopate after 1815 did not differ greatly from that of 1789, except that it contained none of the unbelievers or skeptics that typified the *ancien regime*. It was an important difference. The earlier French hierarchy, like the rest of the aristocracy of that previous age, was strongly influenced by the Enlightenment, and often questioned even the most basic tenets of their faith, as well as religious beliefs in general. Louis XVI, for instance when pressed to nominate a particularly worldly nobleman to the pre-Revolutionary episcopate, had remarked that "at least the Archbishop of Paris should believe in God,"—a fairly accurate comment on the cynicism of the French upper classes of that age.[24]

Because he was in many ways a prince of the *ancien regime* and still retained some of that skepticism, the restored monarch Louis XVIII would not be so acceptable to the zealous French clergy as was his pious brother, the Count of Artois, who eventually succeeded him as Charles X. Nonetheless, Louis XVIII began his reign by granting many concessions to the reactionary clergy and at his restoration gave a charter which proclaimed that "the Catholic, apostolic, and Roman religion is the religion of the State," although the freedom and protection of all forms of worship were also guaranteed.[25] Subsequently, due to clerical influence, restrictions began to appear. A member of the clergy, Abbé Pierre Montesquiou, became Minister of the Interior, and censorship of books and newspapers broadened. In terms of education, the University of France, established by Bonaparte, was dissolved and replaced by a Royal Commission, also headed by a bishop.

24. Ibid. 12.
25. Ibid. 156.

Louis, for his part, had wanted a new concordat and had tried privately to arrange it with Rome. A draft was even prepared. But, while a final document never materialized, several of the articles of that attempted agreement serve to illuminate the intentions of the French regime and the papacy at the time. In particular, these articles stated that the Concordat of 1516, between King Francis I and Pope Leo X, should be revived, superseding that of 1801, along with its Organic Articles. Suppressed dioceses were to be reestablished and added to the existing ones, and all dioceses, chapters, and seminaries were to be endowed with land or capital. The new sees were to be created by a special papal bull. Pius VII, however, withdrew his support for this proposed agreement because he could not accept certain restrictions that it contained regarding the preservation of the Gallican Liberties. He had of course fully realized that more was to be gained by upholding the original agreement made in 1801 with Bonaparte.

During the period of the Bourbon Restoration several developments occurred which demonstrate the further growth of both ecclesiastical and papal influence in France as well as a corresponding increase in ultramontane sentiments. In 1815 the government decreed that Sunday would again be a day of rest, to supersede the secular revolutionary day. Soon after the Chamber of Deputies asked the King to "fortify" religion in France by "a system of Christian and monarchical education" and at the same time removed divorce from the Civil Code. Meanwhile, in what constituted a blow to the Gallican tradition, five bishops of the dissenting "Petite Église" made their submission to Rome. During the same period Joseph de Maistre's influential *Du Pape*, written in support of the doctrine of papal infallibility and against Gallicanism was published. These ideas would soon be echoed in the writings of the Ultramontanist priest and thinker Félicité de Lamennais, who posited a French Catholicism free of the last vestiges of Gallicanism. In his works Lamennais compared even the Bourbons' legitimist position to what he termed the earlier "casesaropapism" of Bonaparte, as both regimes had been too supportive of an independent position for the French Church.

On another level, it was during the Restoration that Jean Vianney, the saintly Curé d'Ars, who became the example the Church officially held up to its pastors, began his career. This is noteworthy because it is indicative of the Catholic revival in France, which the Romantic movement also helped to encourage. It was a religious resurgence that was characterized particularly by the growth of new religious congregations and the extension of domestic "missions" throughout the nation. At the same time, apparently galvanized by the assassination of the reactionary Duke of Berry in 1820, there was also an intensification of extreme royalist and Catholic sentiments and activities. The Church used the occasion to increase its efforts against what it perceived as the growth of secularism in French society, and in education in particular.

When the king appointed a new government in 1821, the influence gained by the ultra-royalists, or "Ultras," and their militant branch, the "Chevaliers de la Foi," was readily apparent. Desiring to see an increased governmental role for the Church and its clergy, the Ultras put their support behind Louis XVIII's reactionary brother and heir, the Count of Artois. When Artois finally did succeed to the throne in 1825 as Charles X, France came closest to the theocratic structure that so many of the Ultramontanist clergy and laity ardently desired. The Law of Sacrilege, for example, which made profanation of the Host a capital offense, was passed, but could not be enforced, its only victim being, it was said, the regime. But the very fact that such a law could be instituted, along with other similar legislation, is itself indicative of how much influence the Church had gained only a few decades after the Revolution. Under Charles X the budget for the Ministry of Cults increased threefold, and ordinations to the priesthood were five times what they had been during the later years of the Empire. Regarding the status of the religious orders and congregations, the laws which previously had required administrative authorization for the establishment of houses of nuns were also removed. Generally, this period was one of wide political support for ecclesiastical authority and the increased role of Rome in national religious affairs.

Yet, a reaction among some of the Gallicans in both the hierarchy and lower clergy was also evident, aimed chiefly at the Jesuits, whose order had been restored in 1814 and who were considered to be the major proponents of Ultramontanism in France. However, it was only after the Revolution of 1830, when the new Orleanist government came to power, that a broader questioning of the status of the Catholic Church in France took place. Anticlericalism again was manifest and eventually reached the point where many clergy had to wear lay attire for their own protection. The new liberal government was strongly encouraged to follow a policy of separation of church and state and supported freedom of education, association, and the press. The Orleanist regime's 1831 Charter described Catholicism again as "the religion of the majority of the French" rather than "the state religion," and the Bonapartist ordinances against the religious orders were revived. Correspondingly, the Ministry of Cults' budget was decreased.

This situation was not to last. It has been said of the Revolution of 1830 that it sought to overturn the throne but "did not go on to smash the altar."[26] The entrenched Ultramontanist faction continued to flourish and soon even liberal Catholics would submit to its influence, accepting with little debate, for example, the terms of Pope Gregory XVI's encyclical of 1832, *Mirari vos*, which condemned the principle of separation of church and state. For its part, Rome, sensing a possible conciliatory trend, sought to develop friendly relations with the Orleanist regime. Later, in terms favorable to the government, the papacy, in 1845, even suppressed the Jesuits in France, prompting the grateful King Louis-Philippe to remark, "the Pope has pulled a thorn from my foot."[27] Meanwhile, the religious orders, despite the ordinances, again began to grow and extend their influence, especially in educational work. A mood of reaction set in, marked in 1833 by the Guizot Ministry's Education Law which stated that primary education was to include "moral and religious instruction" and permitted clerics to teach in state schools. This, however, did not go unchallenged and not surprisingly much of the ensuing debate between church and state in France would center on the Church's role in education. The stage for this quarrel had been set in 1806 with Bonaparte's establishment of the University of France, which gave the state a monopoly over public education. After this the French episcopate usually directed its polemics against the University and the public educational system in general.

26. *Documents Diplomatiques Français*; see also Dansette, vol. 2, 13.
27. Ibid.; see also Felicité de Lamennais, *Affaires de Rome* (Paris, 1836), 98.

Education was not the only area affected by the government's religious policy. During this same period, certain provisions of Bonaparte's Concordat also had a great impact on the status of the lower clergy. By the terms of the Concordat and the Organic Articles, the lower clergy of the second order—priests who were parish assistants—had been placed at extreme disadvantage. Because the Concordat allowed only one parish per canton, 90 percent of these priests could never rise beyond their station to become curés, or pastors. Instead, they had to remain assistants in auxiliary parishes where they lacked security, status, and, with the rise of the bourgeoisie, a certain degree of prestige. Among the peasants, too, the rural clergy often encountered either a growing indifference or an open hostility toward themselves and the Church's teachings. Thus, while the Concordat may have strengthened the position of the hierarchy and higher clergy, and especially those who were Ultramontanists, the lower clergy suffered the consequences of the treaty's parochial restrictions.

For the higher clergy, by contrast, the period encompassing the Second Republic and the Second Empire in many ways could be considered a golden age. In part this was because the Church fortuitously had accepted the Revolution of 1848 and the new provisional government which, in turn, cultivated a friendly policy toward the Church and the clergy. This government clearly acknowledged and accepted whatever influence the clergy still maintained over the electorate. In many districts, for instance, it was the curés who led their congregations to the polls, and the result was an Assembly that was quite respectful toward and even beholden to the Church.

The majority in this first Assembly of the Second Republic were not only Catholic, but (as was the case even among many of the liberals) usually ultramontane. In large part this was because the delegates had been influenced by the writings of such Ultramontanist figures as the noted journalist Charles Montalembert, the Minister of Education Frédéric Falloux, the respected Dominican preacher Abbé Lacordaire, and others who sought an accommodation with the Church. The government also concurred in this policy of accommodation, one result of which was the passage of the so-called "Falloux Law" which allowed the curés, along with the mayors, to supervise the schoolmasters of each commune. The law also allowed the Church to freely open its own schools and the bishops to sit on the governmental Council of Public Instruction.

The pope at the time, Pius IX (1846–1878), as well as the French hierarchy and most French Catholics, accepted the Bonapartist coup of 1851, which was ratified in a plebiscite held in December of that year. Louis-Napoleon, for his part, was well aware of this support and saw to it that further concessions were granted. By a decree of January 1852, congregations of nuns could be authorized by simple executive order while at the same time, the existing congregations of monks, although unauthorized, were allowed to multiply. Meanwhile French bishops were permitted to openly flout the provisions of the Organic Articles and travel into and out of France, usually to visit Rome, as they wished and without government permission. The Organic Articles themselves were in many ways at this point considered a dead letter and, in 1865, the Pope even issued a stinging rebuke to the Gallican Archbishop of Paris, who had defended them in the Senate.[28]

In discussing Church and State relations in France during this period it is also helpful to note briefly the role of the lay Catholic press. Most press activity centered on the figure of Louis Veuillot who, from the early 1840s until his death in 1883, was the editor and main force behind the newspaper *L'Univers*. Because of his strong polemical style and championship of Catholic causes, *L'Univers* became a major factor in the French Catholic world with the hierarchy taking Veuillot's influence quite seriously. He had a wide general audience, but most of his readership was the lower clergy, with whom he was especially popular. Although a number of the bishops were opposed to his extreme Ultramontanism and reactionary rhetoric, as well as to the fact that he was a layman, they were forced to acknowledge the effect he had in Church affairs. Veuillot, through his journal, played a paramount role in Ultramontanist politics, influencing even Rome's approach to the French Church and episcopate during the latter part of the century.

However, the power of the French bishops remained extensive, especially during the period of the Second Empire. One reason, of course,

28. McManners, 78.

was that through the Concordat the hierarchy had gained much control over the lower clergy, even more than was enjoyed by the bishops of the *ancien regime*. During the prerevolutionary era, a parish priest effectively owned his benefice and, once appointed, could not be removed except with great difficulty. Because of this tenure he had a true independence from episcopal authority. At that time, the bishops actually controlled only a few appointments to the benefices themselves. However, the loss of Church property during the Revolution meant that the benefices ceased to exist. Then, when the Concordat was enacted, it created a new system of appointment by declaring that the bishops would nominate the curés, choosing individuals first selected by the government. It was true, that once nominated and approved, the curés had security of tenure and could not be moved. But the Concordat in this case referred only to a very small number of priests, mainly those in the chief towns of each canton. Organic Article 31 made it clear that all other curés in ordinary parishes, known technically as *desservants*, could be removed by the bishop at will, giving the hierarchy extensive control.

Naturally, this new episcopal power did not go unchallenged. In the 1830's the lower clergy already had begun to view Rome as a counterforce to the growing authority of the bishops. At that time, the Pope, Gregory XVI (1831–1846), in reference to the French episcopate's claims, remarked that he "never realized that the French bishops were so many little popes!"[29] And in opposition to the bishops' authority, the lower clergy embraced even more fully the Ultramontanist position to the point that it eventually dominated their entire outlook. As this clergy came to see Rome as the true spiritual center of the Church, they in time also became fervent supporters of the doctrine of papal infallibility. Interestingly, one bishop who was a main opponent of that doctrine when it was promulgated in 1870 was Bishop Felix Dupanloup of Orleans, a prelate who had always tried to impose his authority over his diocese's clergy.

The papacy gave almost unqualified support to Napoleon III's re-

29. Norman Ravitch, *The Catholic Church and the French Nation* (London, 1991), 91.

gime until 1859, when the Emperor decided to back the cause of Italian unification. Up to that point the French hierarchy too had stood strongly behind the government, supporting, for example, its role in the Crimean conflict. Moreover, French clergy at all levels also had generally upheld the anti-republican sentiments of the Pope, a position welcomed by Napoleon III's regime. But, after siding with the Italian national cause, Napoleon III found himself in a much less favorable position vis-à-vis the Church. Then, late in 1859, he sponsored the publication of a pamphlet, *Le Pape et le Congres*, which clarified his position on Italy even further and in essence argued that Pius IX should give up his temporal claims. In rebuttal, Veuillot's ultramontanist *L'Univers* published the full text of the papal encyclical in which Pius had urged the bishops to press for the conservation of the Pope's temporal authority.[30]

Meanwhile the Church in France, and especially its Ultramontanist element, continued to flourish. Records show that in 1861 there were more than 17,000 monks and 89,000 nuns, an increase over the 3,100 and 34,200 recorded in 1851. Ordinations also increased, with the number of priests rising to 56,000 by the end of the decade.[31] At the same time the budget for the Ministry of Cults also increased substantially while, in what amounted to an anti-Gallican move, by 1864, under pressure from Rome, most French dioceses adopted the Roman liturgy over the various domestic rites that had been in frequent use since the Revolution. Additionally, a number of new French sees, including colonial ones, were created by the Pope.

Such facts, however, do not in themselves give the true picture of the Church's role in France in the latter decades of the century. Even before the Second Empire's demise in 1870 there were indications that both a general indifference to religion and a strong anti-clerical sentiment in certain sectors of the population were again on the rise. As the writer Anatole France once observed, "Catholicism was still the most acceptable form of religious indifference to the French."[32] Later, Georges Clemenceau noted similarly that "a combination of Catholic belief with

30. *Documents Diplomatiques Français*; see also McManners, 132.
31. Dansette, vol. 2, 89.   32. Ravitch, 134.

an anticlerical outlook" could serve as a fair description of the view-point of most of his countrymen.[33]

By the late 1870s the number of students in state primary schools had increased and there were indications that education would soon emerge as a major area of conflict issue between the French Church and State. Indeed, it led ultimately to a debate over the very existence of the Concordat itself.

Despite the facts that the first National Assembly of the new Third Republic, elected in 1871, had a Royalist majority and that several pieces of its initial legislation had been favorable to the Church, after the Republican legislative victories of 1876 both the Catholic Church in France and the supporters of the Concordat found themselves on the defensive. Even within the Church there was dissatisfaction with the Concordat, as the limitations it had imposed, especially at the local pastoral level, were, now presenting pastoral difficulties. These difficulties were due to the fact that during the latter part of the nineteenth century the population of the French working classes, mostly in the urban areas, had increased significantly. Accordingly, the average size of urban Catholic parishes rose and with it the need to establish new parishes and appoint additional pastors. But Article 62 of the *Organiques* stated that no new parish could be created in any French territory without the explicit authorization of the government, something the new regime was unwilling to do. In fact, even earlier governments that had been more favorable to the Church had been reluctant to create such new urban parishes, because doing so involved accepting responsibility for the upkeep of new buildings and the payment of additional clerical salaries. Hostile governments, of course, simply refused outright to authorize the new parishes. Thus, for example, while the population of Paris between 1877 and 1906 grew by nearly eight hundred thousand, only one new parish was established there during those years.[34] In most other French cities existing parishes also grew, and their pastors, too, could not care for their congregations, contributing to the fact that

33. Ibid.
34. *Revue de l'histoire de l'Église de France*; see also E. Lacanuet, *L'Église de France sous la Troisième République*, vol. 3 (Paris, 1930), 176.

many French workers in this period were not so much opposed to the Church as simply untouched by it.

In many other ways, too, the early decades of the Third Republic were marked by the growing division between church and state that in 1906 culminated in the unilateral abrogation of the Concordat of 1801. As previously noted, a frequent source of contention was education: who should control it and who should have access to it. After the Republicans gained full control of the government, this point was subsumed into the larger effort to curtail the Church's influence in all areas of French life. Of course, it was often argued that the government could unilaterally abrogate the Concordat at any point. But it was also clear that while the dissolution of the Concordat was an ultimate goal, many felt that for the time being the treaty should be maintained. "The Concordat is a treaty devised to limit the authority of the Church," wrote a French diplomat in 1881, and this was "essential since the Church obeys a foreign power."[35] Earlier, Leon Gambetta, as president of the, Assembly had noted that any major adjustment in the relations between Church and State would have to wait because of "the moral and social state of the country."[36] But one area where an assault on the Church's influence could, it seemed, acceptably take place was in the schools. Arguing against the large role played by the regular clergy—the monks and nuns—in educating French youth, Gambetta questioned their patriotism and declared them to be "a multicolored militia without a fatherland."[37]

At the same time there was also a growing sentiment outside of the government to remove, or at least limit, the Church's role in the educational process. Jean Mace's anticlerical *Ligue de l'Enseignement*, founded in 1866 and devoted to the development of a pedagogical system based on a positivistic model, was perhaps the most outstanding example of this. In particular, he proposed a secular, republican alternative to the moral and religious instruction then presented in French schools by the clergy. Mace and his "Ligue" had great influence on the formulation of what was to be the most important and far-reaching political attempt

35. Ravitch, 91.   36. Ibid., p. 89.
37. Ibid.

to implement its concepts, the Education Law, put forth by the Minister of Public Instruction, Jules Ferry, in 1879. This law had two objectives: to remove the clergy from influential positions in state education and to weaken the system of private education controlled by the Church. Particularly noteworthy was Article 7 of the law, forbidding members of non-authorized congregations to teach. Its main target was the Jesuits. However, while Ferry's legislation was passed in its entirety by the Chamber, the more conservative Senate struck out that particular article. In response, the Government insisted that all non-authorized congregations had to apply for recognition, except the Jesuits, who were to be completely disbanded. Most of the non-authorized congregations, including the Jesuits, ignored that order and remained in the country, leaving the government with the odious task of evicting them. Public opinion was with the congregations, at least in terms of their maintaining their residences. As a consequence, many stayed, and when the furor died down, it was clear that Ferry's law actually had done very little to reduce the Church's role in education. Only much later would Ferry's real aim, the laying of a foundation for a broader educational system — one of "free, obligatory, and lay education" — be realized in France.

While the French government was coming increasingly under anticlerical control, the Cardinal-bishop of Perugia, Italy, Gioacchino Pecci, at the conclave of 1878, was elected as Pope Leo XIII. Of very different temperament from his predecessor, the new pontiff was eager from the onset to reduce the conflict with the French state, and he at once actively sought some means of a possible reconciliation. Meanwhile the policy of secularization continued in France. After 1881, further anticlerical legislation was introduced, and laws were passed that successfully excluded all monks and nuns from teaching in state schools. In the same vein, prayers and crucifixes in public schools were abolished and other laws were amended to allow work on Sundays, to discontinue army and hospital chaplains' posts, and to give mayors of communes control over religious celebrations in their towns. Public prayers at the opening of parliamentary sessions were abandoned and in 1884 divorce was reinstated in the civil code. The trend towards secularization decreased only slightly after the 1885 elections when a substantial Catholic and conservative bloc was returned to Parliament, raising both Catholic and monarchist hopes.

But the prospect of a restored Catholic monarchy in France at this point was unlikely. Aware of that fact, Pope Leo, who in 1889 still had legitimate concerns over the future of the French Church, initiated what came to be known as the *Ralliement*, an appeal to French Catholics to accept and rally to their republican government. The pontiff's hope was that in abandoning the monarchist cause a full rapprochement between Rome and the Third Republic could be achieved. There were of course various other motives behind the Pope's search for accommodation with the French Government. The mutual and growing hostility between the newly unified Kingdom of Italy and the Vatican was then a serious issue, and the support that Germany and Austria-Hungary extended to the Italian government placed the Papacy in a weak diplomatic position. Any improvement in relations with France therefore was seen by Leo as a possible way out of this dilemma. In many ways, Leo XIII was a contrast to his predecessor, Pius IX, who during his long reign had often anathematized the ideas of "modern civilization," including secularism and republicanism. Instead, Leo, who himself was eighty years of age when he initiated his policy of rapprochement with the secular French regime, took another view and sought to patiently move forward his diplomatic efforts, attempting to initiate changes that even Pius, in his later years, had conceded might one day be necessary.

Of course, within the French Church there were also a number of bishops who, for their own reasons, now wanted to come to terms with the Republic. Some of them had in fact come to regard democracy as a truly Christian concept, while others sought a compromise merely out of a sense of expediency. With the Pope, they shared a common sense of political realism and believed that the future of the French Church depended on some form of accommodation with the government.

To begin negotiations with the French government, Leo chose the determined and astute Cardinal Charles Lavigerie of Algiers, a prelate who was to soon become closely identified with the *Ralliement*. Lavigerie worked diligently towards that goal and his diplomatic efforts, publicly and behind the scenes, culminated ultimately in his famous "toast of Algiers," given in October 1890 at a dinner in honor of the

French Mediterranean fleet. In that toast the cardinal proposed that "to rescue the country from disaster," there must be "unqualified adherence" to any established form of government which "was in itself no way contrary to the principles which are necessary to the life of civilized and Christian nations." He ended by declaring moreover, that he was certain that he "would not be disowned by any authorized voice."[38] The speech produced an uproar in France, with the Royalists in particular believing that they had been abandoned by the Church. But Lavigerie was not disowned by any authority and in May 1892 the Pope, who had already been privately informing various individuals of his intentions regarding the French government, finally came out publicly in an interview with a French journalist about his *Ralliement* policy. On that occasion he stated that in his view the only legitimate government in France was the one that the nation had chosen for itself; in this case a republican one.[39] It was a diplomatic move that might have tempted the French Royalists and others who felt abandoned by the Church to agree with a remark made long after by a twentieth-century Roman prelate that "Vatican diplomacy really began with Peter's denial of Christ."[40] In reality, however, what had probably seemed to many to be an insincere or even immoral act of diplomacy based merely on *raison d'état*, was in fact the working out of Leo's deeply held commitment to the earlier Catholic goal of re-Christianizing French society and restoring the Church to its traditional role.

In practice the *Ralliement* meant different things to different individuals, and in time many came to see the Pope's position as only applicable in a general sense, leaving the door open for more conservative interpretations. Later it actually became clear, as in the important election results of 1898, that the *Ralliement* had not significantly affected the political balance, a fact underscored by another event of that year, the publication of Emile Zola's *J'accuse*, which broke the infamous Dreyfus case. It was in fact that case that ultimately demonstrated the impossibility of any real reconciliation between French Catholics and republicans, at least in terms of the preservation of the Concordat and the Church's unique status in France.

38. *Documents Diplomatiques Français*; see also McManners, 72.
39. Ibid., 80.   40. Ibid., 93.

Certainly, the Dreyfus affair and its aftermath was a watershed in the development of church and state relations in France. Just as the Dreyfus issue, at every level, divided the nation, so too it was a unifying point for diverse anticlerical factions within the government. Up to this point, Rome's *Ralliement* policy seemed to have at least been successful in making Catholicism politically respectable in France. Because of this, the bourgeoisie, moderate Republicans, and anticlericals generally had been able, in many ways, to cooperate and avoid any alliance with the extreme Left. But, during the course of the Dreyfus affair, when the Church in the eyes of many was greatly discredited, the French Catholic *rallies* became superfluous in any political alliance. It was possible now to form a coalition of all defenders of republicanism without them and on the basis of anticlericalism alone. In particular, the Socialists were no longer considered dangerous and became allies in a new national cause. Stated another way, to many French it had been the anticlericals, especially of the Left, and not the churchmen, who would finally rescue an innocent man from Devil's Island while on the other hand it was the Catholics, and especially the Church establishment, that had chosen to put expediency above truth and security above justice. Naturally this was an oversimplification, as Catholics too had taken the side of Dreyfus, with even the Pope indicating at various times that he believed in the French officer's innocence. But the press did not report much of this and instead usually wrote of what also in fact seemed to be true, that for every case of Catholic support for Dreyfus, there were many more examples of extreme anti-Dreyfusard and anti-Semitic Catholic statements and acts. Among such things it was reported that more than three hundred Catholic priests had subscribed to the memorial for Colonel Hubert Henry, the army officer who had forged the documents on which Dreyfus had originally been convicted, that a Jesuit journal in Rome had described the Jews as "eternal traitors," and that the French Assumptionist order's paper *La Croix* had stated that the Church's position should not be whether Dreyfus was innocent or guilty, but rather "who will win, the enemies of the army or its friends."[41]

After Dreyfus's second trial in 1899, when he was again found guilty

41. Lecanuet, 200.

of treason, this time "with extenuating circumstances," the outcry for justice as well as an explanation and revenge was overwhelming. The religious congregations, the objects of this revenge, were already pre-destined to be victims. Their teaching role had long been the subject of republican dissatisfaction and now, significantly, other grievances had accumulated against them. The Jesuits especially, with their high military connections, as well as the Assumptionists and Dominicans who had defended the army and had unleashed rabid anti-Semitic and anti-republican rhetoric, proved to be particularly convenient targets.

The French government responded accordingly with an onslaught against the religious orders, led by the Republican minister René Waldeck-Rousseau. To Waldeck-Rousseau, such an attack on the congregations was still within the spirit of Bonaparte's Concordat because in that treaty no provisions had been made for the regular clergy. He considered them to have no roots in secular society and to be a subversive element which looked to Rome, not Paris, for leadership, thereby constituting a menace to the Republic. Waldeck-Rousseau's legislation against the orders was expressed in the Law of 1 July 1901. It stipulated that existing religious corporations, including male and female congregations, had to apply to the government for authorization. If such authorization was refused, their corporate properties were to be auctioned off and their members dispersed.

But early in 1902, while the exact methods of application of that law were being considered, the results of the national elections came in, providing a further and more crucial test for church-state relations. The new prime minister chosen in that election was Emile Combes. A strong anticlerical, Combes was also a convinced positivist and deist and a determined opponent of the Catholic Church. His first task was to put into effect Waldeck-Rousseau's law on the religious congregations. Accordingly, the orders, including the teaching ones, were all immediately dispersed and their schools closed.

Combes went even further. While Waldeck-Rousseau had hoped to maintain good relations with the hierarchy and secular clergy, the new prime minister, preferring to be provocative, froze the salaries of some bishops who had protested the law. In the same spirit he also demanded that the traditionally religious French navy be purged of its Catholic practices. Moreoever, Combes did not even pretend to keep up conciliatory talks with the Vatican while all of this was happening, something other anticlerical governments had usually done. In fact, late in 1902, he deliberately sought a direct confrontation with Rome over the most important of the church-state issues, the right of the French government to nominate bishops. When, in that year, the Pope had refused to accept three candidates sent by Combe's government, the matter was put to the French Chamber as possible grounds for the cancellation of the Concordat and a complete separation of church and state. However, just as this quarrel was taking place Leo XIII died and was succeeded as pontiff by the Patriarch of Venice, Cardinal Giuseppe Sarto, who took the name Pius X. Lacking much of the diplomatic and political experience of his predecessor, the new Pope, who was regarded even during his lifetime as a saint, had chosen as Papal Secretary of State the relatively young Cardinal Merry del Val, son of a Spanish aristocrat and diplomat, who directly challenged the French anticlerical regime.

Previously, other French leaders, including Combes' predecessors in the Third Republic, had usually been able to avoid a controversy over the potentially crucial question of episcopal nominations. Naturally, each government always sought nominees whom it believed would be supportive of its policies, while being aware that this was not always possible. In fact, many candidates, who initially seemed sympathetic to the government, once installed became extreme Ultramontanes. They had been able to conceal their real opinions, something that often was difficult for the government to predict beforehand, until their appointments were secure. As Aristide Briand only half-humorously remarked, "a Minister of Religious Affairs is like a hen sitting on ducks' eggs."[42] Nonetheless, it had become part of the unwritten code of Concordat relations that the French government tried to avoid controversy over such nominations. This was what made the Concordat workable. But after 1902, when the nomination of bishops became a take-it-or-leave-it matter, subject to publicity and public opinion, the system was doomed to break down.

When Combes initiated his hard-line policy, Pius X at first demon-

42. *Journal Officiel de la République Française*; see also McManners, 97.

strated a willingness to be conciliatory. At this point, however, another controversy arose, further complicating the situation. It was not over the issue of new appointments, but over that of undoing established ones. Rome wanted to dismiss two bishops, one a Monsignor Geay of Laval, who had been accused of immorality for having carried on a sentimental correspondence with the superior of a nunnery, and the other a Monsignor Le Nordez of Dijon, who was supposed to have consorted with Freemasons. It should be noted that both were Republican bishops presiding over ultra-royalist sees. In June 1904 they were summoned to Rome and ordered to resign. But, according to the Organic Articles, it was illegal to obey a Roman summons without government permission. Combes responded to the papacy's action by refusing to accept the bishops' resignations, and froze their salaries for leaving France without permission.

Tension between Paris and Rome began to rise steadily. Earlier disputes that had taken place over education, the religious orders, the issue of expelling clergy, and finally the impasse over episcopal nominations, all weakened an arrangement that had existed for a century. The question of the bishops only further exacerbated the situation. But the final blow was actually to be struck over a different matter, one regarding the papacy's status within the newly formed Italian state—the so called "Roman Question."

Briefly, the dispute arose over a courtesy visit made in April 1904 by the French President Loubet to the Italian King in Rome. On that occasion, a state visit to the Pope that Loubet was to have made on the same trip was at the last minute cancelled by Paris, ostensibly over technicalities. In response, the Papal Secretary of State, Merry del Val, drafted a protest which he leaked to the press. This protest, couched in rather insulting tones, implied that, among other things, the Papal Nuncio, or representative, had been instructed by the Vatican to stay in Paris only because the imminent fall of Combes's government was expected. When this was published in *Le Figaro* and other leading French newspapers, there was an immediate and universal outcry in France. Paris recalled its ambassador from the Vatican and suspended relations. Loyal French Catholics, who before had so desperately fought for the schools and for the congregations, now found themselves effectively silenced, while anticlericals openly demanded a complete revision of church-state relations. The very existence of the Concordat was in jeopardy.

But while the anticlericals, in theory, had always sought the eventual abrogation of the Concordat and a complete separation of Church and State, in reality, at least up to the Combes period, little had actually been done to achieve those objectives. One reason for this was the lack of consensus on precisely how this was to be achieved. Precedents in other countries were confusing and contradictory, and many French still agreed with Bonaparte's original contention that the Concordat was the surest way to avoid the encroachments of the Church. Now, however, things were different. Already in 1902 a commission had been set up to examine "all propositions relating to the separation of the Churches and the State, and for the denunciation of the Concordat."[43] Although in 1902 the issue had not been seen as urgent, by 1904 it had become so. As the socialist leader Jean Jaurès announced in the Chamber late that year, it was time "for this great but obsessive problem of the relations of Church and State to be finally settled."[44]

For its part, the French Church was at this time almost completely opposed to the abrogation of the treaty. From the point of view of most of the French hierarchy and clergy any possible advantages that were inherent in freedom from state control were not readily apparent. In fact, in an inquiry made in 1903, only one bishop and a few of the lower clergy, like the progressive Abbé Jules Lemire, an activist and social reformer who also sat in the Chamber of Deputies, clearly favored separation. Meanwhile, the official policy of Rome was to maintain the Concordat at all costs.

In January 1905, while the matter was still being hotly debated, the Combes government fell, having lost public confidence over an issue of favoritism in the military. The end of that government actually made little difference in the progress towards separation which, by now, was considered inevitable. In February, the Minister of Education and Religious Affairs produced an outline for a Law of Separation (the "Law")

43. Lecanuet, 210.
44. Ibid., 211.

that was approved by the Commission. In July, the Commission's proposals were brought to the Chamber by Briand, the president of the Council, and, by a vote of 314 to 233, were approved. Its provisions offered advantages to both sides. At its heart, the proposal proclaimed liberty of conscience and guaranteed the free exercise of all religions, subject only to those regulations deemed necessary for public order. It clearly stated that the Republic neither recognized, nor salaried, nor subsidized any religion. The *budgets des cultes* of the state, the departments, and the communes were to be suppressed, and an official inventory of all Church property was to be taken. The proposal then provided that Church buildings and property (within certain limits that had evolved since the Concordat) were to be taken over by the state. Furthermore, new religious associations, to be known as *associations cultuelles*, and conforming to the "rules of the general organization of the religion whose exercise they propose to ensure" (an important qualifying clause), were to be established and given control of all church buildings and, for a limited time, the seminaries as well. In the interests of the Church, however, ownership of Church property was made contingent on communion with Rome, thereby discouraging schisms. Some other privileges remained, such as the exemption of seminarists from military service, and bishops were now free to come into and go out of the country as they wished. An equitable system of pensions for the clergy was to be provided, and salaries for the pastors of small parishes were to continue for eight more years. The Law was accepted in the Senate in December and, in a year's time, the Law of Separation officially came into effect. As in 1790, the French Parliament had legislated on ecclesiastical matters without consulting the Church. What remained to be seen was the response from the other side.

It had been the intention of the French government to avoid as much open conflict with the Church as possible. During the discussions for the Law, Clemenceau, when sarcastically asked, "is the road to Canossa beautiful?," replied, "I don't know: Briand takes us there in a closed carriage."[45] And clearly, it had been Briand's desire to have the Law passed without the process becoming itself an affirmation of

45. *Journal Officiel de la République Française*; see also Ravitch, 78.

French anticlericalism. In terms of the Law's provisions, nowhere could that issue have been more acute than in Article 4, dealing with the *associations cultuelles*. The choice of words had been unfortunate as *cultuelles* suggested control over the divine services. The term *ecclesiales*, suggested instead, probably would have been better. At any rate, to many, especially on the Left, these *associations* were seen as committees of laymen who, in the old Gallican tradition, would back the parishioners against the curés, the curés against the bishops, and the bishops against the Pope. To the Church, on the other hand, the associations were perceived as an invitation to schism, which made them a stumbling block in the acceptance of the Law. The "essential vice" of the *associations*, wrote the bishops to the President of the Republic in March 1905, "is to create and to impose upon the Catholic Church a purely lay institution."[46]

Fortunately, Briand had both the common sense and the sense of justice to see that the Law of Separation was kept a completely honest document. This was especially important because if it had been completely rejected by the Church the nation could have found itself in a state of undeclared civil war. Even so, the widely divergent opinions within the Chamber on this matter ranged from extreme anticlericalism on the Left to more moderate positions on the Right. Finally, however, even in the case of such controversial sections as Article 4, consensus was achieved and most articles were passed with a large majority.

The Law's opponents were a more homogeneous group than its supporters and included in particular the Catholic press and members of the previously disbanded religious orders. One major reason for opposition to the Law was the manner in which it had been unilaterally imposed. The government had claimed that it was merely abrogating the Law of 18 Germinal Year X, which had originally made the Concordat operative. In fact, as there was no stipulation in the treaty regarding its duration or termination, a unilateral declaration could be considered legitimate. Debate also arose concerning clerical salaries and the status of Church property acquired since the Concordat. These questions were important because the *budget des cultes* had originally been established

46. Ibid.

in the Concordat to compensate for ecclesiastical lands confiscated during the Revolution.

For this reason some serious problems arose regarding interpretations of the "inventories"—the required counting and assessing of Church properties and goods by an ad hoc agency known as the *Direction generale de l'Enregistrement*. During the taking of these inventories so much violence and rioting occurred in certain areas of the countryside and in some urban parishes that the government was, as a consequence, forced to resign. Then, in the new administration, Minister of the Interior Clemenceau decided to pursue a more conciliatory tone. Although previously he had counseled against such a position, Clemenceau now declared that "the counting of candelabra is not worth a single human life."[47] To a large extent, his view reflected the tone of the debates then going on in the Chamber over just how the new law should be applied.

In February 1906 the Church finally gave its official response to the Law. Pius X issued the encyclical *Vehementor nos*, in which he condemned the unilateral separation, arguing that the Law in particular had disregarded the essentially hierarchial nature of the Church. A few days later he consecrated fourteen new French bishops in defiance of the government and used the occasion to reiterate another major objection to the law, that it encouraged schism. But in reality, it seems that at this point Rome actually was prepared to accept the legislation as a foregone conclusion and instead was now concerned with keeping it confined to its stated limits and intentions. "We do not want any new Organic Articles," Pius stated in a private interview.[48]

Meanwhile, the French hierarchy was seeking a way in which the Law could be accepted and implemented with as little loss and disruption as possible. In May 1906, the bishops met in a plenary assembly and, while condemning the principle of the Law, at the same time approved a strategy of finding some *modus vivendi*. They also put forth a proposal to suggest the substitution of new parish councils, to be known as *associations canoniques*, for the *associations cultuelles*, which had

47. *Journal Officiel de la République Française*; see also McManners, 97.
48. Ravitch, 98.

been particularly objectionable because they invited lay control. The bishops then established a commission to administer these matters during the period between the plenary meetings. All the proceedings at the assembly were kept confidential, with only Rome being informed of what transpired. It was now up to the Pope to decide on the bishops' proposals.

The papal decision was made public in August in the encyclical *Gravissimo officii*, in which, to the bishops' consternation, Pius ruled out any of the compromises that they had suggested. All that could be done now on their part was to issue a statement in accord with the encyclical while attempting to care for their Church's immediate financial needs. This would eventually be done by imposing a levy, the *denier du culte*, on the faithful. The French government's response to the papacy's rejection of the Law was to initiate a strategy of wavering between conciliation and harshness. Briand, for example, proposed a one-year grace period for the Law, delaying its effective date until December 1907. But in January of that year, Clemenceau intervened with a harsher policy that pushed forward the evacuation of seminaries and episcopal palaces and the takeover of local edifices and presbyteries. However, in that case too, the possibility of a compromise was also built into the ruling. Exemptions could be made for properties to be used by the *associations cultuelles* or any other such association to be subsequently chartered. Thus, although Rome remained intransigent, the provisions of the Law of Separation were implemented, ending the existence of the century-old Concordat. After 1907 the treaty remained in effect only in the provinces of Alsace and Lorraine, which had been annexed years earlier by Germany.

When the Concordat had originally been arranged none of the chief negotiators, including Bonaparte, could foresee that the agreements that had been made would later serve as a model for treaties defining church-state relations all over Europe and comprise a type of charter to which both secular rulers and Popes would often appeal. For more than a century it remained in place to govern church-state relations through several regimes and papacies. It stands significantly as a hallmark in the evolution of the modern papacy's civil relations, and was a model for a number of subsequent treaties between the Church and other nations. These included concordats signed with Bavaria (1817), Prussia (1821), Switzerland (1845), and Spain (1851). An important concordat was signed with Emperor Francis Joseph of Austria in 1855, and in 1866 another was negotiated with Portugal. After the First World War the Concordat of 1801 would continue to serve as an example for other such treaties, including the concordats signed with Colombia (1918), Bavaria (1929), Czechslovakia (1927) and, of course, with Italy (1929) and Germany (1933).

Perhaps the other real significance of the Concordat of 1801 was in its actual interpretation and application. Until at least the mid-nineteenth century, implementation of the treaty usually had been under the direction of Gallicans who believed that the government's ministry for religious affairs, first set up by Bonaparte, was the successor to the old monarchy. They believed that it had the purpose of controlling the Church in France and, in that regard, saw no break in the continuity between 1682, when the Gallican Articles had been issued, and the treaty of 1801. In this sense Bonaparte's actions were seen as merely a reaffirmation of the Gallican tradition rather than the beginning of a new era in French church-state relations. But as it turned out, the Concordat instead would serve to greatly strengthen the Ultramontanist position and further extend papal control over the French Church.

At another level, it can also be asked, "What effect did the abrogation of the Concordat have on the French Church and on the lives of French Catholics?" Some, like the reformist Abbé Lemire, had hoped that the end of the Concordat would signal the beginning of a reaching-out by the Church to the people, with the clergy no longer being merely agents or functionaries of the state—Bonaparte's "prefects in purple." The Church for the first time would be free and, in time, various social movements within French Catholicism would arise in response to new conditions and needs. In practice, services continued to be held uninterruptedly in the churches, and later, laws were even passed permitting priests to effectively hold title to, and reside in, their rectories. On the other hand, of course, clerical salaries had been completely abolished and, with less prestige now attached to the priestly office, ordinations correspondingly declined while church attendance also continued to drop.

For its part, the French hierarchy now closed ranks and stood even more solidly behind the Pope. An indication of this, and of how Gallicanism had almost fully given way to an Ultramontanist spirit, was perhaps best shown in the French episcopate's nearly unanimous support for Pius X's condemnation of Modernism in 1907. Something of an anti-intellectual mood had developed within the French Church, with the hierarchy finding itself in opposition to any vigorous theological and biblical research or scholarship, although there was a renewal of traditional Catholic literature and writing. And while reforming movements too, such as Le Sillon, were condemned, various other organizations, usually social in nature and inspired by the separation between church and state, were allowed and even encouraged to develop. These included consumers' leagues and clubs for youths, women and veterans. During this period the Catholic trade union movement also grew. However, it is still difficult, in light of these somewhat contradictory elements, to conclude that the aforementioned hopes of such reformers as the Abbé Lemire would be realized. There often remained a certain fear of democracy and a hesitation to support centrist or *popolari*-type factions in France, as is demonstrated by the fact that no specifically Catholic center party ever really developed there. All of this, of course, was to change or come to an end in 1914. With the war, the interests of French society would be redirected and French nationalists and Royalists, Radicals, Republicans and socialists, clericals and anticlericals—in effect everyone—would temporarily forget their differences and join in a *union sacrée* in defense of their homeland. Then, after the war the French Church itself would enter a new era, one characterized by very different issues and ideas regarding church-state relations and ecclesiastical and parochial life.

Mussolini and the Concordat of 1929

FRANK J. COPPA, *St. John's University*

Pius XI (1922–1939) has been described as the pope of the missions, of social and catholic action, of technological innovation and modern mass communications, of concordats and of reconciliation. This Pope, like his immediate predecessors, appreciated the advantages of adjusting the Church's relations with the civil authorities by means of concordats in which the Church surrendered incidentals to preserve essentials. Approval of such agreements represented a compromise on the part of the Church with governments that did not fully recognize its claim to independence. Pius VII (1800–1823), in concluding a concordat with Napoleon, followed Rome's policy of dealing with *de facto* governments without presuming to judge their moral worth.[1] From the fall of Napoleon's empire to the proclamation of Italian unity in 1861, the Church signed some thirty such accords. While Leo XIII (1878–1903) and Pius X (1903–1914) initiated only a few, Pius XI concluded ten from 1922 to 1939, in addition to entering working arrangements with Portugal and Czechoslovakia. Convinced that such agreements

---

1. P. Ferraris, S. J., "Il concordato francese e Il Cardinale Fesch," *Civiltà Cattolica,* anno 87 1 (1936): 497.

h, Pius XI negotiated them with fascist, socialist, and
nes.

distrustful of party politics outside Vatican control and
us XI sought nonpolitical means of safeguarding the
ests. Fearing the vagaries of partisan politics, he preferred
treaties drarted in the form of concordats. Through them Rome sought
to guarantee the life of ecclesiastical organizations in various countries
by making concessions that did not undermine the spiritual functions
of the Church. In these accords the Vatican sought recognition of a
group of Catholic organizations collectively known as Catholic Action,
legal status for church marriages, and the exclusive right to appoint
bishops without any *placet* (consent) from the various signatory governments. For many of the post-World War I regimes, these agreements assured recognition of the government by the Church while
depriving their Catholic citizens of cause for complaint. Often the Vatican attained accommodation and understanding more quickly with
authoritarian regimes, as they were not burdened with the political diversity and anticlericalism that characterized some of the democratic
states. The rapprochement with the Italian regime concretized by Pius
XI in the Lateran Accords, which ended the Roman Question—the
refusal of the papacy to recognize the loss of Rome—was one of the
most significant agreements concluded by the Holy See. Contemporaries quickly perceived it as a historic settlement, and one which paved
the way for the Vatican's 1933 agreement with Nazi Germany. Consequently it warrants consideration.

Motivation for the Lateran Accords, the broader settlement that included the Italian concordat, remains murky, with some charging that
the Concordat of 1929 was an opportunistic maneuver and clerical
intrigue that swept away the whole inheritance of the liberal *Risorgimento*. Fifty years after the fall of Mussolini the entire church-state relationship during the fascist decades remains controversial. Generalizations abound, influenced by political preoccupations and ideological
considerations, with some charging that Catholics were temperamen-
tally authoritarian and found within Fascism a reflection of their ideal
society. Observing that the concept of *Roma caput mundi* was shared by
Pope and Duce alike, and that the nomenclature of Fascism proved no

less Roman than that of the Church, critics deplored, though claimed to understand, the alliance between the Pope, who was infallible, and the Duce, who was always right. Others ridiculed talk of an alleged alliance, perceiving the agreement as nothing more than a truce or "marriage of convenience" that would ultimately end in divorce. Still others denied even this minimal complicity, insisting that from the first, believers preserved serious reservations about the Fascist regime, with few practicing Catholics holding positions of power in the Fascist Party.[2] Given the excesses of the polemical literature and the continuing controversy, a historical assessment is in order.

Relations between Italy and the Vatican had been strained since the *Risorgimento*, during which the Kingdom of Italy had absorbed the Papal States, and the seizure of Rome in 1870 deprived the Vatican of its remaining territory. Pius IX refused to recognize the loss of his state, proclaiming himself a "prisoner" in the Vatican, and his successors followed suit during the next six decades. From their self-imposed "incarceration" they decried the spoilation, calling for the political independence of the papacy and some financial indemnification, while recognizing that a complete restoration of the Papal States was neither possible nor desirable. Over the years Pius IX (1846–1878), Leo XIII (1878–1903), Pius X (1903–1914), Benedict XV (1914–1922), and Pius XI (1922–1939) all rejected the Law of Papal Guarantees of 1871 as inadequate, citing its failure to provide even the most minimal assurances. In their view this Italian law made the papacy dependent on the crown and its ministers and exposed the Church to the will and whim of political action. During World War I, relations did not improve, as Italians resented the alleged pro-Austrian position of the papacy and dubbed Benedict XV (Benedetto XV), who succeeded Pius X in 1914, "Maledetto XV".[3] Sidney Sonnino, the anticlerical Italian foreign min-

2. D.A. Binchey, *Church and State in Fascist Italy* (New York: Oxford University Press, 1941), 85–86; Anthony Rhodes, *The Vatican in the Age of Dictators, 1922–1945*, (New York: Holt, Rinehart and Winston, 1973), 266; John P. McKnight, *The Papacy: A New Appraisal* (London: McGraw Hill, 1953), 141; Giuseppe Dalla Torre, *Azione cattolica e fascismo* (Rome: 1945), 7.

3. J. Derek Holmes, *The Papacy in the Modern World, 1914–1978* (NY: Crossroad Publishing Co., 1981), 3.

ister, was responsible for Article XV of the Treaty of London, which excluded papal participation in the Versailles Peace Conference. The alleged wartime espionage activity of Monsignor Rudolf Gerlach, secret chamberlain to Benedict XV, who from his sanctuary in the Vatican promoted the cause of the Central Powers, angered Italians, and reinforced the anticlericalism of Italy's ministers.

Other difficulties surfaced between Italy and the Vatican during the war, as the Vatican refused to censor the communications of representatives to the Holy See whose countries found themselves at war with Italy. Rumors of Vatican complicity with the Central Powers were rife in Italy, and word soon spread that the Pope had made arrangements to have his states returned should the Allies lose the war. Cardinal Pietro Gasparri, perturbed by these stories, granted a series of interviews to let it be known that such speculation had no foundation, and that the Holy Father sought a solution to the Roman Question not from foreign armies but from an Italian sense of justice. The Holy See revealed its goodwill toward the Italians by protesting the Austrian bombardment of Ravenna and Venice, criticizing the attacks upon these open and undefended cities and their hapless populations.

On the other hand, Pope Benedict was incensed by the Italian seizure of the Palazzo Venezia, the seat of the Austrian embassy to the Holy See, in the summer of 1916. In his letter of protest to the Italian diplomatic representatives attached to the Holy See, Cardinal Gasparri charged that the seizure underscored the vulnerable position of the Holy See under the prevailing conditions, demonstrating that the Law of Guarantees failed to protect the rights of the Universal Church and the Holy See. Likewise the Pope and his secretary of state were disappointed by the Italian response to Benedict's peace note of 1 August 1917, with the Vatican denying that its proposals were "entirely impractical" or that it was inspired by Austria and Germany. Indeed, the Pope sought to have the bishops of Italy explain to their flocks the real motivation for the Holy See's peace efforts.[4]

4. Harry C. Koenig, ed., *Principles for Peace: Selections from Papal Documents from Leo XIII to Pius XII* (Washington, DC: National Catholic Welfare Conference, 1943), 210, 215–216, 227; *Il Corriere d'Italia*, 28 June 1915.

Following the war, relations improved when the Vatican, no less than Italy, showed itself dissatisfied with the peace treaties. While the Italians lamented that "Italy had won the war, but lost the peace," decrying the violation of treaty obligations, the Vatican complained that the treaties of Versailles and St. Germain were inspired by revenge rather than justice.[5] Indeed, the writers of *Civiltà Cattolica* suggested that the 440 articles of the Treaty of Versailles were misnamed "articles of peace" and charged that these articles fostered a future war.[6] Benedict XV dispatched Monsignor Bonaventura Cerretti to Paris while the Peace Conference was in session and the papal envoy met informally with Vittorio Emanuele Orlando, Italy's prime minister. These talks were arranged by Monsignor Francis C. Kelley, a bishop from Oklahoma, who acted as an intermediary.[7] Although little is known of what the two discussed, Cerretti apparently raised the need to transcend Italy's Law of Guarantees. A number of Italy's political figures, and most notably Orlando, sought to tackle the Roman Question by revising the Law of Guarantees, but faced the opposition of the king on the one hand, and the demands of the Vatican on the other. Thus, this early attempt proved abortive.

In 1922, the last year of Benedict's pontificate, the leader of the Fascists reportedly asked Count Carlo Santucci, a personal friend of the Pope, to arrange an interview with the papal secretary of state, Cardinal Gasparri. In the long conversation Mussolini sought to assess the conditions upon which the Vatican could conclude a settlement with the Italian government. Mussolini let it be known he deemed a solution important and promised to give it priority. Some have seen that conversation as the preliminary step in the conclusion of the Lateran Accords of 1929.

Nineteen twenty-two witnessed the accession of Mussolini to power, as well as the election of Pius XI, who followed Benedict XV. Pius XI,

5. Thomas E. Hachey, ed., *Anglo-Vatican Relations 1914–1939: Confidential Annual Reports of the British Ministers to the Holy See* (Boston: G.K. Hall, 1972) 125.

6. "La guerra sociale dopo la pace di Versailles," *La Civiltà Cattolica*, 30 August 1919.

7. Thomas B. Morgan, *A Reporter at the Papal Court: A Narrative of the Reign of Pope Pius XI* (New York: Longmans, Green and Co., 1937), 166.

anxious to end the Roman Question, following his election ventured to the outer balcony of St. Peter's to impart his blessing *urbi et orbi*, to the city and to the world. He was the first Pope since Pius IX to do so. The new Pope deplored the fact that his "own dear land" was missing from the galaxy of powers that surrounded the Holy See. Later, in his Christmas message of 1922, he assured his fellow Italians that their country had nothing to fear from the Holy See.[8] By these and subsequent statements, Pius extended an olive branch to the Italian authorities, revealing his ardent desire for conciliation. Neither he nor his secretary of state, Cardinal Gasparri, believed the Roman Question could be resolved by the laity, much less by the Italian Popular Party.[9]

Three factors influenced the subsequent reconciliation with Italy: the accession of Papa Achille Ratti, who sought some accommodation with his *patria*; the creation of Mussolini's fascist regime following the collapse of the Liberal Italian government, whose Law of Papal Guarantees sanctioned a variant of Cavour's separation of church and state;[10] and the Vatican's disenchantment with Catholic political action and increasing reliance on concordats to assure its rights.

In the second half of the nineteenth century, and the opening decade of the twentieth, the Vatican had tolerated Catholic political action to guarantee the rights of the Church. In his memoirs, Cardinal Gasparri indicated that once Pius X had ended the *non-expedit*, the Catholic Popular Party had spontaneously emerged, without any political intervention on the part of the Holy See either *pro* or *contra* its appearance.[11] This was reconsidered following the Great War, when the Popular Party was deemed potentially detrimental to the papacy's spiritual mission.

Certainly Pius XI, distrustful of secular politics, preferred concordats to preserve Catholicism's position in the state and society. Following the adage that "governments pass away, documents stay," Pius

8. Charles Delzell, ed., *The Papacy and Totalitarianism Between the Two World Wars* (NY: Wiley, 1974), 22.

9. Giovanni Spadolini, ed., *Il Cardinale Gasparri e la Questione Romana con brani delle memorie inedite*, (Florence: Le Monnier, 1973), 53.

10. Maria Elisabeta de Franciscis, *Italy and the Vatican: The 1984 Concordat Between Church and State,* in *Studies in Modern European History,* ed. Frank J. Coppa (New York: Peter Lang, 1989) 2: 207–208.

11. *Il Cardinale Gasparri e la Questione Romana*, 58.

placed his trust in concordats signed with individual governments. In 1924 a concordat was signed with Bavaria providing the Church broad rights, and shortly thereafter talks were opened with Prussia. In 1925 agreements were reached with Latvia and Poland, in 1927 with Romania and Lithuania, and in 1928 the Church concluded an accord with Portugal. All preceded the agreement with the Italians.

In October of 1922, as the Fascists marched on Rome, Pius XI, who had recently been installed in the Chair of Peter, wrote a letter to the bishops of Italy calling for peace.[12] When King Victor Emmanuel appointed Benito Mussolini prime minister at the end of that month, the Vatican, which long maintained that Catholics owed allegiance to the regularly constituted authority, opened communication with the Duce by means of the Jesuit Father Pietro Tacchi Venturi, who considered himself a "good Jesuit and a good fascist."[13] The Catholic *l'Italia* of Milan, which shared some of its writers and editors with the *Osservatore Romano*, early on proved a leading proponent of cordial relations between the Church and Fascist Italy. Subsequently, the Pope did not raise any opposition when the Catholic Popular Party entered Mussolini's first cabinet, contributing to the vote of confidence provided Mussolini's government. In 1923 Mussolini had another secret meeting with Cardinal Gasparri, the Papal Secretary of State, in the Piazza della Pigna.[14] Six years later, an accord was concluded between Rome and the Vatican.

Mussolini, the former Socialist agitator, who was personally hostile to the Church and the papacy's "pretensions," and had brazenly proclaimed that God did not exist, and headed a movement tinged by anticlericalism, nonetheless considered the conflict between the Roman Catholic Church and the Italian state unfortunate for both. Like Napoleon he pragmatically sought its resolution.[15] Paradoxically the

12. "Ora son pochi mesi," in Claudia Carlen, ed., *Papal Pronouncements. A Guide: 1740–1798* (Ann Arbor, Michigan: The Pierian Press, 1990), 2: 89.

13. Manfred Barthel, *The Jesuits: History and Legend of the Society of Jesus*, trans. Mark Howson (New York: William Morrow and Co., 1984), 260; Edward R. Tannenbaum, *The Fascist Experience: Italian Society and Culture, 1922–1945* (New York: Basic Books, Inc., 1972), 186–188.

14. Cesare Rossi, *Mussolini com' era* (Rome: Ruffolo Editore, 1947), 176.

15. Ivon De Begnac, *Palazzo Venezia—Storia di un regime* (Rome: La Rocca, 1950), 433.

figure who had earlier confessed in the *Popolo d'Italia* that he detested all forms of Christianity and favored the revival of pagan worship, assumed a conciliatory stance, donating the Chigi Library to the Vatican. These gestures pleased the bibliophile who wore the tiara. The fact that the Duce closed his first speech in the Parliament by invoking the aid of God, and restored the crucifix to the classroom and the courtroom, likewise sent a positive signal to the Pope.[16] Increasingly Mussolini's movement curtailed its atheistic propaganda and anticlerical agenda. Indeed, part of the Fascist press recognized the persistence of the Roman Question and urged its solution.[17] Years later in 1934, in an interview with one of his biographers, Mussolini confided that he envisioned some sort of a political solution with the Catholic Church from the first days of his government, convinced it would benefit both Church and State.

The Fascists, whose 1919 program had called for the confiscation of Church property, abolition of the privileges of the Catholic religion, and eradication of Catholic influence in the state, once in power restored Catholic instruction in the public schools, while rooting anticlericalism out of the universities and freemasonry out of the Party. Mussolini, who announced that the King and the state authorities would attend a thanksgiving service in Santa Maria degli Angeli, recognized the Catholic University of the Sacred Heart in Milan, while restoring a number of religious houses and exempting the clergy from compulsory military service. The Vatican was pleased that Catholic schools were provided parity with public ones, respect was shown the clergy, and the government provided three million *lire* for the restoration of churches damaged during the war. The fact that the Mussolini government helped to save the Banco di Roma, which was on the verge of collapse, also pleased Pius.[18] In a pastoral letter of 1923 the Arch-

16. L.J.S. Wood, "Mussolini and the Roman Question," *Catholic World* (1924): 66.

17. A good analysis of developments leading to the solution to the Roman Question is provided in Francesco Margiotto Broglio, *Italia e Santa Sede dalla grande guerra alla conciliazione* (Bari: Laterza, 1966).

18. Holmes, 43; *Anglo-Vatican Relations 1914–1939*, 60, 80.; William Teeling, *Pope Pius XI and World Affairs*, (New York: Frederick A. Stokes Co., 1937) 112–113; *New York Times*, 19 February 1923.

bishop of Pisa, a close associate of the Pope, approved the government's policies.[19] Italian Catholics no longer viewed the Duce as the Anti-Christ, and some even sang his praise. The improved climate between Italy and the Vatican led some to speculate that the Pope might exit the walls of his "prison" to pay a visit to Lourdes.[20]

The Duce's words as well as his actions sought to curry the favor of the Church. "We are a Catholic nation," Mussolini expounded, "not only because the vast majority of our people is Catholic, but because Catholicism is inseparable from our history."[21] This represented a remarkable reversal of position for the author of the scurrilous and anti-clerical novel, *The Cardinal's Mistress*. Indeed the British representative to the Vatican recorded that Mussolini had done more than any other statesman since unification to restore Catholicism to its natural place in Italian life.[22] In education the new relationship between Church and State was reflected in the Gentile Reform of 1923, which made concessions to the counterculture of the Church that most Liberals would have deemed inadmissible. Though Mussolini boasted that the Gentile Reform was "the most fascist of reforms," it was welcomed by Catholics who long sought compulsory religious instruction in the state elementary schools.[23] Conservatives in the Church considered Fascism a constructive alternative to a regime dominated by their known enemies: liberalism, freemasonry and socialism.

The new cordiality led *L'Osservatore Romano* to posit that since the new regime defended the Church, the Partito Popolare had lost its reason for existence.[24] Pius's directive of 1924 proclaimed that religious activity should remain outside the political sphere, and formed part of the Pope's broader program of withdrawing the Church from the political arena. He preferred Catholic Action organizations which existed above party politics and sought the defense of religion and morality in public

19. Pietro Maffi, *Lettere, omelie, e discorsi.* (Turin: Società Editrice Internazionale, 1931), 3: 138–139.

20. *New York Times*, 22 March 1923.   21. Cited in Wood, *Catholic World*, 69.

22. *Anglo-Vatican Relations 1914–1939*, 4.

23. Dina Bertoni Jovine, *Storia dell'educazione popolare in Italia* (Bari: Laterza, 1965), 135; Tannenbaum, 154–157.

24. *L'Osservatore Romano*, 17 March 1923; 28 March 1923.

life.[25] The anti-Fascist note struck at the Popular Party's Congress in Turin led to their removal from the Mussolini Cabinet, and provoked the Fascist campaign against Catholic groups while arousing anticlerical outbursts in the Party. Monsignor Enrico Pucci, an intermediary between the regime and the Church, in June 1923 implied that Don Luigi Sturzo, leader of the Popular Party, created problems for the Vatican, and the following month Sturzo resigned as Secretary of the Party.[26] Shortly thereafter he left for London on a Vatican passport. Early the next year Pius forbade the clergy, both secular and regular, from belonging to political parties, while calling for the complete separation of Catholic Action from political Catholicism. It was the beginning of the end of the Popular Party. Neither the Pope nor the Curia regretted its departure.

During the Matteotti crisis of 1924, when Mussolini was condemned by various forces in the country, he received the support of the Church. The *Osservatore Romano* issued an appeal for an end to the recriminations, leaving the administration of law to those responsible— the Fascist regime. Father Enrico Rosa, in the *Civiltà Cattolica*, considered Mussolini and the fascists the lesser of the existing evils.[27] The Cardinal Secretary of State, Gasparri, acknowledged that the Ministry could not be absolved of some responsibility for the agitation and violence, but expressed the conviction that only Mussolini could steer the ship of state into calmer waters, providing the strong hand needed. In December 1924, following the abortive assassination attempt on the Duce, Pius spoke of divine intervention sparing Mussolini's life.[28] Whatever the Vatican's view of the moral basis of Fascism, it determined that Mussolini alone could preserve law and order. Furthermore it applauded his suppression of the freemasons and other such secret soci-

25. For works on Italian Catholic Action see Richard J. Wolff, "Between Pope and Duce: Catholic Students in Fascist Italy," *Studies in Modern European History*, ed. Frank J. Coppa (New York: Peter Lang, 1990) I: xvii.

26. Rhodes, 32; George Seldes, "The Vatican and Nationalism," *The Commonweal*, 1 March 1935: 504–06; *Anglo-Vatican Relations 1914–1939*, 114; Richard Webster, *Christian Democracy in Italy, 1860–1960* (London: Hollis and Carter, 1961), 82.

27. *Civiltà Cattolica*, 16 August 1924.

28. Antonio Pellicani, *Il Papa di tutti, La Chiesa Cattolica, il fascismo, e il razzismo, 1929–1945* (Milan: Sugar Editore, 1964), 10.

eties.[29] In May 1925 the *Osservatore* opposed any collaboration between Catholics and socialists, repudiating those members of the Popular Party who joined the Aventine.[30] In September the Pope personally condemned Catholics who sought to collaborate with the Socialists, calling for their solidarity behind the principles of "faith and religion."[31] Some have suggested that Mussolini survived the Matteotti crisis largely because of the support he received from the Church, which feared revolution and domestic disorder much more than the domestic abuses of Fascism.

In an Allocution of December 1925, Pius paid tribute to the manner in which the Italian authorities facilitated the visits of pilgrims to Rome during the year of jubilee. At the same time he denounced the attempts to take the life of the Duce. He repeated his concern the following year when he announced that all good Catholics prayed for the protection of the man whose life was precious to all Italians.[32] In October the Vatican celebrated the seventh hundredth anniversary of St. Francis of Assisi, the "most Italian of Saints" and in honor of the occasion, the government proclaimed 4 October a national holiday. Pius was represented at the governmental festivities by Cardinal Rafael Merry del Val who praised the Duce and his regime.[33] Preliminaries for a conciliation were thus established.

Certainly, aspects of the regime displeased the Vatican, and the relationship between Catholicism and Fascism was not always harmonious. In a letter to his secretary of state dated 18 February 1926, Pius lambasted Italian ecclesiastical legislation, denouncing as null and void the attempt of the government to enact laws regarding clergy or Church affairs.[34] Pius branded the laws of the *Risorgimento* both erroneous and unjust, insisting on nothing less than the abrogation of the

29. L.G.S. Wood, "Italian Freemasonry," *Commonweal*, 4 March 1925.

30. *Anglo-Vatican Relations 1914–1939*, 62–63, 80.

31. D.A. Binchey, 157–158.

32. Ibid., 74; Eloise Ellery, "Vatican's Censure of the Fascisti," *Current History*, (February 1927), 740.

33. Marc Agostino, *Le Pape Pie XI et l'opinion* (Rome: Ecole Française de Rome, 1991), 354.

34. Amedeo Giannini, *Il cammino della Conciliazione* (Milan: Vita e pensiero, 1946), 40–58.

Law of Guarantees.[35] The *Osservatore* denounced the Law as unworkable and unacceptable.[36] Early in 1927 (24 January) Pius again wrote his secretary of state attacking the Balilla Fascist youth organization. He deplored the attempt of the state to usurp prerogatives of the Church while interfering with its Catholic Action activities.[37] Nonetheless, at the end of 1926 and the beginning of 1927, the Pope prudently did not condemn the Fascist regime, but the conception of the state to which some Fascists subscribed. At the same time he appreciated that the revised law on the Fascist youth organizations provided for a body of chaplains to be attached to these groups.

Preliminaries for an accord between Church and State commenced as early as January 1925 when the Mussolini government nominated a commission for the reform of ecclesiastical legislation. Presided over by the Catholic and Fascist Paolo Mattei Gentile, it included three monsignors. Although the Vatican immediately insisted that the three ecclesiastics participated only to provide technical information, a new age in Church-State relations had clearly dawned.[38] The Vatican also made it clear that it would not, and could not, accept a unilateral revision of Italy's ecclesiastical law but required a bilateral and comprehensive solution. Mussolini understood and proved sensitive to the Pope's position and in a letter of 26 May 1926 to Alfredo Rocco related the Vatican's view. Shortly thereafter Rocco, commenting on the recent papal pronouncements on the revision of the ecclesiastical legislation, indicated that the government intended to reexamine the matter on a wider basis and informed the Holy See that their reconsideration would include the Roman Question.[39]

By the summer of 1926 unofficial, secret talks opened between Italy and the Vatican, with private exchanges between Francesco Pacelli,

35. Gabriele De Rosa, *I conservatori nazionali* (Brescia: Marcelliana, 1962), 141.

36. *L'Osservatore Romano*, 14 October 1927.

37. See "Si e annunciato" of 18 Febraury 1926 and "Abbiamo sotto gli occhi" of 24 January 1927 in Claudia Carlen, ed., *Papal Pronouncements: A Guide: 1740–1798*, 2: 94, 96.

38. "A proposito della commisione per la riforma della legislazione ecclesiastica," *L'Osservatore Romano*, 16–17 February 1925.

39. Renzo De Felice, *Mussolini il Fascista, 1925–1929* (Turin: Einaudi, 1968), 389–390.

brother of Monsignor Eugenio Pacelli, nuncio to Berlin, and Domenico Barone, Councillor of State of the Fascist government. This first phase of the negotiations lasted until the end of December 1926. The second phase ran from early January 1927 to June of that year, but was interrupted in 1928. At the end of May 1928 negotiations were reconvened despite the violence against Catholic action groups and the reservations of the Vatican. When Mussolini and Cardinal Gasparri considered the bases of a possible solution to the Roman Question, the Secretary of State, dubbed the "Giolitti of the Vatican," hinted that there might have to be a change in the Italian electoral law to reach an acceptable accord.[40] Mussolini did not recoil from the suggestion, and encouraged Gasparri to conclude that the Vatican had finally found a figure with whom it could negotiate.[41] In these talks Mussolini posed only one condition: that the Holy See would recognize that the agreement definitely closed the Roman Question. For its part the Vatican asked that the Law of Guarantees be overturned, that its absolute sovereignty should be recognized on the territory it would be accorded, and there be a financial settlement along the lines suggested by the superseded Law of Guarantees.[42]

Pius, likewise, understood that Mussolini could resolve the Roman Question and was prepared to do so.[43] Conversing with Emil Ludwig in 1932, Mussolini confided he considered Cavour's notion of a free church in a free state entirely unworkable, arguing that there were only two possibilities: complete separation of Church and State or else working together on matters of common interest, and he preferred the latter.[44] Vatican representatives made it clear that the Pope considered a concordat regulating Church-State relations in Italy an integral part

40. For a Fascist view of the long negotiation and conciliation consult Carlo Alberto Biggini, *Storia inedita della conciliazione* (Milan: Garzanti, 1942). For a Catholic perspective see Francesco Pacelli, *Diario della Conciliazione* (Vatican City: Libreria Editrice Vaticana, 1959) as well as Angelo Martini, ed., *Studi sulla questione romana e la conciliazione* (Rome: Cinque Lune, 1963).

41. Francois Charles-Roux, *Huit ans au Vatican* (Paris: Flammarion, 1947), 48.

42. De Felice, 392.

43. Luigi Sturzo, *L'Italia e l'ordine internazionale* (Turin: Einaudi, 1946), 113–4.

44. Emil Ludwig, *Talks with Mussolini*, trans. Eden and Cedar Paul (Boston: Little, Brown and Co., 1933), 175–176.

of an overall solution to the Roman Question, and that some territory would have to be accorded to the Pope to assure his independence. Otherwise, he would be perceived as a chaplain in the service of a prince.[45] Pius had said as much in his first encyclical,[46] echoing Pio Nono's position that the papacy required some territory to substantiate its sovereignty.

When word leaked out of the papal demand for territory, the Fascist organ *Foglio d'Ordini* firmly rejected the suggestion, while the Italian Foreign Minister Dino Grandi discounted the idea of a formal concordat.[47] The anticlerical King Victor Emmanuel III had serious reservations about the solution tentatively outlined, complaining it assured neither the dignity of the country nor that of the dynasty.[48]

Within the Fascist party the revolutionary syndicalist wing rejected the contention of the conservative nationalist wing that the Vatican should be courted or that it be granted concessions. Even old line Fascists warned of the dire consequences of the "vaticanization" of Italy, while Fascist intellectuals such as Giovanni Gentile claimed that an Italian recognition of Vatican sovereignty on its territory would prove suicidal. Those Fascists who remained true to their anticlericalism were scandalized by the talk of reconciliation, and considered it an absurd "utopia." They agreed with Giovanni Giolitti, the man who dominated prewar Italy, who had let it be known that he was not prepared to grant the Papacy a plot of territory the size of a postage stamp.[49] Nonetheless, the talks continued. From August to October 1926, the secret, unofficial negotiations made substantial progress so that both sides agreed to continue their clandestine meetings. By the fall, a first draft had been ironed out, and it was revised and refined during the course of 1927. By September 1928, the Holy See, believing a settlement within reach, finally authorized official negotiations. In this third phase the parties had to thrash out the thorny issues of the territory to be accorded the Vati-

45. *L'Osservatore Romano*, 14 October 1927.
46. "Ubi ancano dei consilio," December 23, 1922, in Claudia Carlen, ed., *The Papal Encyclicals, 1903–1939* (Ann Arbor, Michigan Press: 1981), 3, 238.
47. *The New York Times*, 14 October 1927; Rhodes, 39.
48. De Felice, 393.
49. *Il Cardinale Gasparri e la Questione Romana*, 5–6.

can and the amount and mode of payment of the financial settlement. There was also a recognition that both the Pope and the Duce needed some time to prepare their followers for the agreement, which both recognized would provoke controversy.

During the month from 8 January to 9 February 1929 the remaining obstacles were removed and Cardinal Gasparri alerted the diplomatic corps attached to the Vatican of an impending accord. The Italian public was kept in the dark about these developments until the eleventh hour, as were most Fascists. Finally in February 1929, following three years of negotiation, Pius announced that the Vatican had concluded a settlement with Italy, ending a quarrel that had burdened the Papacy for more than half a century. It was signed on 11 February 1929.[50] The Lateran Agreement included three accords: a conciliation treaty that terminated the Roman Question and declared Vatican City to be a neutral and inviolable territory; a concordat, which regulated Church-State relations in Italy, and a financial convention, intended to provide some compensation for Papal territory annexed during the unification.[51] It was a bilateral agreement having the status of a treaty under international law rather than simply an Italian bill, as was the Law of Guarantees, which it superseded. The twenty-seven articles of the political treaty, which dealt with the international status of the papacy and recognized the Kingdom of Italy under the house of Savoy, provided that the Italian state could not intervene in Vatican City, while abrogating the Law of Papal Guarantees of May 1871. Kent Cooper, general manager of the Associated Press, declared this solution of the Roman Question the biggest story of 1929![52] Many deemed it the greatest achievement of Mussolini's Italy.

Article 1 of the Treaty recognized Catholicism as the sole religion of the Italian state. Normally such a provision would have been included only in a concordat; its presence in the treaty reflects Pius XI's determi-

---

50. This was the seventh anniversary of the Pope's coronation and the year of his jubilee, celebrating the 50th anniversary of his ordination to the priesthood.

51. The Italian text can be found in Nino Tripodi, *I Patti lateranese e il fascismo* (Bologna: Capelli, 1960), 267–279. For an analysis of the three documents see Ernesto Rossi, *Il Managnello e l'aspersorio* (Florence: Parenti, 1958), 227–236.

52. Morgan, 269.

nation to have the privileged position of the Catholic Church in Italy guaranteed under international law. Little commented upon by contemporaries or subsequent commentators, this concession represented a substantial surrender on the part of Fascist Italy, which agreed to accept an international intervention in its internal affairs. This extraordinary concession, along with others, belies the conclusion that the Accords benefitted the regime and Mussolini while weakening the Church and the papacy.

Article 2 of the Treaty recognized the sovereignty of the Holy See in the international field, while Article 3 recognized the "exclusive and absolute power and sovereign jurisdiction of the Holy See over the Vatican ..." In Article 7 the Italian government pledged not to permit new construction overlooking Vatican City. Article 8 declared the Supreme Pontiff "sacred and inviolable" and imposed penalties against those who made attempts against him, and Article 11 declared the central bodies of the Catholic Church exempt from all interference on the part of the Italian State. In Article 12 the Italians recognized the right of the Holy See to maintain legations according to the regulations of international law, and in Article 21 they accorded to cardinals the same honors due princes of the blood. Article 24 declared Vatican City a neutral and inviolable territory. While the Holy See promised therein to remain "extraneous to all temporal disputes between states," it retained the right "to bring its moral and spiritual pressure to bear at all times."[53] In part this provision helps to explain the neutral position adopted by Pius XII (1939–1958) during the course of World War II. Article 26 provided for the recognition of the Kingdom of Italy and the Italian recognition of Vatican City.[54]

The treaty did not provide for the claim earlier posed by some for the Vatican to enjoy free passage to the sea by an independent corridor. It was probably put forward by the wily Gasparri as a bargaining chip, and deemed neither essential nor possible by the Pope and his secretary of state. Catholics rejoiced that though the Pope was burdened with a

53. Jonathan Lewis, "Pius XII and the Jews: the myths and the facts," *The Tablet* (London), 25 February 1995.
54. John Hearley, *Pope or Mussolini* (New York: The Macualey Co., 1929), 222–233.

minimum of territory, his sovereignty and freedom were fully assured while the modest indemnity provided by the financial convention assured the economic independence of the Holy See.[55] Pius XI would henceforth be independent of any other entity, a recognized power in the international community. Newspapers such as the *Brooklyn Tablet* emphasized that the Pope sought only a fraction of his former territory because of his fatherly interest towards his Italian children, exacting only that minimum of territory required for his spiritual independence.[56] The ratification of the agreement was followed by the appointment of the first Papal Nuncio to the Italian State, Monsignor Borgongini-Duca, while Count Cesare Maria de Vecchi was named ambassador to the Holy See.[57] The euphoria following the negotiation, notification, and publication proved to be short lived. Critics cited the negative national and international implications of the "alliance" concluded between Duce and Pontiff.

The forty-five articles of the Concordat, which defined the Church's position in Italy, aroused as much controversy as the treaty, which established the sovereignty of the papacy over a territory of some 100 acres.[58] In Article 1 the Italian government assured the Church free exercise of its spiritual power and, recognizing the sacred character of the Eternal City, promised to prevent all that might violate that character. This provision opened the door for Vatican interference in the life and activities of the capital city. Article 2 stipulated that the Holy See could communicate freely with the whole Catholic world without any governmental interference. Article 3 offered the clergy exemption from military service, and Article 4, exemption from jury duty. Article 5 prohibited apostate priests or those under ecclesiastical censure from either teaching or involvement in Italian public service. Article 6 noted that the stipends of ecclesiastics were exempt from charges in the same manner enjoyed by state employees.

55. Arnaldo Cortesi, "Vatican and Italy Sign Pact Recreating a Papal State," *New York Times*, 12 February 1929.

56. "Pope Pius Makes an Explanation," *Brooklyn Tablet*, 16 February 1929.

57. *New York Times*, 7 February 1929; *Anglo-Vatican Relations 1914–1939*, 150, 168.

58. Article VII of the Constitution of the Italian Republic of 1947 confirmed the Lateran Accords. De Franciscis, 215.

Articles 7 and 8 guaranteed the rights of the clergy before the courts while Articles 9 and 10 provided guarantees for Church property. Articles 11 and 12 specified the religious holidays recognized by the state and stipulated their mode of celebration. Articles 13 through 15 regulated the role of the clergy in the military and in the Church of the Pantheon in Rome, while Articles 16 through 18 examined the matter of diocesan and parish boundaries, and 19 through 26 focused on the appointment of bishops and ecclesiastical benefices. In Article 29 the Italian state promised to revise its legislation in ecclesiastical matters to conform to the provisions of the treaty and the Concordat. In Article 36 the government conceded that it considered the teaching of Christian doctrine according to the forms received from the Catholic tradition as the foundation of public education. It further specified that only textbooks approved by ecclesiastical authorities would be used in the public schools for religious training. Articles 38 through 40 recognized the authority of the Church in diocesan universities and seminaries, as well as recognizing the parity of these Catholic schools with state institutions. Finally, Article 44 declared that should any difficulty arise in the interpretation of the concordat, the Holy See and Italy would together work out an amicable solution.[59]

By means of its various provisions the Concordat recognized Catholicism as the religion of state, made religious instruction in the secondary as well as the primary schools compulsory, adopted the Church position that marriage was a sacrament, and sought the harmony of public policy, legislation and moral behavior with Church teaching.[60] The "totalitarian" state was thus constrained to adopt the Church's positions on marriage, divorce, abortion, and homosexuality as well as a host of other issues. Under the Concordat the state agreed to recognize and register all marriages performed by the Church.[61] Article 35 provided that religious schools would be permitted to submit to state examinations, assuring them parity with state schools, while Article 36

59. Hearley, 234–252.
60. See "Il Nostro più" and "Vogliamo anzitutti" in *Papal Pronouncements. A Guide: 1740–1798*, 2: 99.
61. Charles F. Delzell, "Pius XII, Italy, and the Outbreak of War," *The Journal of Contemporary History* 2 (October 1967): 139.

pronounced that the Church provided both the basis and the crown of public education. Articles 37 to 40 further elaborated Catholic rights in the educational realm. The Duce resented the subordination of civil matrimony to the sacrament of marriage provided in article 34, but the Pope threatened to scuttle the entire arrangement if the Catholic position on marriage did not prevail, and got his way.[62] By the Concordat's terms the state assumed the obligation of enforcing canon law upon the Catholic population, while agreeing to revise civil legislation that conflicted with Church teaching in matters of faith and morals. It was thus seen to pledge the state to protect and implement canon law, something the Church had long sought in Italy.[63] The imposition was resented by liberals and Fascists alike.

In the Concordat, the State recognized all the religious holidays of the Church including Sundays, New Year's Day, the Epiphany, St. Joseph's Day, Ascension Day, Corpus Christi, Saint Peter and Paul's Day, the Assumption, All Saints' Day, the Immaculate Conception and Christmas. It provided legitimization for the Catholic demand that education and marriage, as well as other aspects of civil life, reflect Church doctrine, constraining the state to ban excommunicated priests.[64] Priests and even former clergy were placed under the jurisdiction of the Church with special legal rights. Some charged that the agreement was "medieval" in its inspiration, noting that it was the first time that any modern nation had been so extensively placed under the jurisdiction of canon law; others predicted that it might become a misdemeanor punishable by fine or imprisonment for an Italian Catholic to eat meat on Friday.[65] Article 43 provided for the immunity of Catholic Action from Fascist coercion with the understanding that it and similar groups would refrain from all political activity.[66] It was broadly agreed that

62. Tripodi, 164.

63. Arnaldo Cortesi, "Pope Announces Accord with Italy," *New York Times*, 7 February 1929.

64. Francesco Traniello, "Political Catholicism, Catholic Organization, and Catholic Laity in the Reconstruction Year," in *The Formation of the Italian Republic: Proceedings of the International Synmposium on Postwar Italy*, ed. Frank J. Coppa and Margherita Repetto-Alaia. (New York: Peter Lang, 1993), 29.

65. Hearley, 83.   66. Tannenbaum, 190.

Mussolini conceded more to the Church than his liberal predecessors Giolitti, Orlando, Nitti, and others had been willing or able to concede.[67] The separation of the Church and the state of liberal Italy was followed by the clericalization of the Fascist state. The Holy See, in turn, renewed its prohibition on ecclesiastics and religious from enrolling in any political party, thus discouraging the development of political Catholicism in Italy. The Vatican did so because it concluded that no party, Catholic or otherwise, could concede to the Church what the Fascists had surrendered. It was an accurate assessment.

Understandably there were those who decried the terms of the settlement. Critics of the concordat included Jews, Protestants, various intellectuals, liberals, freethinkers, anticlerical fascists, and a number of Catholic and Protestant powers.[68] In the Senate the liberal philosopher and historian Benedetto Croce denounced the concessions accorded the Church on the grounds that "Paris is worth a mass," contrasting Fascist expediency with liberal principle.[69] Mussolini's attempts to quiet the criticism by separating the concordat from the treaty did little to soothe opponents, and was resisted by the Church, which declared the concordat an integral part of the arrangement.[70] At the end of the year Pius reaffirmed that treaty and Concordat formed one "indivisible and inseparable whole" adding that they "either both hold good or both perish."[71] The Vatican was determined to preserve the privileged position of the Church in Italy not only by its concordat with the Italian state, but by the treaty, which had the support of the international community.

Friction between Rome and the Vatican commenced as early as the summer of 1929 as a result of Mussolini's disquieting remarks during the course of parliamentary ratification of these pacts. To reassure his own party that he had not betrayed their program or abandoned the au-

67. "Why the Pope Chose to Sign the Concordat," *New York Times*, 31 March 1929.

68. For a history of the fascist opposition to the pacts see Arnaldo Suriani Cicchetti, "L'Opposizione italiana (1929–1931) ai Patti Lateranensi," *Nuova Antologia*, July 1952.

69. Pellicani, 25.

70. "Ci si e domandato," *Papal Pronouncements. A Guide: 1740–1798*, 2: 99.

71. Carlen, *The Papal Encyclicals*, 3: 346.

thority of the "totalitarian" state, the Duce had recourse to anticlerical rhetoric. The Vatican recognized that the Duce's outburst did not endanger passage of the agreement, and once again its assessment proved accurate. Following the signing of the pacts and prior to their implementation certain formalities had to be concluded, above all approval by the Italian parliament and the final exchange of ratifications. In the Chamber the pacts were discussed on 10 May, and were approved four days later by the overwhelming majority of 357 in favor and only 2 against. During the course of the Senate discussion only the liberal Benedetto Croce spoke against their approval and was part of a small minority in a vote of 316 for and 6 against. Two weeks later on 7 June the final exchange of ratifications took place.

Despite disagreements, Duce and Pontiff were pleased by the settlement. Pius described the concordat as if not the best, then certainly among the best the Vatican had arranged, convinced that Mussolini's intervention had been crucial in securing the agreement, and delighted that finally God had been restored to Italy, and Italy returned to God.[72] Mussolini seconded his sentiment, arguing that henceforth the citizen was a Catholic and the Catholic was a citizen. The Duce could now present himself not only as the savior of the social order but restorer of religious and moral values.[73] When Mussolini appeared before the Chamber to discuss the agreement, throngs packed the Palazzo Montecitorio applauding the Duce's solution.[74] Undeniably the reconciliation provided the Fascist regime considerable respectability and admiration for completing what a score of liberal governments had failed to do for some seven decades. There is a broad consensus that the conclusion of the agreement represented a high point, if not the most important achievement, of the Fascist regime and increased Mussolini's prestige worldwide. Indeed the Jesuit journal the *Civiltà Cattolica* described the Duce as the divine instrument for the long-sought concil-

72. *Il Monitore Ecclesiastico*, March 1929; "Pope Praises Agreement," *New York Times*, 14 Febraury 1929.

73. Arturo Carlo Jemolo, *Cheisa e stato in Italia negli ultimi cento anni* (Turin: Einaudi, 1948), 641.

74. Arnaldo Cortesi, "Mussolini Explains New Vatican Status," *New York Times*, 14 May 1929.

iation.[75] It proved a fit description insofar as no previous or subsequent Italian political figure dared to so compromise the state's authority or grant such broad concessions to the Church and the Vatican. Only the authoritarian Mussolini, who muzzled criticism, could have granted the Church such an advantageous agreement.

On 11 Febraury, the very day that Cardinal Gasparri signed the pacts for the Vatican, Pius addressed parish priests and Lenten speakers in Rome, noting the criticism that would probably be launched against them and indicating that the Holy See did not intend to enter into a polemical debate. Two days later in addressing a group of professors and students from the Catholic University of Milan, Pius asserted that the treaty concluded by the Holy See did not require any justification, arguing that the treaty was its own justification and explanation. Paradoxically, the Pope added that there was an explanation and justification and this was the concordat. The concordat was not only an explanation for the treaty, but a necessary condition.[76] "While the treaty was an essential document of political reconciliation, the concordat is the essential document of spiritual reconciliation," said the Holy Father. "The concordat is thus the instrument which perfects the spiritual union of Italy with the Church."[77] He might have added that it conceded to the Church in Italy privileges it had not enjoyed since unification.

Romans and other Italians waited in the pouring rain in St. Peter's Square to applaud Pius for his efforts, cheering enthusiastically when he appeared, indicating their approval of his actions. Italian public opinion was overwhelmingly favorable. The pontiff despatched a telegram to King Victor Emmanuel III, the first public correspondence between the two, and symbolically opened the bronze doors leading to the Vatican Palace.[78] On 25 July 1929 Pius XI left the confines of the Vatican, the first Pope since 1870 to do so.

Pius informed the Vatican diplomatic corps that the entire world

75. "La Conciliazione fra lo Stato Italiano e la Chiesa," *Civiltà Cattolica*, 2 March 1929.

76. De Felice, 426–427.   77. Morgan, 177.

78. Arnaldo Cortesi, "Pope Becomes Ruler of a State Again," *New York Times*, 8 June 1929.

endorsed the treaty. This was an obvious exaggeration. While approval was not universal, the accords did increase Mussolini's prestige at home and abroad, and contemporaries believed it assured the Duce's place in history.[79] Unquestionably it enhanced his international reputation. In his encyclical at the end of December 1929, assessing the accomplishments of the year, Pius gave settlement of the Roman Question priority. "Once the full sovereignty of the Roman Pontiff was assured, once his rights were recognized and solemnly sanctioned . . ." noted Pius, "We have proof . . . We had not been moved by the vain and selfish desire for an earthly Kingdom, but had always entertained thoughts of peace and not of affliction."[80] He acknowledged that "if all the points agreed upon are conscientiously and faithfully carried out—as there is reason to hope they will be—there is no doubt that the agreement will bring the best results to the Catholic cause, to Our Fatherland, and to all the human family."[81] Pius was pleased because the concordat allowed the Holy See to criticize various aspects of Mussolini's policies, without the response that these were purely internal matters on which the Vatican's protests could not be considered.

Others proved less sanguine in their assessment. The agreement evoked criticism from the opponents of Fascism who found it ironic that the Church should strengthen Mussolini's "totalitarian system." Noting that the financial convention awarded the Holy See one thousand million lire in 5% state bonds, making it one of the largest holders of Italian state bonds, the charge was launched that the Holy See now had a financial stake in the stability and preservation of the odious regime and Pius XI was in Mussolini's pocket. Word spread that the return Mussolini received from his "ruinous concessions" to the Church would not be found in any specific article but in the adherence of the Vatican and the clergy to his regime.[82] It was whispered that the agreements were designed to secure clerical support for Fascism, coupled

79. "The Vatican's Diplomatic Position," *Literary Digest*, 3 August 1929; *New York Times*, 10 March 1939.

80. "Quinquagesimo ante" in Carlen, *The Papal Encyclicals 1903–1939*, 3: 346.

81. "Quinquagesimo ante," December 23, 1929 in *Papal Pronouncements. A Guide: 1740–1798*, 2: 347.

82. See Enzo Tagliacozzo, "Il Concordato va abolito," *Ulisse*, Winter 1958.

with the warning that when the inevitable reaction erupted against the Fascist state, the Church would pay the price for having sprinkled it with holy water.[83] It is true that Pius XI had indicated that he would treat with the devil on behalf of the Church, but it was also true that when he supped with Satan he used a long spoon and proved less than a silent dinner partner. Nonetheless, criticism of the conciliation continued, inspired by both political and ideological considerations.

Even Alcide De Gasperi, the last Secretary of the Partito Popolare, who justified the agreement by putting it into historical perspective, recounting that Pius VII had signed a concordat with the libertine and blasphemous Bonaparte, feared the agreement might lead to an identification of Catholicism with Fascism.[84] He worried it might compromise the Church vis-à-vis the regime. The Duce believed that conciliation would allow him to convert the Church to a national institution, while the pontiff prophesied it would permit the Church to Catholicize the regime.[85] Neither occurred. Pius, who assumed responsibility for the agreement, did not appreciate the reaction the agreement with the Fascist regime would provoke, and even less so the consequences of the concordat with the Nazis, which it inspired.

What did the Church get? What did it give up to get the concessions? And finally, was it worth it? Fifty years after the fall of Mussolini these questions concerning the crucial relationship between Fascism and Catholicism remain polemical and difficult to answer. To be sure Church-State relations have hardly been neglected, and studies of the Vatican and the regime, Pius XI and the Duce, the Roman Question and the Lateran Accords, abound. Unfortunately a good part of the historiography had been written from either a clerical perspective or an anticlerical viewpoint, and both interpretations incline to oversimplification. The assessment of writers who were at once anti-Fascist and anticlerical proved doubly biased. The frameworks provided by such studies have colored much of the subsequent literature, and focused on the

83. Carlton J.H. Hayes, "Italy and the Vatican Agree: II—The Settlement," *The Commonweal*, 3 April 1929, 621.

84. Elisa A. Carrillo, "Alcide De Gasperi and the Lateran Pacts," *The Catholic Historical Review* 49, no. 4 (January 1964): 534–535.

85. De Franciscis, 213; Tannenbaum, 188.

political clash and the practical consensus between the government and the hierarchy, downplaying the complexity of the Catholic world, the confusing nature of Fascism, and the subtleties of the Lateran solution.

The Anglican Archbishop of Durham charged that to purchase the privileges catalogued in the Accords of 1929, the Church was prostituted to the position of handmaiden of the fascist dictatorship.[86] He was not alone in assuming that Mussolini would be compensated for his concessions by subsequent Church support for Mussolini. Undoubtedly, Mussolini reaped benefits from the Accords. Among other things he was able to reduce if not eliminate the opposition against him in part of the hierarchy and the clergy, while removing doubts and reservations that the broader Catholic population still preserved towards his government. The Accords thus enabled Mussolini to broaden the consensus for Fascism.

Salvemini charged that by concluding the concordat the papacy had chosen "reaction rather than progress," likewise warning that the choice would later haunt the Church. Guido Migliori, former leader of the Catholic peasant leagues, lamented that the Concordat contributed to the "inexorable submission of the Pope to the demands of the Regime." For this reason Giuseppe Donati claimed that while the Clerico-Fascists were jubilant, the *Popolari* were distressed by the agreement. From his exile, Francesco Ferrari, former president of the FUCI, the association of Catholic university students, protested that the Concordat represented a "clericalization of public and private institutions" and considered the concordatorial state a confessional one.[87] Carlo Falconi later complained that the agreement imposed canon law over the law of the state.[88] Indeed, in the week following the conclusion of the Concordat the Vatican urged Mussolini to revise his list of candidates for the elections of 1929, complaining of the presence of freemasons, anticlerics, and other "undesirables." Sturzo viewed the reconciliation as a "mixed blessing."[89] Antifascist

86. Binchey, 669.

87. John F. Pollard, *The Vatican and Italian Fascism, 1929–1932: A Study in Conflict* (Cambridge: Cambridge University Press, 1985), 50–56.

88. Carlo Falconi, *The Popes in the Twentieth Century* (Boston: Little, Brown and Co., 1967), 191.

89. Pollard, 55–56.

to the core, and considering the agreement as the logical culmination of the *Risorgimento*, he did not believe that the Accords sanctioned, much less approved of, the Fascist regime.[90]

Alcide de Gaspari, the last Secretary of the Partito Popolare, worried lest the agreement lead to an identification of Catholicism with Fascism, compromising the Church.[91] Giovanni Battista Montini, the future Pope Paul VI, proved even more pessimistic in his assessment:

> Was it worth it to have protested for 60 years for so petty a result? If the liberty of the Pope is not guaranteed by the strong and free faith of the people, what territory and what treaty can do it? We must pray that the Lord helps the Roman Church in this difficulty and does not allow her head to gain a free territory by losing his spiritual one and that of his sons.[92]

Montini, like many Catholics identified with Christian Democracy and the Partito Popolare, worried that the Pope had sacrificed not only political Catholicism but his spiritual independence for a solution to the Roman Question. They sometimes lost sight of the fact that the Roman Question was as much a religious dispute as a political one, with far-reaching implications for the religious life of the peninsula.[93] In fact, Pius XI proclaimed that he would not accept any accord that did not provide for a concordat regulating Church-State relations in Italy while overturning the Law of Papal Guarantees, which provided for a variant of Cavour's separatism.[94] Although the Fascists discounted the notion of a formal concordat, this was the price they reluctantly had to pay for an accord.[95] In the words of Gentile, the Church accepted the treaty in return for the Concordat, while the State accepted the Concordat in return for the treaty.[96] Tracey Koon echoed this sentiment, describing the Accords as a compromise between the Fascist regime and the Catholic Church.[97]

90. Luigi Sturzo, *L'Italia e l'ordine internazionale* (Turin: Einaudi, 1946), 131.

91. Carrillo, 534–35; De Franciscis, 213.

92. Quoted in Richard J. Wolff, "A Re-Examination of the Relationship between Catholicism and Fascism," *Italian Quarterly*, Summer 1982: 70.

93. Binchey, vi.

94. *L'Osservatore Romano*, 14 October 1927.

95. *New York Times*, 14 October 1927; Rhodes, 39; Binchey, 248.

96. Tripodi, 141–142.

97. Tracey H. Koon, *Believe, Obey, Fight* (Chapel Hill: University of North Carolina Press, 1985), 142.

Many fascist intellectuals were as scandalized as the liberals by what they considered a capitulation of state to church.

Catholics were no less divided than the Fascists in their evaluation of, and response to, the settlement. One cannot understand the web of tangled relations, of accommodation and confrontation, without an appreciation of the diversity of Catholicism in Italy. Beyond the Papacy and the ecclesiastical hierarchy there existed an important third element, the Catholic movement, comprising a number of distinct forces and groups held together by a common faith and obedience to the Pope. In the late 1970s and early 1980s, a number of Italian historians including Pier Giorgio Zunino, Pietro Scoppola, Francesco Traniello, Giacomo Martina, and Maria Cristina Guintella explored this Catholic world's relationship to the Fascist Regime.[98] In the words of Giacome Martina, the Church has never been a monolithic bloc and was not so during the Fascist years, and he criticized Croce for identifying Catholic thought with the attitudes of the hierarchy and the Pope, overlooking entirely the wide spectrum of the people of God.[99]

In the United States this view of a varied Catholic response to Fascism has been championed by Richard A. Webster and Richard J. Wolff.[100] In Great Britain John Pollard has argued that the Church was no less complex a protagonist than Fascism. Its response to the Regime was neither simple nor singular, reflecting the interlocking organizations and forces which it housed.[101] Frank Rosengarten concurs, noting that whatever the hierarchy's accommodation with Fascism, even dur-

---

98. Please see Pietro Scoppola and Francesco Traniello, eds., *I Cattolici tra fascismo e democrazia* (Bologna: Il Mulino, 1975) and Pier Giorgio Zunino, *La questione cattolica nella sinistra italiana (1919–1939)* (Bologna: Il Mulino, 1975).

99. Giacomo Martina, "Ecclesiologia prevalente nel pontificato di Pio XI," in *Cattolici e Fascisti in Umbria (1922–1945)*, ed. Alberto Monticone (Bologna: Il Mulino, 1978) 221.

100. In this regard see Richard J. Wolff and Jorg K. Hoensch, *Catholics, the State and the European Radical Right, 1919–1945* (New York: Distributed by Columbia University Press, 1987) and Richard J. Wolff, *Between Pope and Duce: Catholic Students in Fascist Italy, Studies in Modern European History*, ed. Frank J. Coppa (New York: Peter Lang, 1990) as well as Richard A. Webster's *The Cross and the Fasces*, (Stanford: Stanford University Press, 1960) and his *Christian Democracy in Italy, 1860–1960*, (London: Hollis and Carter, 1961).

101. Pollard, 3–4.

ing the so-called period of consensus of the 1930's,[102] various sections of Catholic Action denounced the totalitarian, racist, and anti-Christian features of the regime.[103]

While the Concordat undermined the totalitarian claims of the regime and prohibited the political action the Christian Democrats craved, it provided safeguards for Catholic Action dear to the Pope. Perhaps this is why Pius XI described it as one of the best the Vatican had concluded.[104] Certainly, the concordat did not solve all problems, and subsequent relations between the Catholics and fascists were often strained.[105] Indeed the Duce's speech of 13 May 1929 in the Chamber, which pronounced that the Accords made the Church neither free nor sovereign, and claimed that the Fascist state abandoned little, if anything, in temporal matters while relegating the Church to a secondary position in secular affairs, proved a portent of things to come.[106] The Duce's proclamations that education was solely the state's responsibility angered and aroused the Pope who contested this totalitarian philosophy. Pius XI responded that the "mission" of education belonged first and foremost to the Church and the family.[107] By his spoken and written words, the Pope let it be known that he considered Mussolini's contentions "worse than heretical."[108]

Despite Pius XI's desire to preserve the Lateran Accords, he was not prepared to see the state "swallow up and annihilate the family and the individual," nor educate the young to be "a race of conquerors." The Accords and particularly the Concordat provided the Pope with a legal basis for his opposition to the "totalitarian" regime. In his December 1929 encyclical on the Christian Education of Youth, he upheld the Church's role in education against the pretensions of the emerging totalitarian state. Acknowledging that the state had some role in educa-

102. Renzo De Felice, *Mussolini, Il Duce, Gli anni del consenso, 1929–1936* (Turin: Einaudi, 1974).

103. Frank Rosengarten, *The Italian Anti-Fascist Press (1919–1936)* (Cleveland: Case Western Reserve University, 1968), 55–56.

104. *Il Monitore Ecclesiastico*, March 1929; *L'Osservatore Romano*, 12 February 1929.

105. Giuseppe Rossini, *Il fascismo e la resistenza* (Rome: Cinque Lune, 1955), 48.

106. *New York Times*, 14 May 1929.

107. *Tablet* (London), 25 May 1929.

108. *Tablet* (London), 22 June 1929.

tion, Pius denounced as "unjust and unlawful" all attempts to monopolize education.[109] In fact, Pius proclaimed that "education belongs preeminently to the Church, by reason of a double title in the supernatural order, conferred exclusively upon it by God Himself." Pius XI deemed its claims "absolutely superior therefore to any other title in the natural order."[110] Thus the Pope defended the rights of the Church and family against the totalitarian ambitions of the Fascist regime, decrying the state's attempt to control all education to the detriment of ecclesiastical rights.[111] The papal position distressed Fascist intellectuals such as Giovanni Gentile who recognized that Church and State in Italy were both totalitarian regimes, and foresaw continuing difficulties between the two.[112]

The Catholic university students under Igino Righetti, founder of the *Movimento laureati*, an organization of university graduates, and Giovanni Montini, director of the Italian Catholic University student movement, revealed an ideological opposition to the regime and its institutions. Part of the Fascist press, especially the *Lavoro fascista*, the *Gioventù fascista*, *La Gazzetta del Popolo*, and *La Tribuna*, published articles charging that the organizations in Catholic Action opposed the regime and were directed by former leaders of the anti-Fascist Popular Party, and called for their suppression. When the *Lavoro Fascista*, the organ of Fascist syndicalism, preached that hatred of one's enemies and love of one's friends was a fascist virtue, the *Osservatore Romano* responded that the Gospels taught humanity to love one's enemies, emphasizing the irreconcilable differences between the two.[113]

The Vatican, in turn, was particularly sensitive to Fascist infringement on education and Catholic Action, which had been founded under Pius IX, reorganized by Pope Benedict XV in 1915, and brought under strict clerical supervision by Pius XI in 1923. The Pope consid-

109. "Rappresentanti in Terra," in Claudia Carlen ed., *The Papal Encyclicals 1903–1939* (Milwaukee; The Pierian Press, 1990), 3: 359.

110. Ibid., 3: 355.

111. Joseph Husslein, *Social Wellsprings: Eighteen Encyclicals of Social Reconstruction by Pope Pius XI* (Milwaukee: Bruce Publishing, 1942), 89–121.

112. Giovanni Busnelli, "Cultura e religione in un discorso di Giovanni Gentile," *Civiltà Cattolica*, 3 May 1930.

113. *L'Osservatore Romano*, 3 April 1931.

ered the wide range of Catholic organizations under clerical control apolitical, and resented Mussolini's harassment and Fascist curtailment of their activity, provoking his *Non Abbiamo bisogno* of June 1931, which rejected the Fascist claim to dominate all citizen organizations, youth groups, and private meetings. Denouncing the pagan intentions of the Fascists, the Pope deplored the oath which required the young to execute orders without discussion while complaining that schoolchildren were deliberately diverted from Church services to military and athletic events. Commencing his encyclical by recounting the sad events which troubled Rome and Italy, which had repercussions throughout the Catholic world, Pius protested against "the campaign of false and unjust accusations which preceded the disbanding of the associations of the young people and of university students affiliated to Catholic Action." Deploring the unwarranted dissolutions, Pius protested the other inequities including the calumnies published by the hostile press of the party.

Categorically denying the assertion that these Catholic Action groups had been politically motivated, Pius XI argued that by their very nature and essence, as well as his explicit orders, these organizations remained above and outside all party politics as provided in the Lateran Accords. Although the Pope publically challenged the totalitarian claims of the Fascist regime, he softened his tone somewhat by indicating that he did not mean to condemn the Fascist Party as such but "to condemn all those things in the programme and in the activities of the party which have been found to be contrary to Catholic doctrine and Catholic practice, and therefore incompatible with the Catholic name and profession."[114] The encyclical gained wide currency when it was smuggled out of Italy by an American Monsignor attached to the Vatican's Secretariat of State, Francis Spellman of Boston, and Monsignor Vanneufville, then associated with the news agency HAVAS. Pius thus informed the world he was not prepared to forfeit the young generation to the Fascist regime.[115] To Mussolini's dismay, messages of

114. *Non abbiamo bisogno*, 29 June 1931 in Carlen, *The Papal Encyclicals*, 3: 445–458.

115. Anne Freemantle, ed., *The Papal Encyclicals in their Historical Context*, (New York: G.P. Putnam's Sons, 1956), 249.

support flooded the Vatican and even Protestant countries and circles showed themselves sympathetic to the plight of the Church, to the detriment of Fascism's international reputation. Small wonder that Fascists in the Chamber of Fasces and Corporations denounced the Vatican as Italy's "chronic appendicitis."[116]

Eschewing political action, Pius relied on the collection of Catholic lay organizations in Italy (Catholic Action) to affirm, diffuse, and defend Catholic principles in the state and society. The Duce and anticlerical Fascist party members charged that these organizations, while nominally apolitical, ultimately had a political agenda and served as a rallying point for critics of Fascism, creating a state within the state. Mussolini's government orchestrated a barrage of articles and demonstrations against Catholic activities, suppressing their newspapers while attacking Catholic university groups. By 1930 their bitter campaign had degenerated into virtual warfare.[117] Fascist hoodlums attacked the offices of the Jesuit journal *Civiltà Cattolica* and trampled upon a painting of the Pope.[118] Following the Fascist violence against Catholic Action groups and Mussolini's dissolution of their youth organizations, as well as repeated confiscations of Catholic newspapers and journals, an accord was fashioned on 1 September 1931.[119]

The Accord for Catholic Action focused on three major issues: (1) the organization and leadership of Catholic Action, (2) the aims and objectives of its professional sections, and finally (3) the youth groups of Catholic Action. The first clause proclaimed that Catholic Action was to remain strictly dependent on the bishops who chose its directors, stipulating that these could not be drawn from parties that had in the past been hostile to the regime. The second clause provided that Catholic Action must not include in its membership professional associations and trade unions, adding that its existing internal professional sections must devote themselves to spiritual and religious purposes. Finally, the third clause restricted Catholic Action's youth

116. Delzell, *The Journal of Contemporary History* 2 (October 1967): 154.

117. *New York Times*, 27 May 1931 and 28 May 1931; *Brooklyn Tablet*, 6 June 1931.

118. *New York Times*, 28 May 1931.

119. Dante Germino, *The Italian Fascist Party in Power: A Study in Totalitarian Rule* (Minneapolis: University of Minnesota Press, 1959).

associations to recreational and educational activities of a religious nature, requiring them to refrain from all activities of an athletic or sporting nature.[120]

By its terms Catholic Action could continue, under diocesan control, to engage in educational and recreational activity of a religious nature, but had to boycott all political action while the executive board was dissolved.[121] Catholic youth clubs, rechristened Catholic Action youth organizations, were to be restricted to educational and recreational activities that had strictly religious ends. The Fascists, for their part, promised to arrange their activities so they would not interfere with Sunday services. To improve relations some of the most partisan combatants in the struggle were removed including Father Rosa, Editor of the *Civiltà Cattolica,* and Count Dalla Torre, editor of the *Osservatore Romano*, on the one hand, and Giovanni Giurati, Secretary General of the Fascist Party and Carlo Scozza, head of the Fascist University Students, on the other.[122]

Mussolini announced the struggle had ended with the triumph of the state, and henceforth Catholic Action was practically nonexistent.[123] The contention was sustained by his contemporary George Seldes.[124] It was less than an objective analysis, as was that of the exiled Don Sturzo, who likewise saw it as a victory for Mussolini. Subsequently, Renzo De Felice has concurred with their assessment as have Max Gallo and Tracey H. Koon.[125] The *Avanti* published in Paris at the time, saw it as a capitulation on Mussolini's part, charging in its 6 September 1931 issue that the "Man of Providence" had succumbed to Pius XI. In its view the Vatican had triumphed.[126] Arturo Carlo Jemolo's evaluation considered the agreement a compromise with "neither vic-

---

120. "The September Accords, 1931," in Pollard, 216.

121. The terms of the agreement may be found in Pelicani, at 61–62.

122. *New York Times*, 19 September 1931.

123. Peter C. Kent, *The Pope and the Duce* (New York: St. Martin's, 1981), 120; Galeazzo Ciano, *L'Europa verso La Catastrofe* (Verona: Arnaldo Mondadori, 1948), 81.

124. George Seldes, *Sawdust Ceasar* (New York: Harper and Brothers, 1935), 259.

125. Pollard, 180; Max Gallo, *Mussolini's Italy* (New York: Macmillan Publishing Co. Inc., 1973) 232; Tracey H. Koon, *Believe, Obey, Fight* (Chapel Hill; University of North Carolina Press, 1985), 136–137.

126. Agostino, 481.

tors nor vanquished."[127] The various restrictions on the activities and scope of Catholic Action led some to forget that its very existence and independence were at stake, and on both issues the Vatican rather than the Fascists triumphed. Mussolini failed to eliminate this widespread organization, which remained covertly anti-Fascist and challenged his totalitarian claims. Refusing to submit to the pressure and objectionable features of the Fascists, the *Catholic World* early on proclaimed the Vatican the winner.[128] September 1931 represented a turning point, but it was Mussolini who capitulated on the Catholic Action issue rather than the Pope. The Italian episcopacy, convinced that the 1931 agreement guaranteed the rights of the Church, perceived it as a substantial victory.

Pleased by the 1931 agreement, the Italian bishops quickly moved to reorganize the Catholic organizations in accordance with the new norms. Cardinal Ildefonso Schuster launched an appeal to "evangelize the Kingdom" and hoped that the young would assist in the rechristianization of the country. Meanwhile, Monsignor Gaggia, bishop of Brescia, and Monsignor Ballerini of Pavia undertook initiatives to consolidate and extend the work and functions of their Catholic Action groups.[129] Neither action pleased the Fascists. Nonetheless, in the eyes of some these actions were indicative of a new harmony between the regime and the Church. Others, however, saw the extension of Catholic Action as a non-political entity which might bear political fruit in the future.

The assertion that the agreement of 1931 brought peace between the Church and Regime[130] clearly needs to be examined. To be sure the open conflict of 1930–31 ended, and in January 1932 Pius conferred a papal decoration on the Duce, whom he received in February, exactly three years after the Concordat. This did not prevent the Vatican, that same year, from placing all of Giovanni Gentile's work on the Index, a condemnation of the major theorist of Fascism. The works of Alfredo

127. Arturo Carlo Jemolo, *Church and State in Italy*, trans. David Moore (Oxford: Blackwell, 1960), 258.

128. *Catholic World*, July 1933.

129. Agostino, 479.

130. *L'Osservatore Romano*, 3 September 1931; Tripodi, 160.

Oriani, exalted as a precursor of Fascism, were also condemned. Likewise the Vatican did not hesitate to condemn those aspects of Fascist policy and practice that violated Catholic principles or threatened public morality, expressing its views either in the *Osservatore Romano*, its semi-official journal, or in the Jesuit review *Civiltà Cattolica*.

In his encyclical *Quadragesimo Anno*, published in 1931 on the fortieth anniversary of Leo XIII's *Rerum Novarum*, the Pope praised Catholic corporativism rather than the Fascist variant inspired by Alfredo Rocco. Furthermore, Pius XI also sanctioned Igino Righetti's organization of the militant Catholic University graduates in the Movimento Laureati, which, though independent of Catholic Action, enjoyed the immunity provided by the Pope under Article 43 of the Concordat. Their annual week of retreat attracted lay and clerical anti-Fascists from all over Italy. During the 1930s the FUCI, under the protection of the Pope, in their *Azione Fucina* and the *Studium* publications, championed neoscholasticism and attacked the Fascist philosophy. The Fascist police and prefects were distressed by two clandestine anti-Fascist organizations with strong Catholic connections, the Alleanza Nazionale of Lauro de Bosis and the Movimento Guelfo of Piero Malvestiti.[131] From his sanctuary in the Vatican Library, writing for the bimonthly *Illustrazione Vaticana*, De Gasperi denounced the notion that the Church should accomodate itself to Fascism.[132]

While Mussolini's rhetoric boasted that as soon as a child was old enough to learn, he or she belonged to the state, and that nothing could be out of or against the state, not even religion[133], the reality in Italy was quite different. The FUCI under the protection of the Holy See continued to resist the Fascist notion of Church-State relations.[134] Even in the later 1930s, as repression increased, various Catholic Action groups conducted an ideological campaign against Fascism utilizing clandestine

131. Richard J. Wolff, "The University Under Mussolini: The Fascist-Catholic Struggle for Italian Youth, 1922–1943," *History of Higher Education Annual* 1 (1981); 132–147; Pollard, 150.

132. Richard Webster, *Christian Democracy in Italy 1860–1960*, 132, 140.

133. *New York Times*, 18 June 1931.

134. Tripodi, 160; Richard J. Wolff, "The University Under Mussolini: The Fascist-Catholic Struggle for Italian Youth, 1922–1943," *History of Higher Education Annual* 1 (1981): 134.

publications and discussion groups to condemn the totalitarian, racist, and anti-Christian doctrines of the Regime.[135] Undoubtedly, the greater part of the membership of the Catholic Action organizations were lukewarm in their attitude towards the Regime, and distrustful of it, even though they were not anxious to openly fight it.[136] The Fascist authorities suspected as much. "The Pope equals Catholic Action," noted De Bosis, who considered it "latently anti-fascist," predicting that "When the crisis comes, it will be a valuable rallying point against Fascism."[137]

In July 1935 the Prefect of Treviso denounced Catholic Action as the center of a vast activity preparing leaders for the future, claiming it posed a danger to Fascism. That same year the political police in Milan echoed the concern. "We are not . . . dealing with a political party but we are dealing with a mass organization that could in a few hours become the most powerful and effective political party in Italy," their report warned.[138] Catholic Action groups could be galvanized, as they were when the Pope denounced the anti-Semitic and racist legislation in the later 1930's.[139] In the words of Max Ascoli the Church was sufficiently strong to constrain fanatical and all-pervasive dictatorships to recognize her universal corporate entity.[140]

In the eyes of some, the Vatican's neutrality in the Ethiopian War betrayed a subservience to Fascist Italy. By not condemning the invasion, Pius left the Italian clergy free to support it, and many did. Cardinal Schuster of Milan proclaimed the conquest a virtual crusade, claiming that it opened the area to the Catholic faith and Roman civilization. While Pius did not publicly disapprove of the enthusiasm shown by part of the clergy, the silence of the *Osservatore Romano* leads one to suspect he regretted it. Furthermore, a series of articles in the *Civiltà Cattolica* made it clear that economic necessity did not legitimize colonial expansion.[141] The Fascists recognized the Vatican's reser-

---

135. Rosengarten, 58.

136. Jemolo, *Church and State in Italy, 1850–1950*, 274.

137. Pollard, 151.   138. Ibid., 185.

139. *New York Times*, 17 July 1938; 22 August 1938; 20 September 1938.

140. Max Ascoli, "The Roman Church and Political Action," *Foreign Affairs*, April, 1935, 441.

141. A. Messinio, S.J., "Necessità economica ed espansione coloniale," *Civiltà Cattolica, anno 87* 1 (1936): 390–94.

vations, for they refrained from claiming the Pope's support. Indeed, Mussolini complained that one had to be constantly vigilant vis-à-vis the Church.[142] As early as 1935 Max Ascoli noted the advantages the Church derived from the Accords and the subsequent understanding, noting:

Meantime the Church keeps intact her moral prestige and the hierarchic framework; her legal rights are well guarded; the doors of the spiritual world are wide open; her most loyal and able sons can one by one go to the center of political power and exert some influence and acquire some knowledge.[143]

Renzo De Felice has argued that from the Church's perspective one must differentiate the short-term impact from the long-range implications of the agreement. In the short run, De Felice concludes that the Lateran Accords proved beneficial for the Church, for under its provisions the Holy See obtained both material and religious advantages. Above all, he cites the fact that it enabled the Church to avoid a ruinous division in the Catholic camp in Italy while regularizing the position of Catholic Action, allowing it to play an active role in the country. In the long run, De Felice notes, the conciliation worked to strengthen and legitimize the Fascist regime and thus exposed the Vatican to criticism following the fall of the regime. On the other hand, De Felice observes that if the Church had gone into open opposition against the regime very likely it could not have preserved those Catholic groups and organizations that provided the ruling class in the postwar era. Thus he concluded that even taking a long-range perspective, one cannot fault the Holy See for having signed the agreements.[144]

Despite the advantages provided by the Accords, Pius became progressively disenchanted with the anti-Christian features of Fascism, particularly its hypernationalism and pagan idolatry of the state, and vigorously assailed them. He was aroused by the regime's adoption of a racist and anti-Semitic policy following the issuance of the Aryan Manifesto on 14 July 1938. The next day the Pope branded it "a true

142. See Ciano, 81.
143. Ascoli, *Foreign Affairs*, April 1935, 450.
144. De Felice, 416–417.

form of apostasy" and urged Catholic Action associations to combat it. In September Pius publicly referred to the July manifesto on race as "a gross and grave error" which was "contrary to Catholic doctrine."[145] The Pope condemned racism as contrary to the universality of the faith, while Cardinal Schuster denounced it as an international danger.[146] Part of the Catholic press denounced this Fascist racist policy.[147] On 10 December 1938, Mussolini published a decree forbidding marriage between Italian Aryans and persons of "another race." Pius responded in his Christmas allocution, attacking the measure as a violation of the Concordat. This was undeniably so. The New Year did not bring an improvement in relations, and the Pope was preparing a speech against Fascist abuses when he died on 10 February. The Duce, upon hearing the news, blurted out, "finally that obstinate old man is dead."[148]

In conclusion, how can one assess the policies of the Vatican and Catholicism following the Concordat? First, between the clerico-Fascists of the right, who championed a close alliance of the Fascist regime and the Roman Catholic Church in Italy, and the Christian Democrats of the Left, the Catholic world produced a wide range of responses. Secondly, though the reaction of the Vatican and the rest of the Catholic world to Fascism did not always coincide, there was a connection between the two. Clearly Pius eschewed Catholic political action, preferring to defend and preserve the Catholic presence in Italy and the church organizations by the legal guarantees provided in the Concordat and through the various Catholic groups and societies that collectively formed Catholic Action. Pius assured these Catholic organizations his moral and financial support, virtually forcing the bishops to sponsor them in their dioceses, often in the face of governmental hostility, and offering local branches funds when their resources were

145. Peter C. Kent, "A Tale of Two Popes: Pius XI, Pius XII and the Rome-Berlin Axis," *Journal of Contemporary History* 23 (1988): 600.

146. Camille M. Cianfarra, *The War and The Vatican* (London: Burns, Oates and Washbourne, 1945), 133; *New York Times*, 17 July and 22 July 1938, 12 August and 8 September 1938.

147. *L'Italia*, 15 November 1938.

148. Roger Aubert, *The Church in a Secularized Society: The Christian Centuries*, 5: 557.

insufficient. Since the Church only demanded a Concordat after 1926, one must call into question the notion that from the first the Vatican aspired to the creation of a confessional state. The best evidence suggests that Pius insisted on the Concordat's inclusion in the settlement to counter the increasingly totalitarian state.[149] His policy proved successful. Through a host of Catholic organizations, protected by the Concordat, the Church's principles irrigated almost every sphere of Italian life including the economy, labor, and education.[150]

The protection provided under the Concordat, and especially Article 43, which guaranteed the immunity of Catholic Action groups, assured that one important area of potential political activity remained free of Fascist penetration, allowing the Church to extend its influence in society.[151] It also protected the anti-Fascist FUCI which Pius described as the apple of his eye and the "light of the entire Catholic family."[152] Between 1929 and 1939 Pius did not hesitate to protest against Fascist pretensions in education, and supported by the Concordat, was able to resist Mussolini's quest for ideological hegemony and totalitarian control.[153] As a result of the Pope's efforts, the Church in its structure, activities, and corporate life remained outside the net of the totalitarian state. This enabled Catholicism to compete for the hearts and minds of the young, especially the females on whom Catholic women's groups exercised an enormous influence.[154] The Church was one of the few institutions that Fascism failed to infiltrate or control, and Mus-

149. Pietro Scoppola, paper on "Catholics between Fascism and Democracy" presented before the Matteotti International Symposium at the Italian Cultural Institute and Columbia University, New York, 1975; Pollard, 42–26.

150. Ascoli, *Foreign Affairs*, April 1935, 449.

151. Albert O'Brien, "Italian Youth in Conflict: Catholic Action and Fascist Italy, 1929–1931," *Catholic Historical Review* 68, no.4 (1982).

152. Wolff, History of Higher Education Annual, 140; Richard J. Wolff, "Giovanni Battista Montini and Italian Politics, 1897–1933: The Early Life of Pope Paul VI," *The Catholic Historical Review* 81, no. 2 (April 1985): 245.

153. Richard J. Wolff, "Catholicism, Fascism and Italian Education from the Riforma Gentile to the Carta della Scuola 1922–1939," *History of Education Quarterly*, (Spring 1980): 23.

154. Victoria de Grazia, *How Fascism Ruled Women: Italy, 1922–1945* (Berkeley: University of California Press, 1992), 142, 243.

solini proved unable to make it an instrument of his regime.[155] In foreign affairs, too, the Church preserved its freedom of action, pursuing its own policies, even when its aims paralleled those of the Fascist State.

On the eve of World War II the Regime recognized the Catholic world as a potential competitor in the struggle for control of public institutions and public opinion.[156] At Salò Mussolini admitted that the concessions accorded the Church in the Concordat had been a mistake, acknowledging the need for its revision and calling for greater control over the Church by the State.[157] His realization came too late. Had the Pope relied on direct political action and the Popular party as Sturzo and some of the Christian Democrats hoped, it is likely that the Duce would have reacted sooner, the Church would have faced a more brutal persecution, and the emerging Christian Democrat movement might well have been crushed.[158] As a result of the Vatican's concordat diplomacy this did not occur, so that following the fall of Fascism, Catholic Action remained the most influential mass movement on the peninsula, and played a key role in the post-World War II reconstruction of Italy. Unfortunately the success of the concordat and the Accords in Mussolini's Italy led Pius XI and his Secretary of State Pacelli to conclude they could achieve the same results with Hitler's Germany. They were mistaken.

155. Binchey, 684–685; Webster, *The Cross and the Fasces*, 110–111.

156. Francesco Traniello, "Political Catholicism, Catholic Organization, and Catholic Laity in the Reconstruction Years," *The Formation of the Italian Republic: Proceedings of the International Symposium on Postwar Italy*, ed. Frank J. Coppa and Margherita Repetto-Alaia (New York: Peter Lang, 1993), 29.

157. Denis Mack Smith, *Mussolini* (New York: Knopf, 1982), 311.

158. Webster, *Christian Democracy in Italy*, 111.

The Reich Concordat of 1933
The Church Struggle Against Nazi Germany

JOSEPH A. BIESINGER, *Eastern Kentucky University*

O F THE THIRTY-EIGHT CONCORDATS concluded by the Papacy between 1919 and 1938, none was more controversial or had a greater impact on the reputation and the moral integrity of the Church than that with Nazi Germany. Because of the Reich Concordat, criticisms of the Church have ranged from providing an early and unnecessary international recognition of Hitler's regime, to a lack of resistance against its criminal acts, to providing support for World War II and acquiescing in the Holocaust.[1]

Since communism posed such a grave threat to the Church, Pius XI did not wish to rely on democratic governments to defend the institutions and values of Christian civilization.[2] Despite his awareness of the dangers of totalitarian regimes, Pius XI was optimistic that concordats

---

1. See Ulrich von Hehl, "Kirche und Nationalsozialismus: Ein Forschungsbericht," in *Kirche im Nationalsozialismus*, ed. Geschichtsverein der Diözese Rottenburg-Stuttgart (Sigmaringen: Thorbecke, 1984), 11–29; Ludwig Volk, "Zwischen Geschichtsschreibung und Hochhuthprosa. Kirche und Nationalsozislismus," in *Katholische Kirche im Dritten Reich*, ed. Dieter Albrecht (Mainz: Matthias-Grünewald-Verlag, 1976), 194–210.

2. For Pius XI's attitude toward communism see Ludwig Volk, *Das Reichskonkordat vom 20. Juli 1933* (Mainz: Matthias-Grünewald-Verlag, 1972), 64–65.

with dictators would allow the realization of the Church's apostolic mission.[3] As the Pope and the Curia followed events in Germany during 1931 and 1932, much concern was expressed about the increasing power of the Nazi Party and its ideology, which ran counter to the teachings of the Church. The possibility of Hitler being elected president in the spring of 1932 was considered a threat to world peace. All this notwithstanding, when the new Hitler government offered to negotiate a concordat with the Vatican, Pius XI's "readiness to employ any possible means, even dealing with the Devil himself, if it would accomplish some good," started the Vatican along a path toward a Reich concordat.[4] The success of the Lateran Pact, examined by Coppa, undoubtedly inspired the hope that Hitler might just be another Mussolini, providing the order and social stability required for Christian civilization to withstand the threat of atheistic communism.[5]

Throughout the Weimar Republic the Vatican had attempted to negotiate a concordat with the Reich, but due to the objections in the Reichstag, one was never concluded. The most significant obstacle was the Church's desire to secure the status of confessional schools, and fears by Bavaria and Prussia that their existing treaties, concluded in 1925 and 1929, respectively, might be modified or voided. In 1932 a concordat with Baden had been rapidly negotiated because of fears that Hitler once in power would initiate another *Kulturkampf* against the Church. The earlier resistance by Archbishop Carl Fritz of Freiburg to

3. Derek J. Holmes, *The Papacy in the Modern World, 1914–1978* (New York: Crossroads Publishing Co., 1981), 82, 92–94; Anthony Rhodes, *The Vatican in the Age of the Dictators, 1922–1945* (New York: Holt, Rinehart and Winston, 1973), 213.

4. Stewart A. Stehlin, *Weimar and the Vatican, 1919–1933, German-Vatican Relations in the Interwar Years* (Princeton: Princeton University Press, 1983), 358–367. See the lengthy analysis of the concordat policy of the Church from 1919 to 1933 in Klaus Scholder, *The Churches and the Third Reich*, trans. John Bowden (Philadelphia: Fortress Press, 1988), 1: 52–73, 146–167. On the Pope's willingness to go to any extreme to protect the Church and Christian civilization see Hansjakob Stehle, "Motive des Reichskonkordats," *Aussenpolitik* 7 (1956): 564.

5. Rudolf Lill, "Katholische Kirche und Nationalsozialismus," in *Machtverfall und Machtergreifung*, ed. Rudolf Lill and Heinrich Oberreuter (München: Bayerische Landeszentrale für Politische Bildungsarbeit, 1983), 259; Rhodes, 174.

the Roman centralism a concordat would promote by its protection of the *Codex Juris Canonici*, was overcome after Fritz died. The new Archbishop was Konrad Gröber, who as a friend of Ludwig Kaas, the leader of the Center Party, and Father Leiber, a close advisor to Cardinal Pacelli, supported the Vatican's attempt to conclude a Reich concordat.[6] Another obstacle that contributed to a stalemate during the Republic was the Reich's request for a military chaplaincy, which the Vatican resisted so long as the Reich refused to make concessions to the Church in the areas of church marriages, denominational schools, and state financial contributions.[7] Yet, just as Pacelli had guided the completion of the state concordats, he also continually sought one with the Reich. With Heinrich Brüning in the chancellorship, Pacelli insisted in the summer of 1931 that a concordat be proposed, but was resisted by Brüning. Before Hitler was appointed Chancellor on 30 January 1933 National Socialism had been criticized by episcopal authorities as pagan and anti-Christian in some of its ideas, and seen to be blatantly racist and totalitarian. The German bishops had warned Catholics against Nazism on numerous occasions as far back as 1920 and as recently as February 1931 when the Bavarian bishops had forbidden Catholics to support the party and condemned its pagan ideology.[8] The election campaigns of the Bavarian People's Party and the Center during the elections of 1932 repeatedly emphasized these condemnations.[9]

Like Napoleon and Mussolini, whose aims are examined in the first two essays in this volume, Hitler hoped to harness the Roman Catholic

6. Klaus Scholder, *A Requiem for Hitler*, trans. John Bowden (Philadelphia: Trinity Press, 1989), 66; idem, *Churches*, 1: 391.

7. Stehlin, 430–434.

8. See Ludwig Volk, *Der Bayerische Episkopat und der Nationalsozialismus, 1930–1934*, (Mainz: Matthias-Grünewald-Verlag, 1966), 14–49; Scholder in *Churches*, 1: 132–135 judges these declarations as uncompromisingly opposed to National Socialism, and disagrees with Volk's judgment in *Episkopat* 29 that these were not unanimous; see also Raimund Baumgärtner, *Weltanschuungskampf im Dritten Reich*, (Mainz: Matthias-Grünewald-Verlag, 1977), 138–147, and Donald Dietrich, *Catholic Citizens in the Third Reich: Psycho-social Principles and Moral Reasoning* (New Brunswick, N.J.: Transaction Press, 1988), 1–94.

9. See the study of the 1932 presidential election campaign in Bavaria by Joseph A. Biesinger, *The Presidential Elections in Bavaria and the Reich, 1925–1932* (Ph.D. diss., Rutgers—The State University of New Jersey, 1972), 276–285, 333–339.

Church in the service of his Third Reich. Indeed all three dictators attempted to use concordats to extend their control over the populations of their countries. The concordats provided the regimes with international legitimacy while internally Catholics were required to be politically loyal. The clergy were controlled and their political activity eliminated. Like Napoleon and Mussolini, Hitler, though nominally a Catholic, was not a Christian and had abandoned his Catholic faith in both doctrine and practice. His monism was similar to Napoleon's deism. While Napoleon believed in a supreme intelligence, Hitler appealed to providence. He recognized the Church's influence over so many million Catholic consciences as an obstacle to his totalitarian ambitions.[10] So while Hitler was impressed by the power, the ceremonies, and the organization of the Church, he detested its priesthood and like Napoleon and Mussolini was determined to remove them from politics. The Church was a fundamental obstacle to Hitler's pursuit of a policy of coordination in the building of his Führer state.

Hitler had no intention of directly confronting the Church. "Do not imagine," he said to his friend, Arthur Dinter of Thuringia, who was a strong proponent of *völkish* (popular) religion, "that I shall commit Bismarck's mistake. He was a Protestant and did not know how to handle the Catholic Church."[11] While Bismarck had openly confronted the Catholic Church, Hitler did not intend to do so and planned to use the Church to eliminate the political opposition of the Center Party, which he hated.[12] In a secret meeting with party leaders Hitler was reported by Dinter to have asserted that he would make the Church "the stirrup-holder for the coming Third Reich" and once in power the Vatican would "have little to laugh at."[13] Hitler intended to restrict the Church's

10. Desmond Seward, *Napoleon and Hitler* (New York: Simon and Schuster, 1988), 93–94, 114–15.

11. As cited in Robert d'Harcourt, *Les Catholiques d'Allemagne*, (Paris, 1946), cited in Rhodes, *The Vatican*, 167; Scholder, *Churches*, 1: 381: on Arthur Dinter's ideas, involvement in the Nazi Party, and relationship with Hitler, see pp. 94–98.

12. Ellen Lovell Evans, *The German Center Party, 1870–1933: A Study in Political Catholicism* (Carbondale, Ill.: Southern Illinois University Press, 1981), 55–56. Hitler's animosity toward the Center Party and its alliance with the Marxist Social Democrats was expressed in *Mein Kampf* (New York: Houghton-Mifflin, 1941), 366.

13. W. Gerdemann and Heinrich Winifred, *Christenkreuz und Hakenkreuz*, (Cologne: 1931), n. p. cited in Rhodes, at 168.

organizational activities and eliminate its influence over Catholic youth.[14] The strategy he pursued to obtain a concordat involved both appeasement and smoke-screen tactics.[15] Simultaneously, however, he intended to initiate a new *Kulturkampf*, or *Kirchenkampf*, as it came to be known, which was intended to be much more radical than Bismarck's *Kulturkampf* ever had been. Hitler's *Kirchenkampf* not only involved ideological warfare, but had as its goal the eventual destruction of the Church. In the Kaiserreich the state administration had certainly persecuted the Church, but it did not violate Christian moral norms as was the case in the totalitarian state of National Socialism.[16]

On 1 February, 1933, the occasion of his first radio address to the nation, Hitler attempted to allay Catholic suspicions. He promised to make Christian morality and family the basis of German society and pursue amicable relations with the Holy See. He continued this policy of appeasement during his address to the Reichstag on 23 March.[17] He declared that both Christian confessions were essential foundations of the German nation: he would respect state concordats already negotiated, he would secure the rights of the Church in education, and he would pursue friendly relations with the Papacy. On 26 April Hitler met with the Bishop of Osnabruch, Wilhelm Berning, and Prelate Dr. Johannes Steinmann, the clerical advisor in the Vatican Embassy who had come to present the concerns of diocesan leaders to the Chancellor over the persecution that already afflicted the Church. Again Hitler promised to protect Germany's Christian foundations, reaffirming his desire to cooperate with the Catholic church. In pursuit of his tactics of deceit he hypocritically identified himself as a Catholic, expressing his conviction of "the deep significance of the Christian religion," and even

14. Holmes, 101.

15. Klaus Gotto, Hans Günter Hockerts, and Konrad Repgen, "Nationalsozialistische Herausforderung und kirchliche Antwort. Eine Bilanz," in *Die Katholiken und das Dritte Reich*, ed. Klaus Gotto and Konrad Repgen (Mainz: Matthias-Grünewald-Verlag, 1990), 178.

16. Volk, "Nationalsozialistischer Kirchenkampf und deutscher Episkopat," Ibid., 61.

17. Max Domarus, *Hitler, Speeches and Proclamations, 1932–1945*, vol. 1 (Wauconda, Ill.: Bolchazy-Carducci, 1990), 232–39, 269–96.

renounced his association with the radical ideas of General Erich Lu-
dendorf and Alfred Rosenberg. He went on to state:

My desire is that no confessional conflict arise. I must act correctly to both
confessions. I will not tolerate a *Kulturkampf* . . . I stand by my word. I will
protect the rights and freedom of the church and will not permit them to be
touched. You need have no apprehensions concerning the freedom of the
church.[18]

He also expressed the belief that secular schools were inadequate in
the field of moral instruction and that faith had to be the foundation of
character training. In order to deceive the Church's leaders he promised
to maintain the church-related school system. Concerned with the
buildup of a strong army, it is not surprising that Hitler would say that
the most dedicated soldiers were Christians.

Hitler's concessions were tactical and had the intended goal of securing a concordat with the Vatican. A principal goal of a concordat for
the Nazi leader was the elimination of the Center Party. Although its
influence and prestige had already declined, the votes of the Center
deputies could still have blocked Hitler's legislation, especially that of
the Enabling Act. Hitler also was aware that a concordat would provide
an endorsement of his government by the papacy, which would counter
the opposition and reluctance of Catholics and others to support his
regime.

The bishops initially continued to support the Center Party. Before
the fiercely contested elections on 5 March, Catholics were encouraged
to vote for the Center and Bavarian People's Parties. With the Nazi
success in that election the bishops faced a dilemma. Should they support the government or should they choose to be in opposition to a
government that had emerged through constitutional means? Increasingly, the bishops came under pressure to change their anti-Nazi policy.
The fear of Nazi persecution of the Church prompted Cardinal Adolf
Bertram of Breslau, the presiding bishop of the Fulda bishops' conference, to express his concerns to President Hindenburg. Then, Franz
von Papen, as vice-chancellor and representative of the government,

18. As cited in Ernst C. Helmreich, *The German Churches under Hitler* (Detroit:
Wayne State University Press, 1979), 241.

met with Bertram on 18 March requesting that the Church change its policy against National Socialism. Bertram rebuffed this request and demanded that Hitler should first change his policies.[19] Yet, shortly thereafter, Bertram quickly circulated a draft proposal of a revision of the Church's anti-Nazi position. On 20 March Hitler met with leaders of the Center Party attempting to gain their support by promising "not to abolish the states, to respect the state concordats, the confessional schools, and religious instruction."[20] Then, at the opening session of the Reichstag on 21 March, Hitler staged a great spectacle, known as the "Day of Potsdam," which suggested to Church leaders that National Socialism might play a positive role in the national restoration and that the traditional cooperation between church and state might be restored. During his subsequent Reichstag speech on 23 March, Hitler affirmed the role of Christianity as the "unshakable foundation of the moral and ethical life of our people," promising that the rights of the Catholic Church would not be restricted and good relations with the papacy would be pursued.[21] Events were moving rapidly and the pressures on the leadership of the Church to change policy were great. Draft proposals of a policy change were circulated to all the German bishops by Cardinal Michael Faulhaber and (mainly) by Cardinal Bertram. Although some of the bishops expressed reservations, there was general support for the suggested change of policy. The prohibitions against joining the Nazi Party were to be rescinded. Catholics were also admonished to be obedient to lawful authority and perform their civic duties.

This declaration was a dramatic reversal by the German bishops. Published on 28 March, the new position conditionally withdrew the previous warnings against Nazism and marked the beginning of an attempt by the bishops to cooperate with the regime. The final text

19. See John Zeender's discussion of the bishop's change of position in "The Genesis of the German Concordat of 1933," in *Studies in Catholic History*, N.H. Minnich, Robert B. Eno, S.S., and Robert F. Trisco, eds. (Wilmington, Delaware: Michael Glazier, 1985), 644–649; Scholder, *Churches*, 1: 244.

20. Helmreich, 238.

21. *Dokumente der deutschen Politik und Geschichte von 1848 bis zur Gegenwart*, vol. 4, ed. Johannes Hohlfeld (Berlin: Herbert Wendler & Co., 1954), 30.

differed from Cardinal Bertram's initial draft and did not satisfy the Bavarian bishops' concern with the defense of Catholic political parties and organizations already under attack.[22] Guidelines for the administration of the new policy admonished the Bavarian clergy, for instance, to support the national government, especially in its efforts at spiritual renewal. The general admonition to obedience and "avoidance of whatever might be interpreted as disrespect for the government" was tempered by the duty to criticize error, injustice and acts of violence committed by Nazi party members.[23] Although it is debateable whether this statement of the bishops was a formal recognition of the Nazi regime, it certainly eliminated the restrictions on membership in the Nazi party and participation in the so-called national renewal. As Alphons Nobel, the Catholic editor of Augsburg, wrote, "the positive attitude of the German Catholics to the new state is no longer impeded by religious scruples."[24]

At the end of a plenary meeting of all of the German bishops, on 3 June a joint pastoral message indicated that the Church welcomed the "national awakening" and enthusiastically would support the new regime under the condition that it recognize the rights and freedom of the Church and its insistence on confessional schools and the right of existence of its organizations. It also emphasized the need to support those elements in the Nazi *Weltanschauung*, such as patriotism, obedience to constituted authority, and the emphasis on the common welfare. Yet, the formulation of these statements and the accompanying warnings by the bishops were understood by some contemporaries as unacceptable to the Nazis. In a criticism of Guenther Lewy on this point, Donald Dietrich states that "the June statement was understood at the time to constitute a clear 'no' to National Socialist intentions," and that "both Hochhuth and Lewy failed to understand such statements in their historical context," which limited the validity of their

22. Ludwig Volk, "Zur Kundgebung des deutschen Episkopats vom 28 März 1933," *Stimmen der Zeit* 173 (1963–64), 444–45.

23. Guenter Lewy, *The Catholic Church and Nazi Germany*, (New York: McGraw-Hill, 1964), 40–41.

24. Ibid, 42–43.

criticisms.[25] For Klaus Scholder the Fulda meeting and the pastoral message were a ringing condemnation of National Socialism, but they also were inextricably linked with the concordat. Before the meeting the bishops had been kept in the dark concerning the details of the negotiation. During the meeting they were informed about the concordat by Archbishop Conrad Gröber, debated its merits, and in the end the majority supported his view of the necessity of a treaty.

Were the German bishops pressured from Rome to change their position? There is evidence to conclude that the German bishops did receive some pressure from Rome to be more accommodating to the new regime.[26] Undoubtedly, Hitler's assurances to the Church that its freedom would not be curtailed, that its role in education would not be undermined, that he was a staunch enemy of communism and that peace would be maintained, encouraged both the bishops and the Vatican to take a more positive position.[27] Bertram probably was aware of the negotiations between Catholic officials (likely including Ludwig Kaas) and the government over the Enabling Act. A witness to Pius XI's changed attitude was Cardinal Faulhaber, who had been present at a consistory in Rome during March and reported to the Bavarian bishops:

I found, despite everything, a greater tolerance with regard to the new Government. It is today, moreover, not only in possession of power but it has reached that position by legal methods: indeed it could be said that no revolutionary party has ever come to power in so regular a way. Let us meditate on the words of the Holy Father, who, in a consistory, without mentioning his name, indicated confidence before the whole world in Adolf

25. Dietrich, 108; Lewy, 36–44; Volk, *Stimmen der Zeit* 173 (1963–64): 431–56; idem, "Zwischen Geschichtsschreibung und Hochhuthprosa," *Stimmen der Zeit* 176 (1965): 194–210.

26. Klaus Scholder put forth the thesis that Ludwig Kaas, the Chairman of the Center Party, informed Pacelli that the Hitler government was favorable to a concordat before the change in the bishops' condemnation of Nazism. Scholder relates that Pacelli on 29 March sent confidential information to the German bishops, via the nuncios in Berlin and Munich, to the effect that they were required to change their position toward National Socialism. Bertram had already arrived at this decision earlier at Papen's urging. See Scholder, *Churches*, vol. 1, 382 and Volk, *Reichskondordat*, 87, with whom he disagrees.

27. Holmes, 103; Volk, *Reichskondordat*, 73–79, 84–89; Scholder, *Churches*, 1: 382.

Hitler the statesman who first, after the Pope himself, has raised his voice against Bolshevism.[28]

This report was part of a request sent to the bishops to consider a revision of the Church's position on National Socialism after Hitler's speech and guarantees of 23 March. Though the report had limited circulation, Cardinal Faulhaber made it appear that Pius XI had praised Hitler. The accuracy of Faulhaber's report concerning the Pope's words has been contested, because others present understood the Pope differently.[29] Cardinal Faulhaber's interpretation is contested by Ludwig Volk, a preeminent authority on the events related to the Concordat.[30] The German bishops, Volk emphasizes, had enough pressures from within Germany without a push from Rome to encourage them to lift the ban against National Socialism. The old ban had forbidden Catholics to become members of the Nazi Party, to wear their SA uniforms to church, or be administered the sacraments. With the ban lifted Catholics could now join the party and not fear estrangement from the Church. Perhaps the potential negative ramifications of the ban's reversal were unappreciated by the bishops, especially as they affected the fight of loyal members of the Center and BVP to survive the Nazis' intent to destroy all political parties.

An intense controversy has long existed over who first proposed the negotiation of a concordat with the Hitler government. Was it Vice-Chancellor Franz von Papen, with Hitler's approval, or was it the Vatican through Monsignor Ludwig Kaas, the leader of the Center Party, and Cardinal Secretary of State Eugenio Pacelli? In 1934 Papen claimed that he had discussed the subject with Hitler shortly after 30 January 1933. Statements by Pius XI and Pius XII have maintained that the concordat was sought by the German government and not the Vatican. Father Robert Leiber, the Secretary to Cardinal Pacelli, also testified to

28. Faulhaber an den bayerischen Episkopat, 24 März 1933, in *Akten Kardinal Michael von Faulhabers, 1917–1945*, vol. I, ed. Ludwig Volk (Mainz: Matthias-Grünewald-Verlag, 1975), 672–673.

29. Mary Alice Gallin, O.S.U., "The Cardinal and the State: Faulhaber and the Third Reich," *Journal of Church and State* 12 (1970): 390–391.

30. Ludwig Volk, "Päpstliche Laudatio auf Hitler?," *Stimmen Der Zeit* 173 (1963): 221–29.

the responsibility of the German government for the proposal. Guenther Lewy, however, in his controversial book *The Catholic Church and Nazi Germany*, raised some questions about the consistency of the evidence. His hypothesis is that the Holy See initiated the negotiations in an attempt to fulfill its long-held goal of securing a concordat with the Reich.[31] Klaus Scholder has proposed a similar hypothesis that there was a Hitler-Kaas agreement about a concordat which preceded the Enabling Act, the Bishop's declaration and the trips of both Papen and Kaas to Rome.[32] Nonetheless it is generally accepted, especially by the historians Ludwig Volk, Konrad Repgen, Dieter Albrecht, and John J. Hughes, that Papen and the German government first made the proposal "early in April, 1933 and that the Vatican's initial reaction was receptive but cautious."[33]

Papen left for Rome on 7 April along with Hermann Göring, who was sent along to impress the Vatican with the German government's seriousness about negotiating a concordat. It is interesting, and perhaps not coincidental, that Ludwig Kaas was on the same train, and according to his diary, he and Papen discussed the possible advantages of a concordat. Once in Rome the negotiations began between Papen and Pacelli on Monday 10 April in Holy Week. Since Kaas was present he also participated, and he and Papen prepared a draft treaty that was discussed on Holy Saturday. Central to the answer is the question: Was Kaas's presence in Rome fortuitous or by design? We will never know. Papen took the lead in the negotiations in place of the German Ambassador to the Vatican, Diego von Bergen. When Papen had to return to Berlin on the 18th, it was Kaas and not Bergen who continued the talks with the Vatican. Was this another strange coincidence? Ludwig

31. Lewy, 66.

32. Scholder, *Churches*, I: 240–242; idem.," Altes und Neues zur Vorgeschichte des Reichskonkordats," *Vierteljahrshefte für Zeitgeschichte* 25 (1978), 559–567; Zeender, 655.

33. John J. Hughes, "The Pope's 'Pact With Hitler': Betrayal or Self-Defense?" *Journal of Church and State* 17 (1975): 64; Volk, *Reichskonkordat*: 90–94; Konrad Repgen, "Hitlers Machtergreifung und der deutsche Katholizismus. Versuch einer Bilanz," in *Katholische Kirche im Dritte Reich*, ed. Dieter Albrecht (Mainz: Matthias-Grünewald-Verlag, 1976), 26–27; Dieter Albrecht, "Der Heilige Stuhl und das Dritte Reich," in K. Gotto and K. Repgen, eds., *Die Katholiken*, 36.

Kaas had gained the necessary experience from his active role in nego-tiating concordats with Prussia and Baden. Under these circumstances and considering the gravity of the situation, it is not surprising that the entire draft of the concordat was agreed upon after only four sessions and that the speedy process leading to final ratification was unprece-dented in Vatican history.[34]

Of all the articles in the draft over which there were disagreement, the most contested one was Article 31, which determined the future of the political role of the clergy. Since it was such a thorny issue, the Vat-ican finally decided to submit the draft concordat to the Fulda Bishops' Conference that met from 30 May to 1 June, the first such meeting of all German bishops since 1905. Until this time neither the German bish-ops nor the Center Party had been officially informed or consulted about the details of the concordat. This was a departure from tradi-tional practice. While Pacelli had been optimistic, the German episco-pate was more skeptical about the prospects of a concordat. A distinct minority of the bishops at the conference were resolute opponents of Hitler. At the Fulda Conference Bishop Wilhelm Berning of Os-nabrück and Archbishop Conrad Gröber of Freiburg became the rep-resentatives of the Vatican and were instructed to make the concordat the top priority of the Conference. At this late date the bishops discov-ered that Hitler was demanding in Article 31 the total exclusion of the clergy from politics, a point they refused to concede. There also was op-position to the concordat by Cardinal Karl Joseph Schulte of Cologne and Konrad von Preysing, the Bishop of Eichstätt, though the extent to which their objections were considered is not clear. Nonetheless, for most of the bishops there appeared to be little other choice than to sup-port Rome's initiative, and not to make removing the depolitization ar-

34. J.J. Hughes, "The Reich Concordat 1933: Capitulation or Compromise?" *Aus-tralian Journal of Politics and History* 20 (1974): 165. Citing Alfons Kupper, *Staatliche Akten über die Reichskonkordatsverhandlungen 1933* (Mainz: Matthias-Grünewald-Verlag, 1969), 135, Hughes quotes Bergen as saying that this was a unique treaty and would not have been possible without the help of Monsignor Kaas. Also, in Kupper, *Akten*, 118, Cardinal Pacelli avoided a definitive answer to Bergen's requests for a clear statement of acceptance of Article 31. See Scholder, *Churches*, 1: 385–386 concerning the rapidity of the negotiations as compared with other concordats.

ticle a condition for the concordat's acceptance. The pastoral message of 3 June was drafted by Bishop Gröber and was intended to prepare the German people for the treaty. The bishops sent Bishop Gröber to represent them in the final negotiations in Rome.[35] Papen left for Rome on 29 June to conclude the negotiations. The draft was approved by Pius XI on Sunday, 2 July after two meetings with Pacelli, notwithstanding their concern over the reports of a terror campaign aimed at the Church.

Nazi pressure had begun as early as 8 June, manifested by a large rally of over twenty thousand non-resident Catholic journeymen in Munich. At first the rally was banned by the Bavarian political police, led by Heinrich Himmler, Reinhard Heydrich, and Adolf Wagner.[36] Hitler gave assurances that neither the Church nor the clergy were to be harmed, yet he also expressed the desire that Church associations not demonstrate in the streets for some months. After appeals by Cardinal Michael Faulhaber, the Apprentices' Rally was permitted, but violence by the SA quickly expanded into systematic terror. While Cardinal Faulhaber protested this attack on a Catholic association, the Nazis had produced the intended effect. The Cardinal forbade any further demonstrations in uniforms and formation. By the end of June the persecution of the clergy and Catholic organizations was in high gear. The Center Party and the Catholic Bavarian People's Party (BVP) were confronted by a wave of arrests and dismissals from public office. On 24 June the Congress of Christian Trades Unions was disbanded. Joseph Goebbels publicly demanded that the Center cease delaying its dissolution. During these weeks the persecution against Catholic priests and organizations was especially intense in Bavaria. Whatever the motives behind these actions, it is clear that Hitler's interest in a concordat appeared to be fading. He delayed signing the draft. Inasmuch as most of

35. Scholder, *Churches*, 392–395.
36. Heinrich Himmler an agricultural graduate from Munich, was appointed the Reichsleiter on June 2nd and was the Reichsführer of the SS. In April he had become the Commandant of the Bavarian political police. Reinhard Heydrich, a former naval officer, within three years became chief of the Security Police. Adolf Wagner was the Gauleiter of Munich, Bavarian Minister of the Interior, and the most powerful member of the Bavarian cabinet.

the political parties had already dissolved themselves, it was clear that a concordat was unnecessary to Hitler's goals of eliminating the Center Party and removing the clergy from politics.[37]

As suggested earlier, the relation of the concordat to the Enabling Act and the end of the Center Party has long been debated. There are at least three main schools of interpretation. One alleges that the Center Party was "stabbed in the back" by Kaas, Papen, and the Vatican through the agreement on a concordat; a second school asserts the documentation does not support this conspiracy thesis; and a third interpretation accepts the circumstantial evidence that points to the cooperation of Kaas and Pacelli in trading the Center Party for a concordat. This last interpretation, a modification of that of Klaus Scholder, has been advocated by John Zeender and discounts the likelihood of discovering a "smoking gun" document that would prove or disprove the allegations.[38] Both Kaas, who was a canon lawyer and had been the conservative leader of the Center Party since 1928, and Cardinal Pacelli, the Papal Nuncio to Germany, had performed principal roles in the negotiations of the state concordats with Bavaria, Prussia and Baden and the unsuccessful attempts to conclude a Reich concordat. An indication of Kaas' sentiments favoring a positive relationship between dictatorships and the Church is found in his essay of November 1932 wherein he eulogized Pius XI and Mussolini for restoring harmony to Italy.[39] During that winter, it is thought, both Kaas and Pacelli expressed a "deep desire" for a right-wing coalition in Germany, Kaas preferring a conservative alliance (*Sammlung*) including the National Socialists, the Center Party and the Bavarian People's Party. In fact, Kaas apparently favored a Hitler chancellorship, though not a Fascist dictatorship under a single party. Although Kaas believed in adhering to the constitution, he had, according to Brüning's *Memoiren*, discussed with him the Catholic perspective concerning a "coup d'état", and that "Pacelli had tried to persuade him [Brüning] through Kaas on 1 January 1932 to

37. *Churches*, I: 399–400.

38. Zeender, 617–665. Zeender specifically discusses the lack of records at 637, 657 and 664.

39. See *Churches*, I: 166–67 for a discussion of the significance of this study, and Zeender, 632–635 for a discussion of the Scholder-Repgen debate on this issue.

work toward an understanding with Adolf Hitler"[40] and to include Nazis in his government.[41] At the same time Pacelli believed that the support of the Nazis was necessary to secure a concordat.[42] On 6 March 1933 Kaas met with Papen the day after the Reichstag elections, for the purpose of offering to collaborate with the government. Since Kaas was the *de facto* papal nuncio, it can be inferred that he agreed to promote the support of the Center Party for the Enabling Act in return for the government's initiation of negotiations for a concordat. Kaas is reported to have lobbied hard among Center colleagues for the Enabling Act while only a small minority followed Brüning's opposition.[43] Kaas and Albert Hackelsberger, an industrialist from Baden, were in the forefront of those Centrists who pushed for the Enabling Act.[44] Hackelsberger, a friend of Archbishop Konrad Gröber, had been instrumental in convincing the unwilling Center Party in Baden to vote for the Concordat of 1932. A linkage appears to have existed between Hackelsberger, Kaas, and Gröber in "the German Catholic effort to build up a long-term relationship between their Church and the Nazi regime patterned on the Italian model."[45] These and other factors, John Zeender concludes, suggest that there was a causal connection between the Center's Reichstag vote for the Enabling Act and the beginning of concordat negotiations. It is not difficult to argue that Ludwig Kaas saw the attempt to preserve the Center and the parliamentary system as a hopeless goal under the circumstances which prevailed in Germany and therefore bargained with the Nazis to secure what he had long worked for, the conclusion of a Reich concordat.

An interpretation of the negotiations for the concordat which accepts the statements of Ludwig Kaas and Cardinal Pacelli at face value

40. Ibid., 628 citing Brüning's *Memoiren*, 358–59; Volk, *Reichskonkordat*, 48; Scholder, *Vierteljahrshefte*, 561.

41. Evans, 366–67; Zeender, 628, 631.

42. Zeender, 634 citing Volk's statement at *Reichskonkordat*, 63 that "decisive for Pacelli's church political assessment of the NS movement was its stand on concordats."

43. Outside of circumstantial evidence and the analysis of the persons involved, no direct documentation, that is, no smoking gun, to prove this has been found. See Zeender, 657, 664.

44. Volk, *Bayerische Episkopat*, 115–116.

45. Zeender, 643.

has been the position expressed by the German scholars Ludwig Volk and Konrad Repgen, and accepted by John Jay Hughes. They reject the charge that "the Vatican betrayed its political supporters in Germany by conceding Hitler's demand to exclude the clergy from party politics in order to obtain the Concordat" and assert that it "is not supported by the documentation."[46] Neither Ludwig Kaas, Cardinal Pacelli, nor the Vatican initiated the concordat negotiations. Furthermore they did not trade the Center's support for the Enabling Act for Hitler's willingness to negotiate a concordat.[47] Konrad Repgen, a staunch defender of the good intentions of the Holy See, maintains that not until the dissolution of the parties (22–29 June) did the Vatican give up its position of defending the right of the clergy to participate in politics.[48] The evidence on which this is based is indirect and does not contradict the conclusion that "Kaas and the other Vatican negotiators realized from the beginning of the negotiations that they eventually would have to agree to Hitler's demand that priests be kept out of party politics."[49] Largely through the efforts of Kaas, the Vatican refused to concede the depoliticizing Article 32, which prohibited the clergy from joining any political party until the final negotiations at the beginning of July.[50] With the demise of the Center and Bavarian People's Parties, Hitler no longer needed this concession and could have ended the negotiations. Church leaders then looked to the Concordat as a means to protect the clergy from being required to join the Nazi Party in order to perform their pastoral functions.[51] Church leaders were realistic about what the future held in store and sought a legal "wall of defense" against the persecution they "feared" and "anticipated."[52] That the dissolution of the Catholic parties was neither a goal nor a bargaining chip of the nego-

46. Hughes, *Australian Journal* 20 (1974): 170.

47. See Volk, *Reichskonkordat*, 80–84.

48. Konrad Repgen, "Dokumentation. Zur Vatikanischen Strategie beim Reichskonkordat," *Vierteljahrshefte für Zeitgeschichte* 31 (1983), 529–33.

49. Zeender, 653.

50. Konrad Repgen, "Das Ende der Zentrumspartei und die Entstehung des Reichskonkordats," *Militärseelsorge* 12 (1970): 115, cited by Hughes, *Australian Journal* 20 (1974): 171, note 41.

51. Hughes, *Australian Journal* 20 (1974): 167.

52. Ibid., 171.

tiations is indicated by the recollections of Father Robert Leiber, S.J., Pacelli's private secretary. Pacelli wrote on 15 July 1933 and Leiber stated after the war that Pacelli expressed deep regret that the Center Party had dissolved itself before the Concordat had been signed without any consultation with the Holy See.[53] Scarcely a month after the conclusion of the Concordat, Cardinal Pacelli also told the British minister to the Holy See, Ivone Kirpatrick, that

a pistol had been pointed at his [Pacelli's] head and he had had no alternative. The German Government had offered him concessions, concessions, it must be admitted, wider than any previous German Government would agree to, and he had had to choose between an agreement on their lines and the virtual elimination of the Catholic Church in the Reich.[54]

Why then was it necessary for the Church to consider this offer of a concordat? Could the Church have refused? Probably not without serious repercussions and most predictably it would have faced another *Kulturkampf* with unforseen consequences. It must be remembered that the Pope, Pacelli, and the German episcopate had been concerned about the anti-Christian principles of Nazism and the future attitude of the government toward the Church. Hitler's emergency powers had already removed not only the Reichstag's ability to prevent a concordat, but also removed the guarantees of religious freedom written into the Weimar constitution. All this notwithstanding, the Vatican's initial response to the Hitler government's proposal was noncommital.[55]

To the surprise of the Vatican the German state conceded practically all that Pacelli had demanded in the earlier attempts to secure a Reich concordat, especially in the long-contested area of the Church's control over denominational schools. Under such circumstances the consequences of rejecting the state's offer would have placed the Church in the unenviable position of appearing to be responsible for all of the

53. Pacelli's letter is found in Volk, *Kirchliche Akten*, 162, and Leiber's recollections are found in Robert Leiber, "Reichskonkordat und Ende der Zentrumspartei," *Stimmen der Zeit* 167 (1960): 213–223, both cited by Hughes, *Australian Journal* 20 (1974): 171.

54. Documents on British Foreign Policy, series 2, vol. 5, no. 342 (London: H.M. Stationery Office, 1956), 524f.

55. Kupper, *Staatliche Akten*, No. 53, 118; Hughes, *Australian Journal* 20 (1974): 165.

persecution that threatened to follow. On 1 July, during the final negotiations, Archbishop Konrad Gröber, reputedly the most optimistic
among the German bishops about cooperation with the Nazi state,
wrote to Pacelli concerning his fears of what awaited the Church if the
Concordat was not approved. He said that "everything we have will
soon be smashed. Catholics might say: 'the Holy See could have helped
us and did not.' The government would publish the text of the Concordat and blame the Holy See for blocking the accomplishment of such
a good work."[56] Even Cardinal Faulhaber became fearful. Before June
he had been positive about a concordat, but during that month he had
been threatened, some Bavarian clergy had been arrested, and he began to consider the possible scandal if a concordat were to be signed
while Catholic officials were held in prison by the Nazi regime.[57] Hitler, however, was pressuring the Church into an agreement with tactics
that proved very successful in his later negotiations with other states.
He continued to demand that the clergy remove themselves from politics, and threatened to close Catholic schools and abolish the Catholic youth organizations. In order to be able to defend itself, the
Church had to sign a concordat recognizing the authority of the Reich
government.

Cardinal Pacelli was suspicious of Hitler's motives and expected the
Concordat to be violated. Nonetheless, Pacelli was satisfied with the
negotiations and the final signing. With his usual understatement, he
added the proviso that the German government still needed to fulfill its
provisions. The anti-Catholic persecution in Germany in June and July
had discouraged him and provoked a lack of trust. Yet, since the German government had acccepted the major demands of the Holy See,
the Church's rejection of such a favorable treaty would have led to an
open struggle between Church and State. As Pacelli explained, the
Church was reluctant to provoke a *Kulturkampf*: "A religious war is easy
to start but very difficult to sustain and the Catholics of the country
affected are entitled to know that the supreme government of the

56. Ludwig Volk, *Kirchliche Akten über die Reichskonkordatsverhandlungen, 1933*
(Mainz: Matthias-Grünewald-Verlag, 1969), 92–93.
57. Volk, *Episkopat*, 107.

Church has done everything in its power to spare them the ordeal."[58] The Concordat, then, was motivated by realism.

The final draft of the Concordat, approved by Cardinal Pacelli and the Pope, was taken to Berlin on 3 July. On 8 July the Concordat was initialed. Upon its acceptance by the Vatican in early July, Hitler rescinded the dissolution of those Catholic organizations recognized by the Concordat and canceled any coercive measures initiated against the clergy. In the cabinet meeting scheduled for 14 July Hitler had intended not to entertain any debate or changes to the specifics of the text. When the foreign situation had improved, the objectionable details could be modified Hitler argued. From his perspective he saw the following advantages:

1. That the Vatican had negotiated at all, while they operated, especially in Austria, on the assumption that National Socialism was un-Christian and inimical to the Church.

2. That the Vatican could be persuaded to bring about a good relationship with this purely national German state. He, the Reich Chancellor, would not have considered it possible even a short time ago that the Church would be willing to obligate the bishops to this state. The fact that this had now been done was certainly an unreserved recognition of the present regime.

3. That with the Concordat, the Church withdrew from activity in associations and parties, e.g., abandoned the Christian labor unions. This, too, he, the Reich chancellor, would not have considered possible even a few months ago. Even the dissolution of the Center Party could be termed final only with the conclusion of the Concordat, now that the Vatican had ordered the permanent exclusion of priests from party politics.

4. That the objective which he, the Reich Chancellor, had always been striving for, namely an agreement with the Curia, had been attained so much faster than he had imagined even on 30 January; this was such an indescribable success that all critical misgivings had to be withdrawn in the face of it.[59]

58. Cited in Holmes, 105.
59. *Documents of German Foreign Policy*, series C, vol. 1, 651–653.

The Concordat was signed on 20 July 1933 and the ceremonial exchange of documents took place in the Apostolic Palace of the Vatican on 10 September 1933.[60] The Treaty established a permanent basis for the regulation of relations between the Catholic Church and the German state. Of the thirty-three articles, twenty-one pertained to the rights of the Church. The right of the Church to teach and publicly defend Catholic principles was guaranteed. The right to operate Catholic schools was clearly recognized. The freedom of Church organizations, especially Catholic Youth associations, was safeguarded as long as they were apolitical. It had been so difficult to agree on which religious, cultural and educational organizations were to be protected and which were to be dissolved that Article 31 was left necessarily vague and was to be settled through future negotiations. Explicit pledges safeguarded communications with Rome, canonical regulations governing religious orders, and ecclesiastical property. Bishops were to have the right to approve instructors of religion in the state schools. Actually, privileges that had existed only in predominantly Catholic regions now were extended throughout the Reich, as for instance, the right to make sure that religious education was in accordance with Catholic principles. Catholic parents could even demand the creation of confessional schools whereas the Weimar Constitution (Article 174) had prohibited them (nondenominational school lands). The freedom to make ecclesiastical appointments was also included though limited in some cases by German citizenship or a period of education in Germany. Some consultation with the state was necessary in episcopal appointments, but no right to veto was involved. In a secret military annex it was stipulated that only under the extreme conditions of a general mobilization were seminarians obligated to perform military service. Article 16 of the Treaty required bishops to take a loyalty oath to the Reich government: "Before God and the holy gospels I swear and promise loyalty, as befits

60. William M. Harrigan, "Nazi Germany and the Holy See, 1933–1936," *Catholic Historical Review* 47 (1961): 172–173; Dietrich, 104; Holmes, 105–106; Helmreich, 246–250. The complete text in English can be found in *Documents on German Foreign Policy, 1918–1945*, series C (1933–1937), 80; The Third Reich: First Phase, vol. 1 (Jan. 30–Oct. 14, 1933), 669–679; a summary of its provisions are provided in Hughes, *Church and State* 17 (1975): 78–80.

a bishop, to the German Reich and the Land (state). I swear and promise to respect and cause my clergy to respect the legally constituted government. In dutiful concern for the welfare and interest of the German state I shall in the exercise of my spiritual office labor to preserve it from any harm that might threaten it."[61] The clergy were to have a German education and be German citizens, and religious instruction was to encourage patriotism and loyalty to the state. Article 21 provided that Catholic religious instruction for Catholic pupils would continue in state schools. Instruction was to emphasize a Christian approach to patriotic, civic, and social obligations. Hitler's goal of disbarring the entire Catholic clergy from politics (Article 32) was accepted by the Church, as well as his prohibition of clerics from membership in or even promotion of a political party.

The enthusiasm of the German bishops at the conclusion of the Concordat was widespread if not unanimous. Their expressions of gratitude, however, were couched in language suggesting a lack of confidence that its provisions would be observed. Cardinal Bertram coupled his thanks with the urgent wish that the provisions of the Concordat would be carried out by Hitler in such a way that the Church could cooperate in "the promotion of faith in God, morality, and loyal obedience to the leading authorities," which would rebound with blessing to the welfare of the people and the Fatherland.[62]

The Reich concordat followed the pattern established by the Lateran treaty and not by the concordats concluded with the German states. The state treaties had been negotiated through a process that involved the bishops, clergy, and laity providing advice and influencing the final form of the concordats. The Lateran and Reich Concordats followed "an authoritarian model". The Reich Concordat fulfilled Hitler's goal, already envisioned in 1929, of concluding a treaty with effects similar to what Mussolini had achieved in the Lateran treaties. Hitler had achieved the removal of the clergy from politics. Because of the Enabling Act, the provisions of the Concordat came into force without approval of the Reichstag.[63] In historical perspective the Treaty

61. Hughes, *Church and State* 17 (1975): 79.
62. Scholder, *Churches*, 1: 406.   63. Scholder, *Requiem*, 67.

seemed the most favorable document that the papacy had ever negotiated, though this judgment requires further comparative research.

Cardinal Pacelli, however, refused to accept Hitler's interpretation of
the Concordat as an approval by the Church of the National Socialist
state. In two articles in *Osservatore Romano*, the Cardinal Secretary of
State denied the claims of the Nazis, and emphasized that the clergy
should not cease to work for the welfare of the state, and that canon law
was the foundation of the Treaty. This, he expected, involved the state's
recognition of canon law and even its protection. In no way did it "represent the recognition by the church of the state, but on the contrary
complete recognition by the state of the new church law."[64] Pacelli believed that it also provided Rome the right to intervene in Germany's
domestic affairs and enabled it to challenge Nazi policies. At the beginning of 1934 (31 January) Pacelli reaffirmed that the policy of the
Vatican was to conclude concordats with all forms of government:

It is not for the Catholic Church to reject any form of government or re-
shaping of the organization of the state. She lives in correct and proper relation to States with a variety of governments and of different internal struc-
tures. She has made Concordats with monarchies and republics, with
democracies and totalitarian states. Her Concordats are acts dealing with religion and Church matters and are not simply acts of political significance.[65]

The Concordat provided a legal basis for the protests and defense of
the Church. Nonetheless, in reality the Concordat restrained the bishops from overtly attacking the claims and actions of the Hitler state. It
made the bishops fear that too great a protest could endanger the rights
left unviolated. Finally, although the provisions of the Concordat were
extremely favorable to the Church, the laws needed to implement the
treaty were never passed. Article 31, referring to the Church's organizations, did not specify which were protected. Its provisions were consistently violated.

Cardinal Faulhaber wrote to Hitler on 24 July 1933 expressing both

64. As cited in *Churches*, 1: 407.
65. Promemoria des Heiligen Stuhles an die Deutsche Reichsregierung, den 31.
Januar 1934, in *Der Notenwechsel Zwischen Dem Heiligen Stuhl Und Der Deutschen
Reichsregierung*, ed. Dieter Albrecht (Mainz: Matthias-Grünewald-Verlag, 1965),
1: 69–70; Dietrich, 111; Stehlin, 440.

jubilation and skepticism over the Concordat. He was careful to distinguish that the Concordat had strengthened the international reputation of Germany, and not that of Hitler, the Nazi Party, or the state. After stating that the Concordat could contribute to the moral strength of the German people, Faulhaber expressed the hope that its provisions "will not remain on paper," but would be put into practice. Yet, he also praised Hitler for his farsighted statesmanship, saying "What the old parliaments and parties did not accomplish in sixty years, your far-seeing statesmanship realized in six months of world-historical significance."[66]

Whether or not intended by the Vatican, the Concordat did provide some respectability and prestige to the Nazi state. Through the Concordat Hitler created his one-party state by eliminating the Center Party and destroying the hated power of political Catholicism. In the future the only political activity that legally could take place was within the Nazi Party. The Church, formerly a strong obstacle to Hitler's policy of coordination of power, was now harnessed to the duties of loyalty enunciated in the Concordat.

The ratification of the Concordat on 10 September was welcomed with enthusiasm, although there was some criticism and resistance. Special thanksgiving services were planned in some dioceses. A solemn pontifical mass was celebrated in Berlin by Caesare Orsenigo, the papal nuncio, with Catholic members of the SA and SS in attendance. In the service Hitler was eulogized and the Concordat was hailed as a "symbol of peace and friendship between the Church and state."[67] Some bishops ordered a thanksgiving service, the "Te Deum," to be sung in the parishes of their dioceses, although this generally was not the case, contrary to what Guenther Lewy had claimed.[68] In Bavaria, for example, where the situation was very tense, most of the bishops unanimously replied in the negative to the suggestion of Bishop Michael

66. As cited in Volk, *Bayerische Episkopat*, 121.

67. Dietrich, 137.

68. Ludwig Volk in *Bayerische Episkopat*, 136 claims that Lewy errs on p. 105 of *The Catholic Church and Nazi Germany* where he states that all the dioceses celebrated the event with a thanksgiving service. According to Volk, only the Nuncio in Berlin (Orsenigo) and the Archbishop of Bamberg did so.

Buchberger of Regensburg that a "Te Deum" would pacify the situation. Besides the critical reservations of Cardinal Faulhaber, Sigismund Felix Ow-Felldorf, the Bishop of Passau, wrote "The idea of holding a service of thanksgiving for the Reich concordat is so very repugnant to all my feelings and sensibilities that I would prefer to respond to the suggestion with a strong protest rather than with a simple 'Non placet.'"[69] Criticism of the Concordat was also found among some of the lower clergy in Bavaria while others naturally expected the treaty to protect them.[70]

Before the Concordat was ratified, the persecution of the Church in Bavaria had already soured Cardinal Faulhaber's enthusiasm because some of his clergy were imprisoned during June. The Cardinal protested that over one hundred priests were imprisoned. Some were only mishandled, but some were half beaten to death. The headquarters of Catholic Associations was also attacked. The most dramatic action by the Bavarian Nazi leadership occurred between 25–28 June when almost two thousand Catholics associated with the Bavarian People's Party, which had refused to dissolve itself, were rounded up and imprisoned. In this group were over 150 priests, most of whom were active in local politics, and some of which were opponents of the Nazis. Once the leaders of the BVP dissolved the party, most were released.[71]

Although attacks against Catholic organizations had begun before the Concordat was signed, they intensified afterwards. The Nazis planned to eliminate the Church's influence by restricting its organizations to purely religious activities. Unfortunately for the Church, Arti-

---

69. Ow-Felldorf to Faulhaber, 18 September 1933, *Faulhaber Akten*, I: 766–769. See *Churches*, I: 412 for a general discussion of the celebrations.

70. Lawrence D. Walker, "'Young Priests' as Opponents: Factors Associated with Clerical Opposition to the Nazis in Bavaria, 1933," *The Catholic Historical Review* 65 (July 1979): 409. Walker concludes from his statistical analyses from the records of the Bavarian Political Police that "the mean age of that offending group [was] 49.4 years, [and] that of the non-offending control group [was] 47.3 years," 411. Rather than being younger troublemakers, these clergy were middle-aged and generally exercised authority.

71. Klaus Schönhoven, "Zwischen Anpassung und Ausschaltung. Die Bayerische Volkspartei in der Endphase der Weimarer Republik, 1932/33," *Historische Zeitschrift* 224 (1977): 377; Volk, *Episkopat*, 104–107.

cle 31 of the Concordat, providing for the protection of Catholic organizations and associations by the state, had been left unresolved during
the negotiations. No list of organizations had been included for either
of the two categories: the religious organizations, which were to be provided with total protection, and social and professional organizations,
which were to have protected rights if and when they were merged into
state organizations. It was certainly in the interest of the Nazis to delay
an agreement as long as possible, so that pressures brought on organizations would result in their dissolution.[72]

The assaults on church organizations varied thoughout Germany,
but were most radical and extensive in Bavaria under Gauleiter, Minister of the Interior Adolf Wagner, and the Bavarian political police
under the leadership of Heinrich Himmler and Reinhard Heydrich.
The bans on organizational activities of June 13th and 20th were tight-
ened by the order of 19 September to prohibit all public meetings and
parades of Catholic organizations. Cardinal Berning protested to
Buttmann who pointed out to the Bavarian government that the restriction on the associations was in direct violation of the Church's
rights under the Concordat. After lengthy negotiations between the
state and the Church's representatives, Bishops Wilhelm Berning of
Osnabrück, Nikolaus Bares of Berlin, and Archbishop Conrad Gröber
of Freiburg, certain concessions were made by the bishops to the representatives of the Reich. They did not please some of the other bishops
or the Vatican. When the agreement was submitted to Cardinal Pacelli
he rejected it, as did Hitler, so that the impasse was never overcome.[73]

Although the Nazi regime attempted to coordinate the Catholic
youth organizations into the Hitler Youth (HJ), the Church was relatively more successful in its defense of its youth organizations than it
was with the Catholic press. Church resistance, however, was more
effective when it did not directly challenge the regime and defended
Church doctrines and practices. This has been effectively demonstrated

72. *Churches*, I: 494–95.
73. Ludwig Volk, "Die Fuldaer Bischofskonferenz von Hitlers Machtergreifung bis
zur Enzyklika 'Mit brennender Sorge,'" in *Katholische Kirche und Nationalsozialismus*,
ed. Dieter Albrecht (Mainz: Matthias-Grünewald-Verlag, 1987), 22–23; Helmreich,
271–72.

by Lawrence D. Walker, Barbara Shellenberger and Daniel Horn in their studies of the Church's struggle for its youth organizations against the Nazi attempt to impose its ideology and its dominance on the lives of youth.[74]

Nevertheless, the regime gradually succeeded in undermining the Church's youth programs and eliminating its organizations. Baldur von Schirach, the Reich Youth Leader, on 17 June 1933 prohibited dual membership in Catholic youth organizations and the Hitler Youth. Pressures to join the Hitler Youth increased. In some provinces Catholic Youth members were barred from wearing uniforms and going on organized trips, which made the organizations less attractive and encouraged their members to join the Hitler Youth. Other pressures included the embarrassment administered to seventeen hundred Catholic Youth members in 1935 on their return from an audience with the Pope. They had smuggled their uniforms across the border to wear them in the presence of the Pope. On their return the uniforms were confiscated by customs officials. Many Catholic youth resisted pressures to join the Hitler Youth, since its anti-Catholicism alienated parents and youngsters alike," and "members of the middle class were repelled by its rowdiness, immorality, and low-class tone."[75] The participation of Catholics in the Nazi Young Women's Youth Association (Bund deutscher Mädel) was even lower on average. The Hitler Youth Law of 1 December 1936 officially coordinated Catholic youth organizations into the Hitler Youth, but it was not until 6 February 1939 that the Catholic Young Men's Association (JMV) was finally dissolved by the Gestapo. It was formally ended by the law of 25 March 1939 which made mem-

74. Daniel Horn, "The Struggle for Catholic Youth in Hitler's Germany: An Assessment," *The Catholic Historical Review* 65 (October 1979): 562–63. Recommended by Horn as some of the best studies that emphasize self-defense and the Church struggle over Catholic youth are: Friedrich Zipfel, *Kirchenkampf in Deutschland 1933–1945* (Berlin, Veröffentlichungen der Historischen Kommission zu Berlin beim Friedrich-Meinecke-Institut der Freien Universität Berlin, 1965); Lawrence D. Walker, *Hitler Youth and Catholic Youth, 1935–1936. A Study in Totalitarian Conquest* (Washington, D.C., 1970); and Barbara Schellenberger, *Katholische Jugend und Drittes Reich. Eine Geschichte des Katholischen Jungmännerverbandes 1933–1939 unter besonderer Berücksichtigung der Rheinprovinz* (Berlin: Matthias-Grünewald-Verlag, 1975).

75. *Ibid*, 569.

bership in the Hitler Youth compulsory. Nonetheless, even though the Church had lost out to the Nazis over Catholic youth organizations, from the spiritual perspective its influence was still strong. The Church developed activities that appealed to youth and even trained leaders who could be influential in the Hitler Youth. During the war the Hitler Youth suspended its anticlericalism in order to reduce internal problems and was weakened when many of the leaders of the organization were drafted into the armed forces.[76]

Pressure to bring an end of the Catholic Workers' Associations emerged with the imposition of a ban on 27 April 1934 by Robert Ley, the leader of the German Labor Front, on dual membership in the Catholic and Nazi organizations. Membership in the Front increasingly became necessary for employment.[77] The forced coordination of the Bavarian organizations, however, had already taken place at the end of June 1933 when leaders were arrested and imprisoned along with those of the BVP.[78]

After the elimination of the clergy from politics the only other public voice of political commentary existed in the Catholic daily press. The Catholic press had over three million readers by the beginning of 1933 and the circulation of Catholic journals, including the diocesan gazettes, had a total circulation just under ten million, which actually increased during 1933. Unfortunately, the Concordat said nothing about the press, and apparently neither the Vatican nor the bishops were particularly concerned with the survival of those papers connected with the Catholic parties. Most bishops felt that only the subjects of religion and culture should be discussed in the Catholic press. The suppression of the daily press occurred gradually, with the government controlling the qualifications for journalism and the nature of political news. Finally, on 24 April 1934 the publication of the Catholic dailies was ended on order of the president of the *Reichspressekammer*, Max Amann. One victim of this tragic suppression of a free press was the oldest daily

76. *Ibid*, 564–569, 574; Walker, 146–156; Holmes, 108–109.
77. Lewy, 121; Ulrich von Hehl, *Katholische Kirche und Nationalsozialismus im Erzbistum Köln 1933–1945* (Mainz: Matthias-Grünewald-Verlag, 1977), 69.
78. Dorit-Maria Krenn, *Die Christliche Arbeiterbewegung in Bayern vom Ersten Weltkrieg bis 1933* (Mainz: Matthias-Grünewald-Verlag, 1991), 584–585.

newspaper in Germany, the renowned two hundred-year-old *Augsburger Postzeitung*.[79]

At first, the diocesan weeklies were able to remain exempt from the restrictions imposed by the *Reichspressekammer* which had prohibited any confessional group from publishing a newspaper. In 1936, however, Max Amann initiated a final phase, intended to control or close the diocesan weeklies, which finally culminated at the start of the war. Between 1 January 1934 and 19 October 1939 the weeklies had declined by 71 percent (435 to 134). Some were closed for not complying with the law restricting them to religious issues, while others expired for lack of newsprint. Diocesan gazettes intended for the clergy continued during the war, but were under the surveillance of the Gestapo which sometimes confiscated an edition.[80] In order to remain in print some diocesan papers sought to print statements that were favorable to the regime. It was unfortunate, Bishop Preysing regretfully reported to the bishops in August 1938, that many of the diocesan papers included articles that promoted the ideals and policies of the National Socialist state. Although Preysing recommended that the faithful be made aware that some of the Catholic press did not represent the views of the Church, no action was taken by the bishops to do so.[81]

Some moderation of the attacks on the Church occurred during the plebiscite in the Saar, which was reunited with Germany in March 1935. Afterward, the campaign of persecution resumed on 14 March with the result that forty cloisters, the offices of episcopal administrators, and those of Catholic organizations were ransacked, as were the palaces of the bishops of Würzburg, Rottenburg and Mainz. In 1936 the Nazis began their defamation campaign against priests and religious, arresting and bringing to trial hundreds and driving many others into exile. They were accused of immorality or of violating currency regulations.[82]

79. Dietrich, 145–49; see Lewy, 116–50 for a more extensive treatment, and the most knowledgeable study by Karl Aloys Altmeyer, *Katholische Press unter NS-Diktatur, Die katholischen Zeitungen und Zeitschriften Deutschlands in den Jahren 1933 bis 1945* (Berlin: Morus Verlag, 1962).

80. Dietrich, 153.

81. Lewy, 142–43.

82. Hans Günter Hockerts, *Die Sittlichkeitsprozesse gegen katholische Ordensangehörige und Priester, 1936/1937,* (Mainz: Matthias-Grünewald Verlag, 1971), 48–53.

The Nazi press, for instance, published a cartoon in which two clergy-men, a Catholic and Protestant, were depicted in the midst of bags of gold stating 'Ein feste Burg ist unser Gold!' (A mighty Fortress is our Gold), a pun based on the famous Lutheran hymn, "A mighty fortress is our God." In another cartoon the well-known Vatican Secretary of State, Cardinal Pacelli, was seen to be embracing an extremely large woman who was not only a Jewess, but also French and communist. Not even Pope Pius XI was beyond the reach of such slanderous pro-paganda, as stories from the notorious reign of Alexander Borgia of the Renaissance were allegedly recurring in Rome.[83] This defamation cam-paign and the morality trials were temporarily halted by Hitler in July 1936 because of the upcoming Olympic games.

Catholic schools also came under pressure. Members of the Nazi Party demanded that parents explain why their children attended Catholic schools. Parents were not permitted any official recourse. Over one hundred such incidents were noted by Pacelli. This strategy proved to be so successful that between 1933 and 1937 the percentage of Catholic families in Munich that sent their children to Catholic schools dropped from 65% to 3%. Six hundred teaching nuns were de-clared redundant and dismissed. Catholic teachers in state schools were pressured into resigning from confessional associations.[84]

Once the Concordat was ratified, the bishops' criticism of its wis-dom ended. It already was clear to the bishops that the German Church was in need of a strong defense against the increasing hostility of the Third Reich. The fundamentals of the treaty were accepted, as was the leadership of Rome, although there were continuing disagree-ments over tactics.

83. Holmes, 108.
84. See William M. Harrigan, "Nazi Germany and the Holy See, 1933–1936: The Historical Background of 'Mit brennender Sorge,'" *Catholic Historical Review* 47 (1961): 164–198; Eva Maria Kleinöder, "Der Kampf um die katholische Schule in Bay-ern in der NS-Zeit," in *Das Erzbistum München und Freising in der Zeit der national-sozialistischen Herrschaft*, ed. Georg Schwaiger, I: 639–657; idem., "Verfolgung und Widerstand der katholischen Jugendvereine. Eine Fallstudie über Eichstätt," in *Bay-ern in der NS-Zeit II. Herrschaft und Gesellschaft in Konflikt*, ed. Martin Broszat and Elke Frölich (München: R. Oldenbourg Verlag, 1979), 175–236.

Individual bishops protested violations of the Concordat and opposed some of the Nazi policies that contravened Christian teachings, as did the Fulda bishops' conference and the Vatican. During the visits of many German bishops during October 1934 the Pope was personally informed of their grievances which Cardinal Bertram's 4 October 1933 memorandum summarized. Bertram complained about the totalitarian claims of Nazism and its völkish ideology and their influence both on the state and society. Catholic organizations were suffering state persecution, the Catholic press had lost its freedom, Catholic government employees and clerical religious teachers had been dismissed. The Cardinal opposed the application of the Aryan paragraph to both clerical and lay teachers. Church property and endowments had been sequestered and priests arrested. Catholic confessional schools were threatened. Indoctrination courses in National Socialism were compulsory. Finally, the Cardinal predicted that the first serious conflict would be over the Reich's sterilization law (Law for the Prevention of Offspring with Hereditary Diseases), promulgated 14 July 1933 which violated the Pope's teachings in the 31 December, 1930 encyclical on Christian marriage, *Casti Connubii*. These complaints seriously aggravated the Pope, who wanted to strongly protest the government's violations of the Concordat. Dr. Buttmann was quickly sent to Rome, and extensively discussed the issues with Pacelli, especially their differing interpretations of Article 31. There was no resolution and neither were the views of the bishops included in the implementation ordinance of the sterilization law.[85]

Cardinal Faulhaber emerged as one of the most outspoken opponents of the Nazi regime. His leadership during the struggle, however, manifests some of the problems, dilemmas, and ambiguities of the whole process of episcopal protest under the Concordat. He had been an early supporter of a concordat in the spring of 1933 when he considered it important that the Church protect its schools and organizations and oppose sterilization. As the Nazi Party began to attack

85. Helmreich, 258–59; Scholder, *Churches* I: 496; see Dietrich, 218–19 for an explanation of the theological issues involved in sterilization and its condemnation in *Casti Connubii*.

Catholics, the Cardinal became more critical. Besides condemning the attacks on organizations in Bavaria, he denounced some of the principles of Nazi racial ideology, the theories of the "German Christians" (Protestants who tried to reconcile Christian teachings and Nazi ideology), the closing of Catholic schools, the dismissal of teachers, and the sham trials to which the mostly innocent clergy were subjected. Part of an early counterattack against the Nazi ideology of race and blood occurred during 1933–1934 when Faulhaber delivered five sermons between Advent and New Year's Eve, later published as *Judaism, Christianity and Germanism*.[86] The sermons primarily defended the Old Testament against the Nazi attempt to Aryanize Christianity. Salvation was for all men, he said, and was not based on Germanic blood, but on that of Christ. In the final sermon on 'Christianity and Germanhood,' Cardinal Faulhaber referred to St. Paul's epistle to the Romans (Rom. 10:12), which said that the racial basis of the Old Testament was replaced by faith and baptism, and that Christ was the "Lord of all."[87] Here was a strong denial of the possibility for any racial foundation for Christianity. Unfortunately, he did not consider the sermons a condemnation of contemporaneous anti-Semitism. When asked if he was defending contemporary Jewry Faulhaber replied that he was only defending the Jews and Judaism before Christ, but not those since. Faulhaber, like most of the bishops and laity, were instructed in the Catholic teaching that the Jews were cursed as the killers of Christ, a precept which was not altered until the Second Vatican Council. Inasmuch as the Jews had rejected Christ, they had ceased to be God's chosen people. Faulhaber's failure to carry the principles of his sermons to their conclusion exemplified the ambiguity of his protest and also the failure of all the bishops to speak out on the persecution of the Jews. Even after Jews were being transported to camps, it appeared that "Faulhaber felt no need to speak or act for the Jews and only [spoke] for the Non-Aryan Catholics in the form of petition for mitigation of the harsh conditions of transport and like Cardinal Bertram

86. Michael Cardinal Faulhaber, *Judaism, Christianity and Germany*, trans. Georg D. Smith (New York: Macmillan, 1954).
87. Cited and discussed in Scholder, I, 518–519.

. . . considered as hopeless any intervention with the Nazi government for people of Jewish descent."[88]

Faulhaber's reluctance to defend contemporary Jewry was already evident in early 1933. He rejected the plea of a priest editor to publicly defend the Jews.[89] When the Director of the German Bank in Berlin asked the bishops to intercede on behalf of Jews who were being threatened by new laws that disbarred them from the professions, Cardinal Bertram contacted President Hindenburg, while Faulhaber declined, corresponding to Pacelli that such a defense was "imprudent" and would engender an attack on the Church. Expressly reminiscent of some of the Christian anti-Semitism that was part of his world view, Faulhaber judged that the Jews in their mythical power (contrary to historical fact) could protect themselves.[90]

The domination of the press by the Nazi regime made it easy to alter statements in order to give false impressions about the positions of the clergy. For instance, in November 1933 when Hitler withdrew from the League of Nations and called for a plebiscite, the Fulda bishops' conference was unable to agree on a common statement. Although Faulhaber obtained agreement among the Bavarian bishops to support the plebiscite, their statement also included criticism of the government's hostility toward the Church. The criticism of the government never appeared in the press, while support of the plebiscite did. Unfortunately, there was no forceful and united opposition by the bishops which might have called attention to the "injustices, violence and abuses of human rights" that the Nazis had so far perpetrated.[91]

In the spring of 1937 around the time of the publication of the papal encyclical, *Mit brennender Sorge*, Faulhaber had changed his position to

88. Sister Ethel Mary Tinnemann, "The German Catholic Bishops and the Jewish Question," in *Holocaust Studies Annual*, ed. Jack Fischel and Sanford Pinsker (Greenwood, Fla: The Penkevill Publishing Co. 1986) 2: 70. Tinnemann cites Ludwig Volk's *Akten Faulhabers*, II, 824–825, no. 844, Faulhaber to Bertram, 13 November 1941, 856; no. 851, Faulhaber to Bertram, 1 December 1941.

89. John Zeender, "Germany: The Catholic Church and the Nazi Regime, 1933-1945," in *Catholics, the State and the European Radical Right, 1919–1945*, ed. Richard J. Wolff and Jörg Hoensch (New York: Columbia University Press, 1987), 98.

90. Gallin, *Church and State* 12 (1970): 397; Volk, *Bayerische Episkopat*, 77.

91. Dietrich, 139–142.

favor a policy of public protest instead of petition. By the spring of 1939, however, he had returned to one of accomodation. On 6 March 1939 he told the new Pope, Pius XII (1939–1958), that he now favored making every attempt to improve relations with the German state. If one reviews the major problems that he thought stood in the way of a peaceful relationship it is astounding to see that they were more procedural and legalistic than substantive. Could he possibly have willingly overlooked the continuous violations of the Concordat? The dangers of war? The persecution of Catholics? The persecution of Jews? In his statement he focused on such details as that Hitler meant the swastika only as a national symbol and not as one offensive to the cross, as Pius XI had understood it.[92] Klaus Scholder thinks Faulhaber misinterpreted Hitler's speech of 30 January 1939, when Hitler threatened a future separation of Church and State. Faulhaber thought that Hitler was proposing to refrain from further persecution of the Church. His intent, however, was quite the contrary. The speech was a warning to the Church that Hitler "was ready to reduce the churches to the status of associations and to deprive them of traditional state financial support."[93] Faulhaber may have properly understood Hitler's threat to annihilate the Jewish race in Europe, but he did not comprehend that the Fuhrer intended to destroy Christianity after his victory.

It was in the area of Nazi racist ideology that the Catholic clergy criticized National Socialism, because it was considered to be in the religious sphere delegated to the Church by the Concordat. Considered perhaps the most outspoken opponent of Nazi persecution, the bishop of Münster, Graf von Galen, was especially outspoken in his protests during 1941 against Hitler's euthanasia policy, and the subsequent widespread opposition brought to a halt this taking of innocent lives. Earlier in 1935 Galen had denounced Rosenberg's *The Myth of the Twentieth Century* and the new paganism that it espoused. He protested the inclusion of the book in the libraries of Christian schools. Before any

92. Gallin, 400.

93. Klaus Scholder, "Judaism and Christianity in the Ideology and Politics of National Socialism," in *Judaism and Christianity under the Impact of National Socialism*, ed. Otto dov Kulka and Paul R. Mendes Flohr (Jerusalem: The Historical Society of Israel and the Zalman Shazar Center for Jewish History, 1987), 194.

other bishop, he condemned the killing of Erich Klausner and accused the government of not punishing the perpetrators.[94]

The bishops generally followed the policy which has come to be known as "Eingabenpolitik" or petition politics. In this process the Church leaders would publicly complain of Concordat violations and then privately appeal to the government to desist from such abuses. From 1933 to 1938 the bishops supported this policy of Cardinal Bertram's, though neither unanimously nor enthusiastically. In the first phase of the struggle with the Nazis it was thought that such an approach would be the best defense, and would provide security for schools, youth groups and the press. Soon, however, it became clear to many bishops that National Socialism confronted them with another *Kulturkampf.* While nobody was killed during the Bismarckian *Kulturkampf*, one of the lessons learned from the Church's resistance was that the persecution imposed by the May Laws, which deprived congregations of the ministry of the clergy, had come at too great a price. Consequently, the majority of bishops agreed with Cardinal Bertram that it was best to avoid an open conflict with the government, so that Catholic congregations would again not be deprived of the ministry of clergy. For the bishops this fear of persecution was reinforced by their moral obligation to obey lawful authority, which was a basic principle of the Church's relation to any state and which was reinforced by the loyalty required by the Concordat.[95]

Even though the rights of the Church had been increasingly violated, the pastoral letters between 1933 and 1936 make it clear that the bishops continued to support obedience to legitimate state authority in all things that did not violate divine law.[96] The role of obedience to God's law when the law of the state conflicted with divine law was emphasized in the 1934 letter, but how this would be accomplished was not made clear. Galen, like most of the bishops, believed that all authority, both State and Church, came from God. As late as 1941, during the peak of his criticism of the regime, Galen emphasized, "We Christians

94. Heinrich Portmann, *Cardinal von Galen* (London: Jerrolds, 1957), 63–67, 107–108; Baumgartner, 151–152; Dietrich, 226–228; Tinnemann, 70–71.

95. Dietrich, 136–137, 154.   96. Dietrich, 153; Tinnemann, 66–67.

do not start revolutions."[97] Even when the vicar general from Oldenburg was exiled Galen followed a policy of accommodation, stating
"We stand under force even if we cannot recognize the measures as justified."[98] How were Catholics to understand the Church's expressions of
loyalty in context with its criticisms of the regime? The bishops explained the dilemma by blaming the regime's persecution on Nazi officials rather than Hitler.

Not only were the bishops incompetent to lead a revolution, but the
Pope, according to Pacelli, had sole competence for the interpretation
and observance of the Concordat. In effect, the Concordat had unwittingly produced a dilemma for the bishops. In Article 16 of the Treaty
the bishops were bound to an oath of loyalty to the state, and in Article 30 they were required to pray for the prosperity of the Reich and the
Völk. While pledging their loyalty to the government, the bishops
could only petition for a redress of Concordat violations, with no real
leverage except the threat of public criticism and an appeal to the fidelity of Hitler and the government. Unfortunately, in the minds of the
bishops the Concordat absolved them of political responsibility. They
generally adopted a policy of reserve toward political events and mainly
concerned themselves with problems that were ecclesiastical and moral
in nature, although that generally excluded the persecution of the Jews.
While the Holy See and the episcopate together sought to secure the
rights of the Church under the Concordat, this was only occasionally
successful. Irrespective of the question of whether there was sufficient
popular support for resistance, in the end it was the Concordat that excluded any possibility of a united Catholic action against the regime.[99]

By 1937 the bishops had lost their regular channels of communication with the laity, except through sermons. With the Nazis in control
of the media only abridged pastoral letters and articles uncritical of the

97. Heinrich Portman, *Bischof Graf von Galen spricht! Ein apostolischer kampf und
sein Widerhall* (Freiburg im Breisgau: Herder, 1946), 57.

98. Müller, *Katholische Kirche*, 305, cited in Tinnemann, 71.

99. See Heinz Hürten, "Selbstbehauptung und Widerstand der katholischen
Kirche," in *Der Widerstand gegen den Nationalsozialismus*, ed. Jürgen Schmädeke and
Peter Steinbach (München: Piper Verlag, 1985), 240–253; Scholder, *Churches*, II:
89–90; Scholder, *Requiem*, 99, 131; Dietrich, 138–139.

state could be printed. Even the Church's influence through its educational institutions had practically disappeared, as enrollment in denominational schools had fallen to a low of 4.4 percent even in Catholic Bavaria. The bishops were unsure of what support the faithful would give to any resistance against the state. In December 1936, Bertram wrote to Pacelli that it was impossible to expect a basic change in the attitude of the Nazi Party and the government. With each compromise the Church lessened its ability to resist the state. A case in point emerged from the conference between Hitler and Cardinal Faulhaber at the Obersalzburg on 4 November 1936. Hitler managed to make a favorable impression on Faulhaber. The Cardinal recorded that Hitler manifested a faith in God, though, of course, not in the Catholic Church's divine mission as separate from the state. After the war Faulhaber modified these impressions, asserting that when he talked with Hitler he had "looked Satan in the face." Although the meeting ended on a friendly note, the power of Hitler's countenance, which Faulhaber described as a "dark radiance," cast a spell on Faulhaber that took weeks to shake off. During this meeting Hitler proposed to Faulhaber that if the Church would support the National Socialist struggle against communism (the Spanish Civil War had begun) then Hitler would curtail some of the Reich's violations of the Concordat.[100] Cardinal Faulhaber's pastoral letter of 3 January 1937 responded positively to the offer and pledged the support of the Church for the Führer's struggle against the advance of Bolshevism.

The second phase of the Church's struggle with the Nazi regime

100. See Ludwig Volk, *Akten Faulhabers*, 2: 184–194. Volk's knowledge of this spell-like impact came from another source than the manuscript record of the meeting published in the *Akten*. Perhaps Faulhaber realized that his notes on the meeting with Hitler could be compromised and only recorded favorable judgments. Volk introduces the description of the spell-like impact on Faulhaber in "Kardinal Faulhabers Stellung zur Weimarer Republik und zum NS-Staat" in *Stimmen der Zeit* 177 (1966): 186–187, but does not give his source other than the *Akten*. That Volk's knowledge might have come from some other papers and discussions of Faulhaber's postwar reminiscences is suggested by Otto Gritschneder's review of Volk's *Akten*, where he recounts being a frequent guest of Faulhaber in 1949, when the encounter with Hitler was discussed and elaborated. See Otto Gritschneder's "Kardinal Faulhaber besucht Adolf Hitler," *Münchener Staatsanzeiger* 30 (20 April 1979), 5.

began in 1936 and lasted until 1940 but reached its most dramatic climax with the publication of the encyclical *Mit brennender Sorge*. Having already neutralized Catholic organizations, the Nazi regime aimed at the Church's value system and its identity. During this period the Nazis tried to limit the Church entirely to the liturgical realm, removing it from the life of the individual and society. This phase of the *Kirchenkampf* reached a new dimension in the National Socialist totalitarian drive to dominate the conscience of the individual.[101]

In August 1936 the bishops had requested the Pope to condemn the ongoing persecution of the Church in an apostolic letter.[102] During the years 1935 and 1936 the episcopacy and the Vatican already had made many statements both public and private concerning violations of the Concordat.[103] The Fulda bishops' conference that convened on 12–13 January 1937 complained to the government of seventeen violations of the Concordat. For the outspoken Bishop von Galen, who was an especially strong advocate of a more assertive defense against the persecution of the Church, this was insufficient.[104] Shortly after the Fulda conference a delegation which included Cardinals Faulhaber, Bertram, and Schulte, in addition to Bishops Galen and Preysing, went to Rome to urge the Pope to make a public declaration concerning the ongoing persecution of the Church. The delegation discussed the problems with Pacelli and the Pope, which led to the encyclical. Faulhaber's draft proposal and Pacelli's revisions contributed to its content.[105]

101. Dietrich, 154–156; Gotto et al., "Eine Bilanz," 179.

102. Ludwig Volk, ed., *Akten Deutscher Bischöfe über die Lage der Kirche, 1936–1939* (Mainz: Matthias-Grünewald-Verlag, 1981), 3: 437.

103. Helmreich, 280–83; Dietrich, 155–56. Two protests, one by Cardinal Bertram and another by Cardinal Pacelli, concern violations of Articles 23 and 25 in Prussia: "Kardinal Bertram an Herrn Reichs und Preussischen Minister für Wissenschaft, Erziehung und Volksbildung in Berlin, Breslau, den 18. Februar, 1936"; and "E. Card. Pacelli an Seiner Exzellenz Herrn Dr. Diego von Bergen, Deutscher Botschafter beim Hl. Stuhl Deutsche Botschaft, Rom, de 23 April 1936." Diocesan Archives, Regensburg.

104. See Maria Anna Zumholz, "Clemens August Graf von Galen und der deutsche Episkopat, 1933–1945," in *Clemens August Graf von Galen: Neue Forschungen zum Leben und Wirken des Bischofs von Münster*, ed. Joachim Kuropka (Münster: Verlag Regensburg, 1992), 192–196.

105. See Dieter Albrecht, ed., *Der Notenwechsel Zwischen Dem Heiligen Stuhl Und Der Deutschen Reichsregierung* (Mainz: Matthias-Grünewald-Verlag, 1965), I, 404–443; Helmreich, 280; Heinz-Albert Raem, *Pius XI und der Nationalsozialismus. Die*

With great stealth the papal encyclical *Mit brennender Sorge* was distributed throughout Germany and read from pulpits on 21 March 1937. In keeping with Article 4 of the Concordat pastoral letters and encyclicals could be read from pulpits as well as printed in diocesan *Amtsblätter*, so only copies distributed outside of the churches were confiscated. The encyclical forcefully protested the many violations of the Concordat, reviewed the principles of the Catholic faith, Christian ethics, and the importance of the natural law versus the interests of the state, and condemned the arbitrary "revelations" of Alfred Rosenburg and the exponents of the "so-called myth of blood and race."[106] It was the Church's most forceful and dramatic condemnation of Nazi policy during the Third Reich.

Needless to say the government reacted angrily, condemning the open criticism, and closing the publishing houses that remained. It is possible that earlier Hitler had considered a more moderate political solution to the relations between Church and State. With the publication of the encyclical, however, Hitler concluded that Catholicism had declared war on the Nazi ideology and there no longer was any hope of compromise. A storm of Nazi propaganda followed. In his May Day address Hitler found it intolerable that any authority should criticize and attack the morality of the German state. Goebbels's understanding of Hitler's intent was that the Church had to be bent into a servant of the state. Outlined in five stages, the campaign against the Church was to include expropriation of Church assets; dissolution of religious orders and monasteries; restriction on entrance to theological studies; prohibition of education by clergy; and elimination of clerical celibacy.[107] The promulgation of the encyclical even prompted Hitler's Minister of

---

Enzyklika "Mit brennender Sorge" vom 14 März 1937 (Paderborn: Ferdinand Schöningh, 1979), 32–45.

106. See Ludwig Volk, "Die Enzyklika *Mit brennender Sorge*," in *Katholische Kirche und Nationalsozialismus*, ed. Dieter Albrecht, et al. (Mainz: Matthias-Grünewald-Verlag, 1987), 34–55.

107. See Elke Frölik, *Die Tagebücher von Joseph Goebbels*, teil I. bd. 3, 1937–1939 (München: K.G. Saur, 1987), 97–98, 128–129; Hans Günther Hockerts, "Die nationalsozialistische Kirchenpolitik im neuen Licht der Goebbels-Tagebücher," in *Aus Politik und Zeitgeschichte, Beilage zur Wochenzeitung, Das Parlament*, (1983) B, no. 30 (1983): 30; Raem, 216–29.

Ecclesiastical Affairs to consider abrogating the Concordat.[108] Yet, Hitler's tactics so vacillated that the settlement of the whole Church-Reich conflict with both Evangelical and Catholic churches, which he had planned to announce on Reformation Day, 31 October 1937, never occurred. Neither his speech nor his note to the Vatican abrogating the Concordat were ever delivered. Both Hitler and the Curia preferred to retain the Concordat.[109] In 1938 Nazi intentions remained a secret. It was recognized that the provisions of the Reich Concordat and the preceding concordats with Bavaria, Prussia and Baden ran counter to the educational goals and ideology of National Socialism. Instructions sent from the Foreign Ministry to provincial governors stated that "in our relations with organs of the Catholic Church we also avoid all reference to provisions under the Concordats or discussions of alleged violations of Concordats."[110] Some provisions were observed by the government, though by 1938 the Foreign Ministry still had not clearly defined its attitude. In writing to the Armed Forces Supreme Command Headquarters on 28 January 1939 Martin Borman, the Chief of Staff to Rudolf Hess, stated that the majority of clergy of "both Churches stand, in accordance with the attitude of those Churches, in concealed or open opposition to National Socialism and the State led by it."[111] A similarly critical attitude was expressed by Reinhard Heydrich, chief of the security police and head of Reich Security Main Office (RHSA), who in his 1938 annual report in the *Sicherheitshauptamt* criticized all the churches for not only being hostile to the regime but trying to bring about the collapse of the Third Reich, citing "the hostility constantly displayed by the Vatican, the negative attitude of the bishops towards the *Anschluss* as typified by the conduct of Bishop Sproll of Württemberg, the attempt to make the Catholic Eucharistic Congress in Budapest a demonstration of united opposition to Germany, and the continued accusations of Godlessness and of destruction of church life made by Church leaders in their pastoral letters."[112]

---

108. Scholder, *Requiem*, 112.
109. John S. Conway, *The Nazi Persecution of the Churches, 1933–1945* (New York: Basic Books, 1968) 203, 215–16.
110. Ibid, 216–17.   111. Ibid., 217.
112. Zipfel, 458, note 1: 61, 458, cited in Conway, 218.

In 1937 and 1938 the government increased its pressures on the Church, though all denominations were being affected by the same laws. By comparison the Protestant churches were worse off. The Catholic Church was spared any attempt to control its hierarchy or to threaten the authority of the bishops over the laity. The government's demand for an oath of loyalty may have troubled some Protestant clergymen, but was a non-issue for the Catholic bishops who were bound to comply by Article 16 of the Concordat. One very effective device used against the Catholic Church by Heinrich Himmler was the confiscation and sequestration of church properties. In the Rhineland during 1939 Catholic institutions were placed under the control of an SS-sponsored welfare society. Some institutions were confiscated for the purpose of serving as Nazi maternity homes and schools for indoctrination. In Wiesbaden by April 1940 up to 30 million Reichsmarcks worth of church property were transferred.[113] Of greater religious impact, and indicative of the extremity of Nazi goals, were the increasingly exaggerated fabrications against the clergy in the morality trials. The clergy were also prohibited from conducting religious instruction in community and vocational schools. Private schools were abolished or taken over by the state. In the spring of 1939 the denominational schools were converted into interdenominational ones and members of religious orders were denied the right to serve as teachers. Even crucifixes and religious pictures were requested to be removed from classrooms in Oldenburg and Bavaria, which led to mass protests and criticism by the Bavarian bishops on 26 July 1941. In this case the Nazis backed down in a clear victory for the Church.[114]

The notorious arrest and conviction of the popular Jesuit preacher Rupert Mayer in Munich was one example of the government's prosecution of the clergy.[115] In 1937 Father Mayer had intensified his criti-

---

113. Helmreich, 286–87; Conway, 245.

114. Ian Kershaw, *Popular Opinion and Political Dissent in the Third Reich: Bavaria, 1933–1945* (Oxford: Clarendon Press, 1983), 340–57.

115. On 24 January 1937 Fr. Mayer gave his famous sermon in the St. Michaels-Kirche in Munich. See "Pater Rupert Mayer vor dem Sondergericht," *Dokumente der Verhandlung vor dem Sondergericht zu München am 22 und 23 Juli, 1937*, ed. Otto Gritschneder (München: Verlag Anton Pustet, 1965).

cism and was increasingly influential in Munich. His campaign of protest against the closing of Catholic schools and his unwillingness to compromise made him a "thorn in the side of the National Socialists." He harshly judged his more cooperative clerical colleagues. In May and June of 1937 he was prohibited from preaching, arrested, imprisoned, released; he obeyed the government's prohibition, preached again, then was imprisoned for four months in 1938. At the beginning of the war he was again imprisoned in Oranienberg. Fearful that Father Mayer might become a martyr if he died due to illness, his captors transfered him to the Benedictine Monastery at Ettal in the Bavarian Alps on 7 August 1941.[116] Rupert Mayer survived the regime.

Even after the pronouncement of the encyclical and the increased Nazi repression of the Church, Cardinal Bertram decided to continue his policy of petition and negotiation.[117] The continuation of such a policy, however, was considered useless by Cardinal Faulhaber, as well as the new bishop of Berlin, Konrad von Preysing, Bishop von Galen of Münster, and Bishop Michael Rackl of Eichstätt, who all favored publicly protesting against the regime. For example, in a letter of 18 October 1937, Preysing judged the Church to be a paralyzed institution in a war of annihilation. He rejected the policy of subtle diplomacy with "delicate diplomatic language" as ineffective, and emphasized that the bishops needed to publicize the aggressions of the state and party so that both clergy and laity be informed, and mobilize opposition.[118]

116. Anton Koerbling S.J., *Father Rupert Mayer* (München: Schnell and Steiner, 1956), 143, 146, 149, 150, 180; Vince Lapomarda, *The Jesuits and the Third Reich* (Lampeter, U.K: The Edwin Mellen Press, 1989), 11, 17–18, 38; see Wilhelm Sandfuchs, "Fur die Rechte der Kirche und die Freiheit, Pater Rupert Mayer SJ unerschrochener Bekenner und Glaubenszeuge im Kirchenkampf" and Roman Bleistein, "Die Jesuiten in der Erzdiözese München und Freising," II, 489–512 in Georg Schwaiger, ed. *Das Erzbistum München und Freising in der Zeit der Nationalsozialistischen Herrschaft* (München: Schnell and Steiner, 1984) II, pp. 186–211, 489–512.

117. See Ludwig Volk, "Nationalsozialistische Kirchenkampf und deutsche Episkopat," in *Die Katholiken und das Dritte Reich*, eds. Klaus Gotto and Konrad Repgen (Mainz: Matthias-Grünewald-Verlag, 1990), 60–63.

118. Dietrich, 158. On Preysing's position and motives in this conflict with Bertram see Walter Adolph, *Geheime Aufzeichnungen aus dem nationalsozialistischen Kirchenkampf, 1935–1943*, ed. Ulrich von Hehl (Mainz: Matthias-Grünewald-Verlag, 1979), 170f.

Preysing pointed to three noteworthy examples of opposition to the regime among Catholics: the successful resistance against the removal of crucifixes from the schools in Oldenburg;[119] a large demonstration in Eichstätt during April 1937 over the arrest of a cathedral priest who had protested the morality trials;[120] and an impressive street demonstration in Munich during June 1937 protesting the imprisonment of Father Mayer.[121] In all these instances, protests had forced reversal or moderation of the government's actions.

Bishop von Galen also strongly advocated in 1936 and 1937 that the bishops break the "wall of silence" that shrouded the struggle between Church and State.[122] Cardinal Pacelli agreed with the group of protest-oriented bishops, no longer thinking that the "bishops' conciliatory negotiations would be successful."[123] Yet Bertram and most of the bishops were opposed to an open conflict with the regime, for fear, as Bertram expressed it, that "the faithful would again have to die without a priest," as they did during the Bismarckian *Kulturkampf*.[124] So Bertram rejected Preysing's proposal for a change of policy, aware that the majority of the bishops, and in the end the Holy See, supported him. Since the government was aware that the episcopacy would not mobilize public opinion against the regime, it fearlessly pursued its anti-Christian propaganda and repression of the Church. Preysing had become so discouraged that it was only the Pope who forstalled Preysing's resignation

119. See Jeremy Noakes, "The Oldenburg Crucifix Struggle of November 1936: A Case Study of Opposition in the Third Reich," in *The Shaping of the Nazi State*, ed. Peter Stachura (New York: Barnes & Noble, 1978), 210–233.

120. Helmut Witetschek, ed., *Die kirchliche Lage in Bayern nach den Regierungspräsidentenberichten, 1933–1943. Regierungsbezirk, Ober-und Mittelfranken* (Mainz: Matthias-Grünewald-Verlag, 1967), 175f.

121.Schwaiger, II, 44f.

122. Volk, *Akten Faulhabers*, II, 115; idem., *Akten deutscher Bischöfe*, IV, 208; for an analysis of Bishop Galen's position on publicly criticizing the Nazi regime for its persecution of the Church see Maria Anna Zumholz, "Clemens August Graf von Galen und der deutsche Episkopat 1933–1945," in *Clemens August Graf von Galen: Neue Forschungen zum Leben und Wirken des Bischofs von Münster*, ed. Joachim Kuropka (Münster: Verlag Regensberg, 1992), 179–220.

123. Dietrich, 158.

124. Ludwig Volk, "Adolf Bertram (1859–1945)," in *Zeitgeschichte in Lebensbildern*, ed. Rudolf Morsey (Mainz: Matthias-Grünewald-Verlag, 1973), I, 282.

from the conference and his episcopal see. By the beginning of the war the divisions in the episcopate had almost come to an open breach. The next episcopal conference in August 1940 became so tense after Preysing's opening remarks that Bertram left the meeting, which was then ended. Instead of a change of leadership or policy, the assembly was reconvened under Bertram.[125]

Perhaps the last chance to change course and pursue a policy of public criticism of the regime was lost in 1941. This favorable opportunity grew out of popular protest against the euthanasia program pursued by the regime and the medical establishment against the relatives of Aryan Germans. The T-4 program had as its goal the murdering of the mentally ill and congenitally deformed. Of course, the origin of the program went back to the sterilization policy enacted in 1933. In late October 1939 after the beginning of the war Hitler issued the order to eliminate the so-called racially inferior population, otherwise described as persons with a "life unworthy of living."[126] Earlier there had been criticisms and protests but they were either too vague or too private. For instance, Pius XII's first encyclical, *Summi Pontificatus*, of October 1939, generally warned against the state usurping the position of God as the arbiter of the moral order, but said nothing specific about euthanasia.[127] The *Osservatore Romano* of 6 December 1940 condemned the policy as contrary to both natural and divine law. Both Bishop Gröber on 1 August 1940 and Cardinal Faulhaber on 6 November 1940 privately protested the killings to Hitler's Minister of Justice, Dr. Franz Gürtner, Faulhaber justifying his protest on the basis of Article 16 of the Concordat which required Faulhaber to take an oath to protect the Reich against any harm.[128] It was, however, Bishop von Galen who spoke out in three famous sermons (13 and 29 July and 3 August 1941) against the

125. Dietrich, 164–65; Scholder, *Requiem*, 162.
126. Henry Friedlander, *The Origins of Nazi Genocide: From Euthanasia to the Final Solution* (Chapel Hill: University of North Carolina Press, 1995), 64; see Dietrich, 224–27, for a discussion of this decision.
127. *The Papal Encyclicals in Their Historical Context*, ed. Anne Fremantle (New York: Mentor Books, 1956), 265–269.
128. Faulhaber an Gürtner, München, 6 November 1940, *Akten Faulhabers*, II, 689–694.

execution of the mentally ill and took the courageous step of initiating legal charges of murder based on paragraph 139 of the German Criminal Code. His renown and high position probably protected him from the Gestapo's retribution. Galen's sermons seriously affected German public opinion and even that of some soldiers. Other bishops now followed Galen's example with public denunciations of euthanasia. In the end Hitler stopped the killings within Germany and moved the program eastward. The successful protest unmistakably proved that a strong united opposition which the Nazis feared could produce an alteration in government policy. In Daniel Goldhagen's recent evaluation of this case he profiles this as a model of successful protest that might have been used to save Jewish lives.[129] Unfortunately, the episcopal leadership either saw their successful protest against euthanasia as concerning a unique moral issue that had no parallels requiring such an outspoken effort (such as the extermination of the Jewish race) or they ignored the lessons that might have been learned from their success.

At the Fulda bishops' conference in 1941 a draft of a pastoral letter was formulated under the direction of Bishops Preysing, Berning, and Gröber. Its language was clear and bold. The pastoral letter, which had the support of twenty bishops, protested the policy of euthanasia, the persecutions in Poland, and the closing of monasteries and houses of religious orders. It lacked a discussion of the Jewish question, but it did ask "the one decisive question . . . : 'What is our duty in the present moment? What does conscience require? What does God, what do German believers expect of their bishops?'"[130] During the conference it was proposed that both Catholic and Protestant churches join in appealing to the Reich government to stop its persecution of the churches. This failed. Early in 1942 Bertram also hindered the promulgation of the pastoral letter, effectively ending any possibility of what might have

---

129. Daniel J. Goldhagen, *Hitler's Willing Executioners and the Holocaust* (New York: Alfred A. Knopf, 1966), 119 where he states "Germans (1) recognized this slaughter to be wrong, (2) expressed their views about it, (3) openly protested for an end to the killing, (4) suffered no retribution for having expressed their views and for pressing their demands, and (5) succeeded in producing a formal cessation of the killing program, and saving German lives."

130. Scholder, *Requiem*, 134.

been a significant turning point in the compromising and ineffectual episcopal policy toward the Third Reich.[131]

At the 1943 Fulda conference Konrad Preysing proposed that the bishops protest the treatment of deported Jews. Preysing's proposal had been drafted by Margarete Sommer, the episcopacy's advisor on Jewish affairs and executive director of the Special Relief Office in the Berlin diocese. This office was organized to help both Catholic Jews (those Jews who had converted to Catholicism) and non-Catholic Jews. Sommer was informed that the fate of "transported" Jews was death. Her "Draft for the Petition Favoring the Jews" (August 1943) which was presented to the bishops, concerned the recognition of the rights of all Jews who were deported. Most of the bishops, however, were not convinced that non-Catholics subject to deportation were their concern. The evidence in support of the draft failed to convince Cardinal Bertram, whose support was essential for the conference's endorsement. Preysing warned the bishops that God would hold them accountable for their silence. Preysing also urged Pope Pius XII to provide leadership and require the German bishops to confront the Nazi regime on this issue, but the Pope left the responsibility in the hands of the bishops, who remained silent.[132]

That the leadership of the German Church was in the hands of a Cardinal whose secretiveness elicited bitter complaints from Dr. Negwer, the Dean of the Breslau Cathedral chapter, which prompted Walter Adolf on 19 June 1937 to ask: "Is it not a disaster that a seventy-nine-year-old autocratic and mistrustful old man should guide the helm of our church in Germany in so decisive an hour?"[133] The mantle of au-

131. Scholder, *Requiem*, 162–63; See Volk, *Akten deutsche Bischöfe*, 4: 564–567; idem. (ed.), *Akten Faulhabers*, 2: 759, 826, 833, 838, 850, 888, 936; Walter Adolph, *Hirtenamt und Hitler-Diktatur*, 2nd ed. (Berlin: Morus-Verlag, 1965), 169–71; idem., *Kardinal Preysing*, 159–65; for the history of the pastoral letter see Volk, "Die Fuldaer Bischofskonferenz von der Enzyklika *Mit brennender Sorge* bis zum Ende der NS-Herrschaft," in *Katholische Kirche und Nationalsozialismus*, ed. Dieter Albrecht et al. (Mainz: Matthias-Grünewald-Verlag, 1987), 56–82.

132. Michael Phayer, "The Catholic Resistance Circle in Berlin and German Catholic Bishops during the Holocaust," *Holocaust and Genocide Studies* 7 (Fall 1993), 216–24.

133. Walter Adolf, *Geheime Aufzeichungen aus dem nationalsozialistischen Kirchenkampf 1935–1943*, ed. Ulrich von Hehl (Mainz: Matthias-Grünewald Verlag, 1979), 133.

thority in this hierarchical system unfortunately fell on a bishop whose bureaucratic and diplomatic style proved a failure in the face of mounting violations of the Concordat and the Jewish question. In the name of all the bishops Bertram had begun to send birthday greetings to Hitler by 1935. The continuation of these greetings to Hitler even with the escalating repression of the Church also was an expression of "petition politics." On the occasion of Hitler's fiftieth birthday, 20 April 1939, and again in 1940, Bertram congratulated Hitler on behalf of the entire episcopate using the occasion to express loyalty to the Catholic head of state and to remind him of the complaints that Catholics had with the government. Bertram was not alone, however, in his congratulations in 1939 for even Pius XII sent a message through Nuncio Orsenigo.[134] Cardinal Preysing, however, became so upset over the greeting in 1940 that he resigned from his position as *Pressereferat* of the bishop's conference.[135] The Pope did not support his challenge to Bertram's leadership.[136] Yet, perhaps tactical concerns were not Bertram's primary motivation for continuing a policy of petition. Certainly the obligations of the Concordat reinforced Bertram's natural obedience and loyalty to authority. His official behavior at the end of the war was certainly surprising; after learning of the death of Adolf Hitler, he continued to express his loyalty, requesting parish priests to offer a solemn requiem mass in memory of the Führer.

Due to his revisionist and expansionist foreign policy, Hitler needed to promote national unity and not alienate foreign opinion during 1938 and 1939. With the outbreak of World War II increased pressures were brought to bear on the Church for its support of the regime and the war. The Catholic bishops proclaimed their support of the invasion of Poland. Although a truce was declared, it turned out to be a false *Burgfrieden*, as it only lasted until the conquest of France had

134. Dietrich, 160–162. Volk and Scholder disagree on the purpose of the 1940 greeting: Volk says it was an attempt to bring the complaints of Catholics to the head of state, while Scholder believes this was an expression of loyalty to a German Catholic head of state in wartime. See Volk, *Katholische Kirche im Dritte Reich*, 75, and Sholder, *Requiem*, 162; see also Adolph, *Hirtenamt*, 161–63.

135. Adolph, *Hirtenamt*, 164–68.

136. Burkhart Schneider, ed., *Die Briefe Pius XII An Die Deutschen Bischöfe 1939–1944* (Mainz: Matthias-Grünewald Verlag, 1966), 31–32, 70–75, 108–11.

166   JOSEPH A. BIESINGER

ended.[137] Then the *Kirchenkampf* continued with a renewal of restrictions, prohibitions, incarcerations and surveillance. Reinhard Heyrich initiated some of the new measures, such as closing down churches that were too far from air raid shelters. Most church publishing facilities were closed by June 1941. Church bells were melted down. Commanders of SD units were instructed to conduct surveillance on all aspects of the lives of the bishops. Informants placed in diocesan offices compromised the secrecy of files and archives; they were to report conflicts and weaknesses of the bishops. Priests were prohibited from entering hospitals unless requested and approved. In Saxony all religious education was suspended. In Berlin prayers were prohibited during school assemblies. Confiscation of monastic properties and non-parochial institutions expanded. From 1941 onward the anti-church campaign was aimed at Christianity itself. The belief that Christianity and National Socialism were irreconcilable was acknowledged both by Borman and Hitler, though Hitler decided to delay the suppression of Christianity until the end of the war.[138] As Hitler remarked, a synthesis between Christianity and National Socialism was no longer a possibility for "Pure Christianity . . . was merely wholehearted Bolshevism, under a tinsel of metaphysics."[139]

As Germany expanded, the regime decided not to recognize the applicability of the Concordat in annexed and conquered territories. Neither the German bishops nor for that matter the Minister for Church Affairs were allowed to exercise any authority over the churches in these areas. In June, 1942 Hitler denied the papal nuncio, Cesare Orsegnio, any jurisdiction or rights of visitation in the occupied territories. Neither were protests from Orsegnio, or directly from the Vatican, concerning atrocities against Polish priests or the Jews, considered to be in the Vatican's jurisdiction. Vatican representatives were not even allowed to enter Poland, and the existing Nunciatures in Amsterdam and Brussels were closed.[140]

137. See Heinz Hürten, *Deutsche Katholiken 1918–1945* (Paderborn: Ferdinand Schöningh, 1992), 460–78.
138. Conway, 236–39, 243–44, 254–60; Lill, 262; Adolf, *Hirtenamt*, 77–84; Dietrich, 142–45, 166.
139. As cited in Conway, 253.
140. Conway, 303–9; John F. Morley, *Vatican Diplomacy and the Jews during the Holocaust, 1939–1943* (New York: KTAV, 1980), 120–28.

The pastoral letters of the German bishops in 1942 and 1943, and the sermons of the newly elected Archbishop Joseph Frings of Cologne, have often been cited as evidence of public protest against the genocidal policy directed against the Jews. Pastorals and sermons of note by Archbishop Frings include those concerning the foundation of human rights (12 December 1942). Frings condemned the killing of innocents of non-Aryan blood, who were probably understood by Catholics to be Jews (25 December 1943 and 12 March 1944).[141] Generally, the episcopal statements condemned the Nazi racial ideology. All of these statements, however, were mild theological pronouncements, and markedly different from those which were so successful in stopping euthanasia. The Jews were not clearly identified as the "foreign peoples" or the people of an "alien race and descent." The pastoral of December 1942 did, however, defend human rights as sacred, founded on divine law and not based on blood or subject to the state which was a challenge to the legality of the treatment of the Jews.[142] Had the bishops been willing to lead a public protest, as they had against euthanasia, there is evidence that some mobilization could have occurred, although it is unlikely that the deportations could have been stopped.[143] Nevertheless, the bishops failed to educate German Catholics against both their overt and latent anti-Semitism and, perhaps considering the Jewish question a political one, refrained from involving themselves with this inasmuch as it was prohibited by the Concordat and probably would have triggered government retribution.

An example of the kind of retribution that was possible occurred in Holland, and it most likely chilled any desire by the German bishops to make a clear statement of protest about the persecution of the Jews. The bishops were aware that the Nazis had retaliated against the pastoral issued by the Dutch bishops in July 1942 that condemned the deportation of Jews. Catholic Jews such as Edith Stein were immediately rounded up and shipped to Auschwitz. Edith Stein (1891–1942) had been an assistant to the phenomenologist philosopher Edmund Husserl,

141. Hehl, *Erzbistum Köln*, 234; Lill, 265; *Akten Faulhabers*, II: 883–88.
142. Phayer, *Holocaust and Genocide Studies* 7 (1993): 224.
143. Dietrich, 238–39; Phayer, *Holocaust and Genocide Studies* 7 (1993): 216–20.

converted to Catholicism in 1922, during 1934 became a Carmelite nun in Cologne, and fled to Echt, Holland after *Kristallnacht* in 1938.[144] A total of forty thousand Jews were deported.[145]

The so-called "Decalogue Pastoral" of the Fulda bishops, completed in September 1943, treated of the Ten Commandments, and especially the Fifth. Euthanasia was condemned, as was killing allegedly in the interest of the common welfare and the execution of defenseless prisoners of war and "people of alien race and descent." Although Germans probably understood this as referring to the Jews, the Nazis were not explicitly accused of killing them. Some bishops even modified the public reading of the pastoral to omit the statement on race. Certainly, what was lacking in the pastoral was a clear accusation and condemnation that the Nazis were in fact perpetrating the genocide of the Jews.[146]

Lack of information was not a justifiable excuse. The bishops had considerable information or could have informed themselves. Konrad Gröber's denial after the war that he had knowledge of the Holocaust was perhaps motivated by not wanting to be informed, so he could avoid moral responsibility. It is the judgment of Saul Friedlander that if the bishops had knowledge, they would probably have felt like traitors. Bishop Heinrich Wienken provides us with an example of the complexity of assessing the consequences of having knowledge about the fate of the Jews. Not only was Wienken informed of the death camps, he also hid (Catholic) Jews in Berlin. He refrained, however, from involvement in the Kreisau Circle, and did not support an episco-

---

144. Edith Stein (1891–1942) was born of Jewish parents, became an assistant to the philosopher Edmund Husserl, and converted to Catholicism in 1922. Professionally, she was a teacher and lecturer. In 1934 she became a Carmelite nun in the convent in Cologne taking the name Sister Teresa Benedicta of the Cross. After the *Kristallnacht* pogrom in 1938, fearing the Nazis might close the convent, she fled to the Carmel in Echt, Holland. In reprisal for the outspoken condemnation of Nazi anti-Semitism by the Dutch bishops in their pastoral, she and other clergy were taken to Auschwitz where she was executed about 10 August 1942. Her most important philosophical work was *Bounded and Unbounded Being* in the phenomenological school of Edmund Husserl. Her most mature spiritual writing, though unfinished, was her study of St. John of the Cross, *Science of the Cross*. She was beatified in 1987 and canonized in 1998.

145. Tinnemann, 66; Lewy, 304–5.   146. Tinnemann, 62.

pal confrontation with Nazism. He apparently wanted to remain on good terms with the regime in order to help imprisoned priests.[147]

In contrast to the diplomatic language and petition policy of the bishops, the lower clergy were less conciliatory and often hostile, openly making derogatory and sometimes vulgar remarks about the regime. During a religious lesson one priest reportedly blamed Hitler for the actions of the Nazi party and its officials. Another priest allegedly remarked in a private conversation that the Führer needed Rosenberg and others to attack the Church because he was too cowardly to do it himself. The attempt to disassociate Rosenberg's views from the official position of the Party was evidently unsuccessful.[148] It was unfortunate, one priest commented, that some brownshirts had not been killed in a brawl, while another priest threatened to break the skulls of "SS bastards." In other examples, the Nazi brown shirt was likened to a pile of manure, and Göring and Röhm were denounced as homosexuals. Whatever the real thinking of the priests, few of the cases accused Hitler of responsibility for the persecution of the Church. Like the bishops, it is thought that most of the lower clergy publicly accepted the belief that Nazi church policy was the work of Nazi fanatics and not Hitler.[149]

Against the measures of the Gestapo the Church was generally helpless. Among the bishops only Johannes Sprol of Rottenburg was prosecuted by the regime, though his sentence was never carried out. The imprisonment of the lower clergy in Dachau, where most of the interned ones were held, could not be stopped with any success.[150] Bernard Lichtenberg, the Dean of St. Hedwig's Cathedral in Berlin, was imprisoned for two years for his public criticism of the regime's anti-Jewish policies. He paid with his life while being transported to Dachau in 1943. During the period 1933–1945 the Nazi regime used co-

---

147. Phayer, *Holocaust and Genocide Studies* 7 (1993): 225, 229.

148. Ian Kershaw, *The Hitler Myth: Image and Reality in the Third Reich* (Oxford: Oxford University Press, 1990), 113–114.

149. Holmes, 109–110; Kershaw, *Hitler Myth*, 115.

150. For the experiences of priests in Dachau see Karl Hausberger, "Das Konzentrationslager Dachau," Schwaiger, 1: 77–134 and Johann Maria Lenz, *Christus in Dachau* (Wien: Buchversand, "Libri Catholici," 1957).

ercive measures against one-third, or 7,155, of the secular clergy, and one-fifth, or 866, of the clergy of religious orders—a total of 8,021 clerics. It is estimated that about one-third, or 34.5 percent, of the total offenses prosecuted (22,703) involved criticism of the regime, political unreliability, and behavior hostile to the state.[151] Out of some 1,860 priests in the archdiocese of Cologne, some sixty were interned for a considerable time. Of all the German clergy interned, 418 died while interned; from Cologne twenty died, from München-Freising fourteen, from Breslau thirty-seven, and the largest group (fifty-seven) from Sudetenland.[152]

Throughout the history of the Third Reich the Holy See strongly and repeatedly protested the numerous violations of the Concordat. Vatican radio and the *Osservatore Romano* denounced the doctrines and the violence of the Nazis. At least fifty-five diplomatic notes including lengthy Promemoria were authored by Cardinal Pacelli, according to his secretary, Father Robert Leiber. Most never received a reply.[153] Pacelli was the inspiration and the energy behind this extensive *Notenwechsel* and the editor, Dieter Albrecht, is convinced that they reflect his personality and will. While the Concordat was a defensive wall, it was in the correspondence and the memorandums that the diplomatic battles were waged. These memorandums, besides being protests against the violations of the Concordat, were also analytical essays which Pacelli used as a platform to apply the teachings of the Catholic church on government, ethics and society. This correspondence also reflects his realism and objectivity.[154]

On 19 October 1933 in the first of these detailed Promemoria Pacelli protested the violence and restrictions directed against Catholic Youth organizations, the repression of the Catholic press, and the dismissal of

151. Ulrich von Hehl, *Priester unter Hitlers Terror: Eine Biographische und Statistische Erhebung* (Mainz: Matthias-Grünewald Verlag, 1984), XLII–III, LII–LXIV.

152. Ibid., LVIII, LXXIX–LXXX; Hehl, *Katholische Kirche*, 221–225.

153. Robert Leiber, S.J., "Mit brennender Sorge, März 1937–März 1962," *Stimmen der Zeit* 169 (1961–62): 419.

154. Ibid.; Albrecht, *Notenwechsel*, I, XVII, XXII–XXIV; Robert Leiber, S.J., "Pius XII," *Stimmen der Zeit* 163 (1958–59): 84–85.

Catholic government officials. He repeated these complaints in April, September, and December, 1934. Should the persecution continue, Pacelli threatened, Pius XI would publicly denounce it. He was concerned that the world was watching and would misunderstand the Vatican's forbearance. The persecution was already of "greater harshness and arbitrariness" than that which had existed under Bismarck's *Kulturkampf*.[155] Pacelli was to repeat his criticism of this expanding persecution of the Church in his Promemoria of 29 January 1936 wherein he summarized all of the government's violations, which the regime continued to deny, and then instructed German officials about the state's obligation to concern itself with the welfare of its people.[156]

During 1934 Cardinal Pacelli was still hopeful that negotiations would successfully resolve the conflict with the Reich. The most important Promemoria before 1937 was that of 14 May 1934, in which the Nazi regime was criticized more extensively than earlier. At the same time it was intended to function as a support for the negotiating position of the German bishops and facilitate a peace settlement. Pacelli's tactics involved the threat of an open break with the Reich in order to bring pressure on the German government to settle the outstanding issues of the conflict.[157]

Catholics, the memorandum reminded the government, were disappointed in their hopes of cooperation between Church and state. The Chancellor's message of peace on the day of the Enabling Act was being ignored, Pacelli wrote. A central theme of the Promemoria was its insistence on the Church's freedom to live and propagate its own *Weltanschauung*, which was repeated in future notes.[158] This freedom had become threatened by National Socialist party leaders who en-

155. Albrecht, *Notenwechsel*, I: 7–14; Leiber, *Stimmen der Zeit* 169 (1961–62): 420–23. Pacelli negotiated with Buttmann in February 1934 proposing an eight-point resolution to the problems. A protest was also made to the *Reichspresskammer* concerning Amann's regulations of 24 April 1935.

156. Albrecht, *Notenwechsel*, I, XXI–XXII, 310; Leiber, *Stimmen der Zeit* 169 (1961–62): 423–24. These issues were also reviewed in communications of September, October and December 1933; May 1934; January 1935; and January, March, and April 1936.

157. Scholder, *Churches*, II: 178–79.

158. Leiber, *Stimmen der Zeit*, 169 (1961–62): 421.

forced their worldview through the organizations of an unprecedented authoritarian state. He challenged the Nazi claim to total allegiance of Catholics who were admittedly responsible to support the state, but were required first to obey God's law in the religious sphere. Pacelli complained that Catholics were being treated unjustly when the government accused them of willful disobedience to the state when they actually were obeying God's law and teachings of the church and were unable to obey the state.[159] Fundamental errors were involved in the false claims and practices of the totalitarian state which Pius XI had already condemned in April, 1931. "Power," the Pope had written, was unthinkable without norms," and human norms were unthinkable without being anchored in divine norms."[160]

The attack on Catholic schools drew Pacelli's ire in October 1933 and February 1935, and he condemned the hatred in Nazi propaganda against the confessional schools in the Promemoria of 10 July 1935. A proposal of thirteen resolutions in January 1936 to mediate the conflict over the confessional schools was unsuccessful. The closing of Catholic schools was protested by a whole series of notes in 1936/1937. The Nazis proceeded in their campaign and by 1939 had closed over ten thousand schools in the old Reich. The prohibition against the teaching of religion by the clergy and their participation in Catholic Youth organizations was protested by Pacelli in eight notes from October 1933 to June 1937. The surveillance of sermons and other restrictions on the use of the pulpit, restrictions on seminarians, and the imprisonment of the clergy were repeatedly protested from September 1933 to April 1936.

At a stormy meeting with Pius XI at a New Year's reception for the Diplomatic Corps in 1936, Ambassador Bergen was confronted by an angry Pope who told him of the "resentment" and "embitterment" that had become pervasive in Vatican circles. Not only was the German government in violation of its solemn declarations and engaged in a persecution of the Catholic church, Pius informed him, but was intent on destroying it. After a follow-up meeting with the more conciliatory secretary of state, Bergen communicated to the Foreign Office his judg-

159. Albrecht, *Notenwechsel*, 1: 127–28, 130–31.
160. Ibid., 146.

ment that "Cardinal Pacelli constantly strives to pacify, and to exert a moderating influence on the Pope who is difficult to manage and influence."[161] In response to another episode created by Cardinal Mundelein of Chicago, who had made a provocative speech attacking Hitler and Nazi Germany, Pacelli "emphatically assured [Bergen that] normal and friendly relations . . . would be restored as soon as possible."[162] This apparent difference in attitude toward Germany between the Pope and his secretary of state was evident after the Austrian *Anschluss* and concerning the question of Danzig, Pacelli "repeatedly protested his fervent wish for peace with Germany."[163] The secretary of state's conciliatory attitude should not, however, distort our understanding of the Vatican's strong condemnation of National Socialism. In a letter to Cardinal Schulte of Cologne Pacelli displayed no illusions about the Nazis and their aims, referring to them as "false prophets with the pride of Lucifer," and as "bearers of a new Faith and a new Evangile," who were attempting to create "a mendacious antimony between faithfulness to the Church and to the Fatherland."[164]

In 1936 the Pope described both Nazism and Communism as the enemies of truth and justice. He accused National Socialists of employing the methods of the Communists. Pope Pius XI also refused a requested papal audience to the German Minister of Justice because the German government permitted public insults and lies about him. The encyclical *Mit brenndender Sorge* in March of 1937 was Pius XI's most forceful protest. By 1938 the Pope was recognized by the western democracies as a leader in the fight against Nazism and Fascism, and it was hoped that he might be of help in the struggle to maintain world peace.[165] Throughout 1938 relations between the Vatican and the Reich

161. Ambassador Bergen to Foreign Minister Neurath, Rome, 4 January 1936, in *Documents on German Foreign Policy, 1918–1945*, Series C, 1933–1937, vol 4, April 1935–March 1936, no. 482, 963–67.

162. George O. Kent, "Pope Pius XII and Germany: Some Aspects of German-Vatican Relations, 1933–1943," *American Historical Review* 70 (October 1964): 63.

163. Ibid., 63–64.

164. Pacelli to Schulte, Vatican City, 12 March, 1935, in Volk, *Akten deutscher Bischöfe*, 2: 113–17.

165. Owen Chadwick, *Britain and the Vatican during the Second World War* (Cambridge: Cambridge University Press, 1988), 20.

did not improve as the Pope condemned the errors of exaggerated nationalism and absolute claims of the totalitarian state.[166]

With the election of Pacelli as Pius XII in March of 1939 there was a relaxation of tensions between the Vatican and the Reich. That April the Pope avoided the condemnations of his predecessor in his address to a group of German pilgrims.[167] The German Ambassador informed his government that Pius XII was prepared to make concessions and favored a public truce so long as vital Church institutions and Church principles were not endangered.[168] Indeed, following the outbreak of war in September 1939, a truce of sorts was established, and the Vatican's protests of the violations of the Concordat were temporarily suspended.[169] Perhaps, Pacelli had become convinced that a continuation of the confrontational tactics of dramatic pronouncements like *Mit brennender Sorge* would not only fail to stop the Nazis, but would serve to increase the persecution of the Church in Germany.

On 27 October 1939 Pius issued his first encyclical, *Summi Pontificatus*, in which he condemned the invasion of Poland, but did so in generalizations lacking specific condemnations of German aggression. Although Heydrich considered the encyclical as a criticism of Germany, the Poles were extremely disappointed. Nonetheless, he did not abandon his prudent diplomatic policy. He followed the example of Pope Benedict XV during the First World War who followed a policy of strict neutrality, avoiding direct intervention on either side, and whose 1917 peace initiative failed to bring an end to the conflict. Based on the first Vatican Council of 1870 Pius XII considered it his primary duty to maintain the unity of the Church. More recently, in Article 24 of the Lateran Treaties, the Pope had committed himself to neutrality in international conflicts.[170] Even though this was the case, it is difficult to

166. Pius XI, "Le Missioni e il nazionalismo" to the Students of the College of the Propagation of the Faith in Rome, 21 August 1938, in *Principles for Peace. Selections from Papal Documents from Leo XIII to Pius XII*. ed. Harry C. Koenig (Washington, D.C., 1943), 545.

167. Kent, *American Historical Review* 70 (October 1964): 65.

168. William M. Harrigan, "Pius XII's Efforts to Effect a Detente in German-Vatican Relations, 1939," *Catholic Historical Review* 49 (July 1963): 184.

169. Kent, *American Historical Review* 70 (October 1964): 66.

170. Dieter Albrecht, "Der Heilege Stuhl und das Dritte Reich," in *Die Katholiken*

understand why at the end of 1940, when the Vatican received reports of the euthanasia program in Germany, no formal protest was lodged. Although the Pope was advised by some cardinals to denounce the persecution of the Church in Germany as his predecessor had done, Pius did not do so and to the consternation of many remained silent.[171] The Pope's silence was inspired, it was reported, by his concern not to harm Germany's war effort against the Soviet Union.

When the church policy measures in the Reich had become visibly more severe, Pius XII had believed that he could no longer be responsible for further silence on the subject. However, when the war against Soviet Russia began he had refrained from the step considered necessary in order not to injure Germany and her allies in this phase that was so decisive for the fate of the world. To go beyond this and to take sides publicly and unequivocally in the fight against Soviet Russia had been made impossible for him by Germany.[172]

In September 1941, President Franklin D. Roosevelt dispatched a special Representative, Myron C. Taylor, to the Vatican. His assistant and charge d'affaires in the Vatican, Harold Tittman, repeatedly pointed out to Pius the danger to his moral leadership incurred by his failure to denounce the notorious violations of the moral and natural law by the Nazis.[173] In his Christmas message of 1942 Pius did express generalized sympathy for those who "without any fault on their part, sometimes only because of their nationality or race, have been consigned to death or to a slow decline."[174] Although this statement can be interpreted as expressing concern for the treatment of the Jews, the Pope never publicly identified as Jews those whom he described as suffering and being exterminated. He refused to say more, and Vatican officials defended his stance, asserting:

---

und das Dritte Reich, ed. K. Gotto and K. Repgen (Mainz: Matthias-Grünewald-Verlag, 1990), 42.

171. *Documents on German Foreign Policy*, ser. C, vol. 1, no. 501; Kent, *American Historical Review* 70 (October 1964): 67; Rhodes, 237.

172. *Documents on German Foreign Policy*, ser. D, vol. 13, no. 309, cited in Kent, *American Historical Review* 70 (October 1964): 70.

173. Kent, *American Historical Review* 70 (October 1964): 71.

174. Koenig, 804.

There is constant pressure on the Holy See from the Axis powers to denounce alleged Allied atrocities and, because of its silence, the Holy See is
often accused of being pro-Ally. The Holy See could not very well, therefore,
condemn Nazi atrocities on the one hand without saying something, for instance, about Russian cruelties on the other.[175]

The Pope's silence has been a prominent issue for Holocaust historians. As John S. Conway has recently pointed out, "two of the arguments most frequently advanced in the postwar debates (for and against
Pius XII) were wholly mistaken: first, that the Vatican lacked information about what enormities were being committed, or second that it
lacked compassion."[176] Since these were inaccurate then what considerations might have motivated the Pope in the formulation of his statements? First of all, the Vatican had experienced a remarkable lack of
success in receiving answers to its protests over violations of the Concordat. Also, Pius XII had come to question the effectiveness of his
public statements and feared the possible additional suffering that
might be exacted by the Nazis in retaliation for a strong criticism. Undoubtedly, as John S. Conway points out, "a sense of frustration, disil-
lusionment and failure was markedly to affect the Vatican's efforts to assist the victims of the war, including those efforts launched on behalf of
the Jews."[177] The Vatican's attempts to help Catholic Jews emigrate were
frustrated even by those Catholic countries, like Brazil, that placed almost insurmountable restrictions on immigrants. Papal documents reveal that restrictions on and persecution of the Jews spread even though
papal representatives made efforts to ameliorate their treatment. While
the prestige of the papacy had certainly been insufficient to counteract
anti-Semitism in Germany, the disregard of papal representations in
Slovakia where the President was a priest highlighted the Vatican's lack
of influence to effect a change in policy in favor of the Jews. That
neither the President not the clergy in the Slovakian parliament opposed the legalization of Jewish deportations in March 1942 deepened

175. Kent, *American Historical Review* 70 (October 1964): 71.
176. John S. Conway, "The Vatican, Germany and the Holocaust," in *Papal Diplomacy in the Modern Age*, ed. Peter C. Kent and John F. Pollard (Westport, Conn.:
Praeger Publishers, 1994), 115.
177. Conway, "Vatican," 110.

the pessimism of Monsignor Domenico Tardini of the Vatican and prompted him to write, "It is a great misfortune that the President of Slovakia is a priest. Everyone knows that the Holy See cannot Bring Hitler to heel. But who will understand that we can't even control a priest?"[178]

There is some evidence that the Pope had the intention of making a strong statement concerning the Jews. According to the 1983 testimony of Sister Pascalina Lehnert (1894–1984), who was Pius' secretary and confidant, the Pope had prepared a strong condemnation of Nazi atrocities in the Netherlands. After being informed of the deportations, Pius became deeply disturbed at the Nazi potential for retaliation. He is reported to have said, "I wanted this protest to be published this very afternoon. But then I thought that if forty thousand people ended up in the death camps because of the Dutch bishops' words, Hitler would intern at least two hundred thousand for those of the pope."[179]

According to the German reports, the Vatican's principal concern was the Bolshevization of Europe. It was reluctant to speak out against German conduct in Poland, even though its President in exile implored "may the voice of the Holy Father . . . finally break [through] the silence of death."[180] According to Ernst von Weizsacker, who replaced Bergen at the Vatican, Pius sought: a "speedy conclusion of the war" and "a permanent peace."[181] Having few illusions about National Socialism, he had none about Bolshevism. On the other hand, the Vatican refused to support Hitler's invasion of Russia. Cardinal Domenico Tardini explained that while Communism was the worst enemy of the Church, it was not the only one.[182]

Pius XII, anxious first to avoid war and then determined to mediate a peace, pursued a policy of conciliation vis-à-vis Germany in contrast

---

178. *Ibid.*, 113.

179. Timothy G. McCarthy, *The Catholic Tradition: Before and after Vatican II, 1878–1993* (Chicago: Loyola University Press, 1994), 13.

180. John Lukacs, "The Diplomacy of the Holy See During World War II," *Catholic Historical Review* 60 (July 1974): 277.

181. Kent, *American Historical Review* 70 (October 1964): 78.

182. Hansjakob Stehle, *Eastern Politics of the Vatican* (Athens, Ohio: Ohio State University Press, 1981), 209.

to his predecessor's policy of confrontation.[183] During these difficult years both Pius XI and Pius XII sought to protect the interests of the Vatican. Neither proved completely successful.

In 1945 Pius XII confirmed the wisdom of Vatican policy that the Reich Concordat, even with its shortcomings, had prevented greater evils and was the best policy for the Church in its struggle with Nazi Germany.[184] Even if he had privately questioned the wisdom of the Concordat through the years of persecution from 1933 to 1945, he chose to proclaim victory at the end of the struggle. Nonetheless, the Reich Concordat had failed to protect the Church and worked more to the advantage of National Socialism by harnessing the Church's loyalty in support of the National Socialist state. Had Hitler won the war, the destruction of the institutional Church was high on his priority list. Only the Allied victory made the Concordat policy appear to be a success.

The Pope's triumphalism also extended to the denial of collective guilt of the German people for not opposing the Nazi regime and especially the Holocaust. Even before the end of the war the Pope had been outspoken against the judgment of collective guilt. His interpretation of the Nazi years was that it was a life-and-death struggle between the Church and the dictatorship. The failures of the bishops, especially in not clearly protesting the genocide of the Jews, were ignored. While in 1943 Pius XII had not supported von Galen and Preysing in their attempt to change the episcopal policy, after the war he honored them, elevating them to the cardinalate to emphasize the Church's opposition to Nazi Germany.[185]

What judgment did the German Church itself make after the war about its role during the Third Reich?[186] In their Fulda letter of August

183. Harrigan, *Catholic Historical Review* 49 (July 1963): 190.

184. Holmes, 105–106.

185. Michael Phayer, "German Catholic Bishops, the Vatican, and the Holocaust in the Postwar Era," in *The Netherlands and Nazi Genocide: Papers of the 21st Annual Scholar's Conference*, edited by G. Jan Colijn and Marcia S. Littell (New York: The Edwin Mellen Press, 1992), 179.

186. For a detailed analysis of the postwar position of the German bishops on the question of responsibility for their failure to protest the Holocaust see Frank Buscher and Michael Phayer, "German Catholic Bishops and the Holocaust, 1940–1953," *German Studies Review*, IX (October, 1988): 463–484.

1945 the bishops, on the encouragement of Konrad Preysing, admitted to the guilt of individual Germans but avoided the controversial issue of the collective guilt of Germans for the war and the Holocaust. A debate over the issue raged through 1947, but then ended with the onset of the Cold War and the opposition of the bishops to the denazification process. Certainly, the opposition of Pius XII to collective guilt and his belief that German Catholics had been "martyrs" and opponents of Nazism contributed to this change. In the judgment of Michael Phayer, "Most postwar statements of Church leaders . . . called attention to the persecution of the Church itself. Seldom were Catholics thought of as perpetrators of the Holocaust or as bystanders who should have intervened."[187] Catholic theology emphasized individual, not collective, sin, guilt, salvation or damnation. So Church leaders focused on the guilt of Nazi leaders who were considered to be the perpetrators and bearers of responsibility for the Holocaust. The participation of the bishops in denazification, Michael Phayer believes, was intended more to deflect any responsibility that Germans might have had in cooperation with the Nazi regime. In 1948 the postwar debate over guilt and restitution came to an end.[188]

During the fifties the Concordat was continued by the Federal Republic and Germans became the first line of defense against the danger of communism in the Cold War. The bishops of the Nazi era defended their accommodation and capitulation to the Nazi regime as the path of prudence and therefore morally correct, whereas those who resisted were seen as reckless and morally wrong.[189] Beginning in 1959, however, a change of attitude took place. According to Michael Phayer, the German episcopacy "now recognized German guilt for the Holocaust. Second, they blamed Catholic Germans, and especially church leaders, for not having spoken out against the murderous Nazi regime. Third, they felt profound sorrow for the Jewish people, and were able to express empathy publicly and appropriately."[190] A number of factors were instrumental in creating this change. Of primary importance was the

187. Phayer, *Holocaust and Genocide Studies*, 7 (1993): 153.

188. Phayer, "The German Catholic Church After the Holocaust," *Holocaust and Genocide Studies* 10 (1996): 161.

189. *Ibid*, 156.   190. *Ibid*, 161.

death of Pius XII, with whom the bishops had been reluctant to disagree. Another obstacle was removed with the death of most of the German bishops who served during the Nazi period. Other factors included the war crimes trials conducted by German courts, which exposed the public to the horrors of the Holocaust. The trial of Adolf Eichmann also provoked a general recognition and admission of guilt of Germans as perpetrators of the Holocaust. At the Second Vatican Council (1962–1964) German bishops apologized for the Holocaust, admitting that it was a German crime. The formulation of *Nostra Aetate* also removed the theological basis for Christian anti-Semitism and the condemnation of the Jewish people collectively as the killers of Christ. The general synod of German bishops of November 1975 acknowledged the general Catholic responsibility during the Third Reich for the Church's focus on the protection of its institutions and community, and that the Church was guilty for remaining silent concerning the crimes against the Jews. On numerous anniversaries of *Kristallnacht* (9 November 1938) individual German bishops expressed repentance for not protesting the pogrom. In May 1980 the ecumenical commission of the German Church made a formal statement of repentance.[191] In the judgment of Hans Kung, however, this statement by the Catholic episcopal conference in 1980 still was an ambiguous "confession of its own historical complicity" in the Holocaust. Rather, it was at the 1975 Synod, under the influence of the theologians and laity that formulated the "Declaration of the Joint Synod of Catholic Dioceses of the Federal Republic of Germany" (22 November 1975), that a clear admission of guilt was made for complicity in the Nazis' attempt to systematically exterminate the Jewish people.[192]

The Catholic Church has traditionally tried to accommodate itself to the state, and its Concordat policy was intended to protect the rights and the freedom of the Church to pursue its mission of ministering to

191. *Ibid*, 161–63; Phayer, *Netherlands*, 182–187; for the texts of the bishops' statements in 1980 see *Die Kirchen und das Judentum: Dokumente von 1945 bis 1985*, ed. Rolf Rendtorff and Hans Hermann Henrix (München: Chr. Kaiser Verlag, 1989), 260–280.
192. Hans Kung, *Judaism: Between Yesterday and Tomorrow* (New York: Continuum, 1996), 265–266.

the faithful. The Reich Concordat did not intend to give legitimacy to the Nazi regime, though that was a consequence. The regime intended to restrict and then strangle the Church's influence in society. Given the nature of the Nazi regime, with its competing power centers between Hitler's subordinates, the failure of the Concordat was a foregone conclusion. The Church found it difficult to have its grievances over the numerous Concordat violations satisfied. Some officials had no power to alter policy and others were the perpetrators. Hitler was never seen as the problem. The majority of the episcopacy wanted to avoid an open conflict like that of the *Kulturkampf*, and feared the consequences of the elimination of the ministrations of the clergy. They were confronted by many dilemmas, and a growing number believed that they had to risk challenges to the state, but because of their loyalty to legal authority, their timidity, legal-mindedness, and unwillingness to risk the dangers of resistance and opposition, they failed that higher standard of resisting evil.

Three Controversial Concordats
A Commentary

STEWART A. STEHLIN, *New York University*

THERE HAVE been numerous concordats in the annals of church-state relations, the first most probably the treaty concluded between Pope Calixtus and Henry V in 1122 to settle the Investiture Controversy. Angelo Mercati's 1954 edition of *Raccolta de concordati* lists 148 and since then more have been added. They generally were concluded to terminate a state of hostility between Church and State and restore peace in a given country. The three concordats examined in the present volume mark high points of this policy and can be viewed as part of the larger Church-State conflict in which each institution sought to redefine its identity in the modern world, chronicling tensions in these relations that run from the dawn of the modern age to the present day. The three treaties have some things in common: all were signed by the Vatican with strong leaders of authoritarian governments, all provided a measure of peace to countries divided over aspects of the Church-State conflict, and finally all three were intended by the secular leaders to be used to enhance the power and prestige of their own regimes. However there were differences both in how the treaties were approached and in the results obtained.

As indicated in the first essay, Napoleon sought to bring internal peace to France and stability to his regime by coming to terms with the

Vatican. William Roberts rightly points to the advantages which the Emperor gained by concluding this treaty. It should be noted that the French ruler had something to bargain with that neither Mussolini nor Hitler possessed. He had a schismatic church, with its own hierarchy and claims to validity, which he could threaten to support in order to frighten the Vatican. Granted, the Constitutional Church had been losing ground as the majority of the faithful expressed their desire to reconcile themselves with the See of Peter; granted, too, that Rome as well as impartial observers might rightfully question the value of Napoleon's support of the Constitutional Church. But in diplomacy it is often not the reality but the perception of it and of alternate possibilities that is often most important. With a national leader that had already frequently surprised and outflanked the opposition on the battlefield and in the conference room, there was no certainty that he might not be willing to use the Constitutional Church to press Rome for concessions or at least make the Vatican more accommodating.

Once signed, the French Concordat was immediately used as a model for the Vatican's negotiations with other states such as the Kingdom of Italy, Bavaria, and Wurttemberg, and even for those of the twentieth century. There are, in fact, structural similarities in the texts of the concordats discussed in this volume, based on the Vatican's perceived needs. There was, however, more opposition in France to the Concordat at its inception than to the two modern-day treaties discussed in this book. Intellectuals, die-hard republicans, and the army were the major groups in which this dissatisfaction was centered. In fact the Prussian minister in Paris commented "that of all the operations which Bonaparte has carried through, that of the legal reestablishment of religion is the one which has most exercised all the constancy of his will and all the resources of his mind."[1]

Nevertheless in 1801 when the Concordat was ratified, it appeared as if the Emperor had negotiated a good settlement and had forced the papacy to accede to his demands. This was the view in the short run. Napoleon had gained religious peace at home, and by adding the Or-

1. Robert B. Holtman, *The Napoleonic Revolution* (Philadelphia: J.B. Lippincott, 1967), 126.

ganic Articles to the original agreement he had even regained some of the Gallican liberties so prized by former French rulers. Napoleon's concordat also had more staying power that the other two, which is another criterion for evaluating its success. But if we look at it in another perspective, it was the Pope rather than the Emperor who triumphed. In fact the Concordat increased the power of the Pope in France as the 1929 agreement did in Italy. Upon completion of the treaty the entire French hierarchy was asked to resign and the Pope consecrated or confirmed in office those he chose. He was thus able to liquidate the old hierarchy at one stroke of the pen, a maneuver which would have been the envy of most of his predecessors. True, it was the Emperor who now nominated all the bishops, but they were installed by or received their confirmation from Rome, according the Pontiff a crucial veto power.

Another victory for Rome was the fact that the religious orders were not mentioned in the Concordat, Napoleon apparently believing that they were not central to his plan for state control. Although religious orders had to receive authorization from the government to be established, once they had been given that permission, and since there was no qualifying mention of them in the Concordat, they were responsible not to local secular or religious officials but solely to the Pope. As a result, many orders again flourished as many émigré religious returned to France. Thus instead of cutting the ground out from under religion, Napoleon unwittingly helped to facilitate the nineteenth-century religious revival in France.

Finally, the Organic Articles, intended to weaken the concessions made to Rome in the treaty and allow power to remain in the hands of the secular authorities, worked slowly and subtly to produce the very opposite results. The rather brash demands and insistence on state control made in the Articles, to which Pius was forced to agree, cast the Pontiff in the role of an underdog and increased both opposition to the state and sympathy for Rome among the populace and did much to unite the clergy behind their spiritual leader. The hierarchy and clergy thus became increasingly ultramontane since Rome was perceived as a protective shield against what they deemed the unnecessary and gallingly close supervision by the state. In other words, both the Pope's advantages as specified in the Concordat and his apparent defeat, as evidenced by the concessions he was forced to grant the state, contributed to the Ultramontanist attitudes of the clergy and eventually to French support for the declaration of papal infallibility in 1870.

The Lateran Accords, like the French Concordat but unlike the German treaty, dealt with a country which was overwhelmingly Catholic, but like the German concordat, concerned gaining not only internal peace within the state but diplomatic prestige for the regime. This had not been a major consideration for Napoleon since his government already had recognition and his prestige was considerable at that moment. Frank Coppa reveals that Mussolini, like Napoleon before him and Hitler afterwards, hoped to use the Church for his own purposes. As Coppa shows, Mussolini had little more success than Napoleon in doing so.

It is true that by reversing the tide of anti-clericalism, a favorite theme of the Liberals, the Duce combated Liberals and freemasons who opposed him and in return expected to gain the gratitude of the Vatican and the support of the Church. Coppa reveals that superficially, at least, the Duce's gamble succeeded since the Vatican supported, if only by its silence, many of Mussolini's actions in its belief that he was the man to provide law and order to society. Undeniably, for Mussolini the settlement appeared beneficial, for it established some stability at home and cut a Gordian knot by ending the embarrassment of two governments in Rome that officially did not talk to one another. However, the Vatican gained more than it gave, for it secured its independent status by means of an international agreement and placed itself in a position to challenge the pretensions of the totalitarian state by means of the Concordat and Treaty, which reorganized Catholicism as the religion of state. Furthermore, the Vatican was now free to send and receive foreign dignitaries without the danger of a caesaro-papistic situation developing, because the spiritual leader of a multinational religion was himself a citizen of one of Europe's nation-states.

As Coppa rightly points out, the post-1918 era can rightly be called the era of concordats. Pius XI saw great value in the guarantees such treaties afforded, viewing them as the most suitable means to regulate Church-State relations. The Italian Accords did not provide a complete success for either party, as had been the case to some degree with the treaty of 1801, since the agreement with the Duce faced problems almost immediately, starting with the crisis of its implementation. Shortly after the conclusion of the Accords Mussolini stated, "we have not resurrected the Temporal Power of the Pope, we have buried it."[2] Even concerning matters of education, where despite the concessions promised in the concordat he was soon to say "education must belong to us; these children must, of course, be educated in our religion, but we need to integrate this education, we need to give youth the sense of victory, of power, of conquest . . . "[3]— hardly Christian sentiments, as Pius XI did not hesitate to proclaim. However, the rhetoric of Mussolini's Italy did not always mirror the reality, as Coppa shows.

The Accords settled the territorial claims of the papacy but not its spiritual claims to the souls of Italian Catholics, and the Church was forced to protest against Fascist violations of the agreement. However, thanks to the Lateran Accords, in many ways the Church's position in Fascist Italy was stronger than it had been in the preceding liberal age, 1861–1922. Having constrained Mussolini to conclude a concordat which guaranteed the Church a public position in social life and assured its role in education, the Vatican now had the means to intervene in Italian life, to the dismay of anticlerical Fascists and convinced liberals. Nonetheless, the Accords tainted the Vatican with the disrepute of Fascism, as many people both within the Church and outside questioned how the institution which purported to be the world's greatest moral authority could have made a treaty with an immoral regime that professed an ideology antithetical to the Church's teaching. In the age of liberal democracies, especially after 1945, public opinion asked not only *what* occurred, as they did in the nineteenth century, but also, increasingly, *why*.

The consequences of the *Reichskonkordat* in Germany were in many ways similar to those of the Lateran Accords in Italy, provoking even greater controversy. In the short run, Hitler was able to gain acceptance and prestige for his regime. But unlike the other two treaties, where the concordat was meant to heal a schism or rift between Church and

2. Benito Mussolini. Speech to the Chamber of Deputies, 13 May 1929, *Opera Omnia di Benito Mussolini* (Florence: La Fenice, 1958), 24: 74.
3. Ibid., 75–76.

State, here, with no formal rift, it was meant to divide the opponents of the State from the Vatican and to weaken the opposition to the Nazi regime. Hitler sought to make diplomatic capital out of the treaty by claiming that the Vatican's conclusion of the agreement with him provided recognition to his government. This was not so, since the treaty was between the Holy See and the Reich, regardless of the regime, and not with the Nazi State. Furthermore, the Holy See was not the first sovereign entity to arrange an agreement with the Nazi regime. That dubious distinction goes to Stalin's Soviet regime, which concluded a trade agreement with Hitler's Germany in early May 1933. This was followed by the Four Power Pact between Germany, England, France, and Italy signed in Rome in July 1933, prior to the signing of the Reich Concordat.[4] From the Vatican's perspective, if Hitler's government fell — and there was no definite reason in July 1933 to believe that it would have greater lasting power than the previous governments in the revolving door cabinet intrigues of the last days of Weimar Germany— if it fell, the Vatican still had a treaty with Germany. If on the other hand the regime were to last, then at least the Curia had a legal basis on which to raise protests should it deem them necessary.

In the short run the *Konkordat* was a success for the Nazis because it gave Hitler what he wanted. German documents indicate that during the spring of 1933 Hitler commanded his negotiators that the treaty be signed, whatever the price.[5] Concede anything, promises could always be disputed later. From the Vatican's viewpoint the treaty was considered a qualified victory for it offered many things that had eluded Curia officials in their negotiations during the Weimar period. On the other hand, as Joseph Biesinger correctly emphasizes, the *Konkordat* was now seen as a necessity, for it gave the Church that legal basis needed to protest violations without which Berlin could justifiably claim that actions which the State took against the Church were an internal affair and that Vatican complaints were foreign interference. This was Papal

4. John Jay Hughes, "The Pope's Pact with Hitler: Betrayal or Self-Defense," *Journal of Church and State* 17 (winter 1975): 69.

5. Germany, Auswärtiges Amt, *Documents on German Foreign Policy, 1918–1945*, series C, vol. I (Washington, D.C.: U.S. Government Printing Office, 1957), especially the minutes of the Cabinet meeting, 14 July 1933, 651–653.

Secretary of State Eugenio Pacelli's perception of the Concordat's value in 1933 when he told the British charge d'affaires in Berlin that he was under no illusion about the nature of the regime. Pacelli recognized that the Nazis would violate the articles of the agreement, but as he wryly said, hopefully not all at the same time.[6]

The treaty, however, created the legal basis for resistance to the regime, which the Vatican regrettably did not utilize to the fullest and hence missed an excellent opportunity to display its moral stature to the world. But the Concordat did help to preserve the Church intact and protect some of its organizations scheduled for certain destruction by the Nazis. The fact that the Church did indeed survive more intact than almost any other comparably large institution in Germany during the oppressive Nazi regime was in part due to the 1933 Concordat. But as in the case of the French concordat of 1801 and the Italian agreement of 1929, disagreements erupted after the Concordat's ratification; as in the earlier agreements, the honeymoon proved short. The disagreements were so serious that one observer commented, we should not call this sort of treaty a *con*cordat but rather a *dis*cordat. Part of these Church-State difficulties, I suggest, can be traced to the post-Versailles-era mentality, which sanctioned an excessive legalism in dealing with international as well as many national problems, encouraging the Vatican to virtually restrict itself to this method for solving Church-State problems. A legally binding treaty seemed to the Vatican to be the best, or at times, as was the case with Germany, virtually the only method of salvaging something for the Church in dealing with authoritarian regimes. The breakdown of the agreement also implied an assumption by Curial officials, made by virtually all the statesmen of the era, that they were dealing with rational and responsible leaders negotiating to some degree in good faith—an error that proved equally fatal when dealing with non-ecclesiastical affairs.

What can be the conclusions drawn from the experiences described within these essays? In the long run, I believe we can say that the first of the concordats, that with Napoleonic France, perhaps yielded overall

6. Great Britain, Foreign Office, Public Record Office 371/16727/5452, Kirkpatrick to Foreign Secretary Simon, 19 August 1933.

the best results for the Vatican; the last, that with Hitler's Germany, the worst, especially since it most acutely touched the issue of the Church's morality. In an era when both sides were seeking to define their identity in the modern age of the nation-state, both sides learned something from the experience of concluding concordats. The state learned that despite the growth of a secular society, despite the attacks of agnostic indifference, Marxist materialism, and Freudian skepticism, the Church cannot be omitted from society. The three governments found they could not ignore the role of religion and found it necessary to come to terms with it in order to bring internal peace to the country.

The Vatican, for its part, observed to its dismay that concordats are not always effective, and in fact are at times detrimental, for they limit the Church's activities once they are specified and defined in the treaties. It learned that by practicing the policy of Pius XI, *i.e.*, dealing with the Devil himself if it would help the Church,[7] many times the Church came out singed by too close contact with the Devil's helpers, for the Church simply overestimated the willingness of the opposing powers to cooperate. Finally, the Vatican learned that no matter how good its intentions, the consequences of disregarding the true nature of a negotiating partner can allow the future to be built on false premises, and may leave the Church tainted with the stigma associated with an authoritarian regime once its true nature has been revealed. In the postwar period the Church has confronted sharp criticism, especially for its dealings with Mussolini and Hitler, and has had to struggle to live down its concordat policy of the 1920s and 1930s.

Today the theological debate over Church-State relations in the modern world continues. But there has been a transition, certainly noticeable since Vatican II, from viewing the Vatican solely as a governmental institution in the tradition of Innocent III to one of a more pastoral nature typified by the pontificate of John XXIII. Certainly the modern papacy, despite its continued role in world affairs, especially in Eastern Europe, seems to emphasize the *cura animarum* and to appeal

7. Pius XI is said on one occasion to have stated his readiness to employ any possible means, even dealing with the Devil himself if it would accomplish some good and help the Church. Hansjokob Stehle, "Motive des Reichskonkordats," *Aussenpolitik* 7 (1956): 564.

to idealism rather than rely on treaties and accords. The Vatican seems to realize there is more authority in underlining spiritual rather than international laws.

It is understandable that nowadays there is a wariness in the Curia to engage in all-encompassing concordats; rather, there is a willingness to let them lapse or to renegotiate old ones, concentrating more on individual, specific questions. There is also a tendency to rely more on the local hierarchy to work within the laws of the State in order to pursue the mission of the Church. The Vatican is leaning more toward the argument that the Church should eschew pacts with civil society in order better to carry out its spiritual mission, to refrain from being overtly associated with agreements belonging to the political order and maneuverings of normal diplomacy while urging its adherents, especially in free and pluralistic societies, to influence their governments, and to exhort the hierarchy, enhanced with a new self-confidence and influence represented by national episcopal conferences, to do the same. All of this, of course, tends to diminish the value of concordats. The controversy over such treaties will continue, as will the tensions over Church-State relations. Perhaps these relations have in part been redefined on the basis of the lessons learned from past concordats and especially those with Napoleonic France, Mussolini's Italy, and Hitler's Germany.

Appendix
Texts of the Concordats

1. Convention between the French Government and His Holiness Pius VII[1]

The Government of the Republic recognizes that the Catholic, Apostolic and Roman religion is the religion of the great majority of French citizens. His Holiness equally recognizes that this same religion has derived, and derives at the present time, the greatest good and the greatest glory from the establishment of Catholic worship in France, and from the personal profession of it by the Consuls of the Republic. Consequently, following this mutual recognition, as much as for the good of religion as for the maintenance of internal tranquillity, they have agreed as follows:

ART 1. The Catholic, Apostolic and Roman religion shall be freely exercised in France; its worship shall be public, conforming itself with police regulations which the Government shall judge necessary for public tranquillity.

ART 2. The Holy See, in concert with the Government, shall make a new circumscription of the French dioceses.

ART 3. His Holiness shall declare to those holding French bishoprics that he expects from them in firm confidence, for the sake of peace and unity, every kind of sacrifice, even that of their Sees. After this exhortation, if they refuse this sacrifice commanded for the benefit of the Church (a refusal, however, which His Holiness does not expect), provision shall be made for the appointment of new officials to govern these newly divided bishoprics in the following manner:

ART 4. The First Consul of the Republic shall nominate, within three

---

1. J. Hastings, ed. *The Encyclopedia of Religion & Ethics* (New York: Scribner, 1911), vol. 3.

months from the publication of the bull of His Holiness, to the archbish-oprics and bishoprics under the new arrangement. His Holiness shall confer canonical institutions, according to the forms established by agreement with France before the change of government.

ART 5. Nominations to bishoprics which shall be vacant immediately shall likewise be made by the First Consul, and canonical institution shall be given by the Holy See in conformity with the preceding article.

ART 6. The bishops, before entering upon their duties, shall take directly at the hands of the First Consul the oath of fidelity which was in use before the change of government, expressed in the following terms: "I swear and promise to God, on the Holy Gospels, to be obedient and faithful to the Government established by the constitution of the French Republic. I promise also to have no dealings, to be present at no council, to belong to no league, whether at home or abroad, which may be contrary to the public peace; and if, in my dioceses or elsewhere, I learn that anything is being plotted to the prejudice of the State, I will make it known to the Govern-ment."

ART 7. The ecclesiastics of the second order shall take the same oath at the hands of the civil authorities named by the Government.

ART 8. The following form of prayer shall be recited at the end of the Mass, in all the churches of France: "Domine salvam fac Rempublicam; Domine, miros fac Consules."

ART 9. The bishops shall make a new circumscription of the parishes of their dioceses, which shall have no effect without the consent of the Gov-ernment.

ART 10. The bishops shall nominate to the curacies. Their choice shall fall only upon persons acceptable to the Government.

ART 11. The bishops may have a Chapter in their Cathedral, and a Semi-nary for their diocese, but the Government shall not be obliged to endow them.

ART 12. All churches, metropolitan, cathedral, parish and others not ecularized, necessary for the worship, shall be placed at the disposal of the bishops.

ART 13. His Holiness, for the sake of peace and the happy re-establish-ment of the Catholic religion, declares that neither he nor his successors shall in anyway trouble those who have acquired alienated ecclesiastical property; and that consequently the possession of this same property, and the rights and revenues attached to it shall remain unchanged in their hands or in those of their assignees.

ART 14. The Government shall guarantee an adequate salary to the bishops and clergy whose dioceses and parishes shall be introduced in the new division.

ART 15. The Government shall at the same time take measures to enable French Catholics, if they wish, to endow churches.

ART 16. His Holiness recognizes in the First Consul of the Republic the same rights and prerogatives as the old Government enjoyed.

ART 17. It is agreed between the contracting parties that, in case any one of the successors of the First Consul now acting shall not be a Catholic, the rights and prerogatives mentioned in the article above, and the nomination to bishoprics, shall be regulated, with respect to him, by a fresh convention.

2. The Concordat of the Lateran Pacts of 1929[1]

In the name of the Most Holy Trinity,
considering:

That from the beginning of the negotiations between the Holy See and Italy to settle the 'Roman Question' , the Holy See itself proposed that the Treaty dealing with the said Question was to be accompanied, as a necessary complement, by a Concordat intended to regulate the conditions of religion and of the Church in Italy:

That to-day the Treaty for the settlement of the 'Roman Question' has been concluded and signed:

His Holiness the Supreme Pontiff Pius XI and his Majesty Victor Emmanuel III, King of Italy, have decided to make a Concordat, and for this purpose they have nominated the same plenipotentiaries as for the stipulation of the Treaty, that is, on His Holiness's side, His Most Reverend Eminence the Cardinal Pietro Gasparri, His Secretary of State, and on His Majesty's side His Excellency the Knight Benito Mussolini, Prime Minister and Head of the Government, who, having exchanged their full powers and having found them in good and due form, have agreed as per the following articles:

ART 1. Italy, as per Art 1 of the Treaty, guarantees to the Catholic Church the free exercise of the spiritual power, the free and public exercise of wor-

1. John F. Pollard, *The Vatican and Italian Fascism, 1929–32, A Study in Conflict* (Cambridge: Cambridge University Press, 1985), 204–14.

ship, and also of its jurisdiction on religious matters in conformity to the rules of this Concordat; when necessary, it guarantees to all ecclesiastics, for the acts of their spiritual ministry, the support of its authorities. In consideration of the sacred character of the Eternal City, Episcopal See of the Supreme Pontiff, center of the Catholic world and goal of pilgrimages, the Italian Government will take care to prevent in Rome anything that might clash with that character.

ART 2. The Holy See shall communicate and correspond freely with the bishops, the clergy and the whole Catholic world without any interference from the Italian Government. In the same way, for all that concerns their pastoral ministry, the bishops can communicate and correspond freely with their clergy and with all the faithful. The Holy See, as well as the bishops can freely publish and also affix inside or outside the doors of the buildings dedicated to worship or to the offices of their ministry, all instructions, orders, pastoral letters, diocesan bulletins and other communications concerning the spiritual government of their flock, that they may deem within the limits of their competency. These publications and notices and generally speaking all the acts and documents referring to the spiritual government of the faithful will not be subject to fiscal dues. The above publications in regard to the Holy See can be made in any language and those of the bishops in Italian or Latin, but beside the Italian text the ecclesiastical authority can add a translation in other languages. The ecclesiastical authorities can have collections taken at the entrance of and inside the churches or other buildings belonging to them without any interference from civil authorities.

ART 3. All theological students, scholastics in their last two years previous to their courses in theology who intend taking orders, and the novices of religious houses can, on request, delay year by year the fulfilling of their military service until their 26th year of age. Clerics ordained *in sacris* and those who have taken vows are exempt from military service, except in case of a general mobilisation. In such a case priests pass into the Armed Forces of the State, but they retain the ecclesiastical dress in order to carry on their sacred ministry under the ecclesiastical jurisdiction of the military Ordinary as per Art 14. All other clerics and members of religious orders are in preference drafted into the auxiliary military corps. Nevertheless, even in case of general mobilisation, all priests having the care of souls are exempt from answering the summons. As such are considered all bishops, parish priests and their assistants, vicars and all priests permanently in charge of churches open to the public.

ART 4. All clerics and members of religious orders are exempt from jury service.

ART 5. No ecclesiastic can be appointed to, or remain in any post or office of the Italian State or of any pubic body under its jurisdiction, without the *nihil obstat* (permission) of the Ordinary of the diocese. The withdrawal of the *nihil obstat* deprives the ecclesiastic of the capacity to continue to hold the appointment or position assumed. In any case no apostate or censored clergy can be appointed or kept in any teaching position, office or employment in which they would be in direct contact with the public.

ART 6. All salaries and other emoluments enjoyed by ecclesiastics in virtue of their office are exempt from seizure to the same extent as the salaries and emoluments of State employees.

ART 7. Ecclesiastics cannot be compelled by magistrates or other authorities to supply information concerning persons or matters with which they have become acquainted through their holy ministry.

ART 8. In the case of an ecclesiastic being charged before a magistrate with any penal offense, the Public Prosecutor must immediately inform the bishop of the diocese in whose territory he exercises jurisdiction: he must also transmit immediately to the bishop the result of the preliminary investigation and, when it takes place, also the sentence ending the trial, both in the first instance and on appeal. In case of arrest the ecclesiastic or religious is treated with the respect due to his state and to his hierarchical rank. When an ecclesiastic or member of a religious order is sentenced, the terms [sic] of imprisonment is spent, where possible, apart from ordinary criminals, unless the competent Ordinary has reduced the condemned man to the rank of a layman.

ART 9. As a rule, all buildings open to worship are exempt from requisition and occupation. If serious public necessities should require the occupation of a building open to the public, the authority that proceeds to the occupation must previously make arrangements with the Ordinary, unless reasons of absolute urgency prevent it. In such a case the acting authority must inform the Ordinary at once. Except in cases of urgent necessity, police forces in the execution of their duties cannot enter buildings open to worship, unless previous notice has been given to the ecclesiastical authorities.

ART 10. No building open to worship can be demolished for any reason, unless previously agreed upon with the competent ecclesiastical authority.

ART 11. The State recognizes all holidays of obligation prescribed by the Church, which are the following: all Sundays, New Year's Day, the Epiphany (January 6th), St. Joseph's Day (March 19th), Ascension Day, Corpus

Christi, S.S. Peter and Paul's Day (June 29th), the Assumption of the Blessed Virgin (August 15th), All Saints' Day (November 1st), the Immaculate Conception (December 8th), and Christmas Day (December 25th).

ART 12. On all Sundays and holidays of obligation, in Capitular Churches the celebrant of the Conventual Mass will sing a prayer for the prosperity of the King of Italy and of the Italian State, according to the rules of sacred liturgy.

ART 13. The Italian Government will forward to the Holy See the complete list of ecclesiastics appointed for the spiritual direction of the military forces of the State, as soon as it has been officially approved. The selection of ecclesiastics to whom the supervision of the service of spiritual assistance is entrusted (Military Ordinary, Vicars and Inspectors) will be made in confidence to the Italian Government by the Holy See. If the Italian Government has any reason for objecting to the selection, it will notify the Holy See, which will proceed to make another appointment. The military Ordinary will have the rank of an archbishop. The military chaplains are nominated by the competent authority of the Italian State, on the designation of the military Ordinary.

ART 14. The Italian land, sea and air forces enjoy, regarding religious duties, all privileges and dispensations approved by the Canon Law. The military chaplains, in regard to the troops, have parish competence. They exercise their sacred ministry under the jurisdiction of the military Ordinary assisted by his own Curia. The military Ordinary has the jurisdiction even over the religious personnel, masculine and feminine, employed in Military hospitals.

ART 15. The military archbishop will be attached to the Chapter of the Pantheon Church in Rome, constituting with it the clergy to whom the religious services of the said basilica is entrusted. This clergy is authorized to arrange for all religious services, even outside Rome, which in accordance with ecclesiastical rules may be required by the State or the Royal Household. The Holy See consents to confer on all the Canons members of the Pantheon Chapter the dignity of protonotaries *ad instar durante munere*. Each one will be nominated by the Cardinal Vicar of Rome, on presentation by His Majesty the King of Italy, after the confidential indication of the candidate. The Holy See reserves to itself the power to transfer the present staff to another Church.

ART 16. The High Contracting Parties will proceed with mutual accord by means of mixed commissions, to a revision of the territory of the dioceses, so as to make them, if possible, co-terminous with that of the provinces of the

Kingdom. It is agreed that the Holy See will institute the diocese of Zara, and that no part of the territory under the sovereignty of the Kingdom of Italy will depend upon a bishop whose see is in a territory subject to the sovereignty of another State; and that no diocese of the Kingdom will include zones of territory subject to the sovereignty of another State. The same principle will be observed for all parishes, existing or to be made, in zones near the frontiers of the State. All alteration that it may be necessary to make in the future in the frontiers of a diocese after the previously mentioned arrangement, will be decided by the Holy See in consultation with the Italian Government and in conformity with the above mentioned rules, except such small alterations as may be for spiritual objects.

ART 17. The reduction of the dioceses that will result from the application of the preceding article will be effected little by little as the said dioceses fall vacant. It is understood that this reduction will not imply the suppression either of the titles or of the Chapters of the dioceses, that will be preserved although they will be so grouped as to make the diocesan centre correspond with the chief town of the province. The above mentioned reductions will leave untouched all the economic resources of the dioceses and of all other ecclesiastical bodies existing in the same, including the amounts paid at present by the Italian State.

ART 18. If, by order of the ecclesiastical authority, it becomes necessary to group together, temporarily or permanently, several parishes, either entrusting them to one rector assisted by one or more vice rectors, or collecting together several priests in the same presbytery, the State will maintain unaltered the financial treatment due to the said parishes.

ART 19. The appointment of archbishops and bishops pertains to the Holy See. Before proceeding to nominate an archbishop, a diocesan bishop, or a coadjutor *cum jure successionis,* the Holy See will notify to the Italian Government the name of the selected ecclesiastic in order to ascertain whether the said Government has any political reasons for objecting to the nomination. All arrangements concerning this will be made with the greatest possible speed and every reserve, so as to keep secret the name of the candidate until the nomination is made.

ART 20. All bishops, before taking possession of their diocese, will take an oath of fealty to the Head of the State, according to the following formula: "Before God and His Holy Gospel I swear and promise as is fitting in a Bishop, fealty to the Italian State. I swear and promise to respect, and to make respected by my clergy the King and the Government established according to the constitutional laws of the State. Further, I swear and promise not to take part in any agreement, nor to be present at any meeting, which may injure the Italian State and public order, and that I will not permit my clergy to do so. Desirous of promoting the welfare and the interests of the Italian State I will seek to avoid any course that may injure it."

ART 21. The provision of the ecclesiastical benefices pertains to the ecclesiastical authority. The appointment of priests to be invested with parish benefices must be communicated privately by the competent ecclesiastical authority to the Italian Government, and cannot take effect until thirty days after the communication. In the mean time the Italian Government, if serious reasons are opposed to the appointment, will privately inform the ecclesiastical authority, when, if agreement cannot be reached, it will refer the case to the Holy See. If serious reasons make the permanent tenure of an ecclesiastic in a parochial benefice undesirable, the Italian Government will notify these reasons to the Ordinary, who, in mutual agreement with the Government, will take the appropriate measures within three months. In the case of divergency between the Ordinary and the Government, the Holy See will entrust the solution of the question to two ecclesiastics chosen by itself, who, in agreement with two delegates of the Italian Government will arrive at a definite decision.

ART 22. Ecclesiastics who are not Italian subjects cannot be invested with benefices existing in Italy. The occupiers of dioceses and parishes must also speak the Italian language. If necessary, they may be assisted by co-adjutors who, besides Italian, understand and speak also the language in use in the district, so as to give religious assistance to the faithful in their own language, according to the rules of the Church.

ART 23. The rules laid down in Arts. 16, 17, 19, 20, 21 and 22 do not apply to Rome and the suburbicarian dioceses. It is also understood that should the Holy See proceed to a new arrangement of the said dioceses the amounts at present paid by the Italian Government either as stipends or to other ecclesiastical institutions will remain unaltered.

ART 24. The *exequatur*, the royal *placet*, and all other imperial or royal appointments to ecclesiastical benefices or offices are abolished, except in the cases laid down in Art. 29, letter (g).

ART 25. The Italian State renounces the sovereign prerogative of the Royal Patronage over major and minor benefices. The "regalia" on major and minor benefices is abolished. The "pensionable third" in the provinces of the ex-kingdom of the two Sicilies is also abolished. The State and the administrations dependent in it, cease to be responsible for any financial obligation.

ART 26. The appointment of ecclesiastics to major or minor benefices or of those who may temporarily represent the vacant see or benefice, takes effect from the date of the ecclesiastical nomination and must be officially communicated to the Government. The administration and the enjoyment of the income during the vacancy is settled in accordance with the rules of Canon Law. In case of bad administration the Italian State, after coming to an agreement with the ecclesiastical authority, may proceed to the seizure of the temporalities of the benefice, handing over the net income to the nominee, or, lacking him, to the benefice itself.

A R T 27. The Basilicas of the Holy House in Loreto, of St. Francis in Assisi and of St. Anthony in Padua, with all buildings and workshops dependent, except those of purely lay character, will be handed over to the Holy See and their management will wholly pertain to the said See. All other bodies of any nature directly controlled in Italy by the Holy See, including colleges for missionaries, will equally be free from any State interference or conversion. None the less all Italian laws regarding acquisitions by moral bodies remain in force.

Regarding the possessions owned at the present by the said Sanctuaries, a mixed Commission will proceed to their division, taking into consideration the rights of their parties and the endowments necessary to the said purely lay institutions.

The unrestricted control of the ecclesiastical authority will take the place of the civil administration existing in all other Sanctuaries, without prejudice to the division of possessions contemplated in the preceding article, where this is the case.

A R T 28. To tranquilize consciences, the Holy See will grant full forgiveness to all those who, in consequence of the Italian laws against ecclesiastical patrimony, find themselves in possession of ecclesiastical properties. With this object the Holy See will give the necessary instructions to the Ordinaries.

A R T 29. The Italian State will revise its legislation, in so far as it refers to ecclesiastical matters, so as to reform and complete it, putting it into harmony with the principles the treaty stipulated with the Holy See and this Concordat.

The following have been agreed upon between the two High Contracting Parties:

a. While the juridical personality of the ecclesiastical bodies recognized up to the present by the Italian laws (Holy See, dioceses, chapters, seminaries, parishes, etc.) remains unaltered, such personality will be recognized also for churches open to public worship, that do not possess it already, including those previously owned by suppressed ecclesiastical bodies, in which case they will enjoy the income that at present the Maintainance Fund assigns to each of them. Except when prescribed in Art. 27, the Boards of Administration, wherever they exist and whatever their name, even if composed totally or mainly of laymen, may not interfere in regard to divine worship, and the appointment of their members must be made in consultation with the ecclesiastical authorities.

b. Judicial personality will be recognized to the religious associations, with or without vows, approved by the Holy See, that have their principal residence in the kingdom, and are represented there, juridically and materially by persons who are Italian subjects domiciled in Italy. Juridical personality will also be recognized to Italian religious provinces within the limits of the territory of the State and its Colonies, as well as to associations having their mother-house abroad, as long as they fulfill the same conditions. Juridical personality will also be recognized to religious Houses when by the special rules of their Orders the capacity of acquiring and owning property is guaranteed to them. Moreover, juridical personality will be recognized in the case of residences of Generals of religious orders and to the head offices of foreign religious associations. All Associations and religious Houses, which already have juridical personality, will retain it. All legal acts regarding the transfer of properties already owned by the associations, from their present nominal owners, will be exempt from any duty or tax.

c. All confraternities having purely or mainly religious aims are not subject to any further definition of aims, and will depend upon ecclesiastical authority for their direction and administration.

d. Religious foundations of every kind are admitted, so long as they correspond with the religious needs of the population and do not cause any financial burden to the State. This rule applies also to foundations already existing *de facto*.

e. In the civil administration of the ecclesiastical patrimony arising from the confiscation laws, the boards of the administration will be composed as to one half by members nominated by the ecclesiastical authority. The same applies to the religious foundations of the new provinces.

f. All action taken up to now by ecclesiastical or religious bodies not in conformity with civil laws, may be recognized and legalized on the request of the Ordinary within three years from the coming into effect of this Concordat.

g. The Italian State renounces the privileges of ecclesiastical jurisdictional exemption of the Palatine clergy throughout Italy, except for such clergy appointed to the churches of the Santa Sindona in Turin, of Superga of the Sudario in Rome and of the chapels appertaining to the residential palaces of the Sovereigns and of the Royal Princes, while all other nominations and appointments to benefices and offices will be ruled by the preceding articles.

A special commission will assign to each Palatine basilica or church an adequate endowment according to the rules laid down for the sanctuaries in Art. 27.

h. Leaving unaltered all fiscal privileges already granted by the Italian laws to ecclesiastical institutions, all institutions with a strictly religious aim are put on an equality, for fiscal purposes, with those having a benevolent or educational scope. The special 30 per cent. tax imposed by Art. 18 of the law August 15th 1867, No. 3848, the concomital quota of articles 31 of the law July 7th 1866, No. 3036 and 20 of law August 15th, 1867, No. 3848, are abolished, as well as the tax on the transfer of usufruct of the goods constituting the endowment of benefices and other ecclesiastical bodies, as per Art. 1 of the Royal Decree, December 30th, 1923, No. 3270; so that in future no special tribute can be imposed upon the possessions of the Church. The 'professional' tax and the 'patent' tax instituted by the Royal Decree, No. 2538, of November 15th, 1923, in place of the suppressed tax on shops and re-selling, will not be imposed on priests in respect of the exercise of their clerical mission, nor any other similar tax.

i. The wearing of ecclesiastical or religious dress by seculars, or by clerics or religious to whom this has been forbidden by a permanent decision of the competent ecclesiastical authority (which in such case should be officially communicated to the Italian Government), is forbidden and punished with the same penalties as are inflicted for the illegal wearing of military uniforms.

ART 30. The administration, both ordinary and extraordinary, of the properties owned by any ecclesiastical institutions or religious association is carried on under the supervision and control of the competent Church authorities, excluding any interference from the Italian State, and without any obligation to subject to conversion any estate or building.

The Italian State recognizes to all ecclesiastical institutions and religious associations the capacity of acquiring possessions within the limits of the civil law ruling acquisitions by moral bodies.

The Italian State, until new agreements ordain otherwise, will continue to make up the deficiencies in the incomes of the ecclesiastical benefices with sums corresponding to an amount not inferior to the real value fixed by the laws now in vigor. In consideration of this, the patrimonial administration of the said benefices, in regard to all acts and contracts outside ordinary administration, will take place with the concurrence of the Italian State, and in the case of a vacancy the delivery of the possessions will be made in the presence of a representative of the Government, and an official report will be made of the fact. The episcopal stipends of the suburbicarian dioceses and the endowments of the Chapters and parishes of Rome and of the said dioceses will not be subject to the above conditions.

As regards the above, the amount of the incomes that are paid to the recipients of the benefices out of the said stipends and endowments will appear from a statement rendered yearly under his own responsibility by the suburbicarian bishop for the dioceses, and by the Cardinal Vicar for the city of Rome.

ART 31. The erection of new ecclesiastical bodies or religious associations will be made by the ecclesiastical authority according to the rules of Canon Law. Their recognition for civil effects will be granted by the civil authorities.

ART 32. The recognitions and authorizations contemplated by the present Concordat and by the Treaty will take place according to the rules of civil law, which will have to be put in harmony with the prescriptions of the Concordat and of the Treaty.

ART 33. The charge of the Catacombs existing in the subsoil of Rome and in other parts of the Kingdom is reserved to the Holy See, with the onus of custody, upkeep and preservation. The Holy See can therefore, while observing the laws of the State and the rights of third parties, proceed to the needful excavations and to the transfer of the holy bodies.

ART 34. The Italian State wishing to restore to the institution of matrimony, which is the basis of the family, the dignity it deserves considering the Catholic tradition of the nation, recognizes the civil effects of the sacrament of marriage as laid down by Canon Law. The publication of the banns must be carried out, not only in the parish church but also by the municipality. Immediately after the ceremony the parish priest will explain to the married couple the civil effects of marriage, reading to them the articles of the civil code concerning the rights and the duties of husband and wife, and he will draw up the marriage certificate, a complete copy of which must be forwarded within five days to the Commune, in order that it may be entered in the registers of the Civil Status.

All causes concerning nullity of marriage and dispensations from marriages celebrated but not consummated, are reserved to the authority of the ecclesiastical courts. The decisions and verdicts, when they have been made absolute, shall be reported to the Supreme Court of the Segnatura which will verify whether the rules of Canon Law in regard to the competency of the judge, the summoning and legal defense or the contumacy of the parties concerned, have been compiled with. The said decisions and final verdicts with the decrees of the Supreme Court of the Segnatura shall be transmitted to the Court of Appeal of the appropriate district, which with an Order of the Council of Judges will pronounce them effective for civil purposes and will order them to be duly noted in the registers of the Civil Status in the margin of the certificate of marriage.

As regards all cases of personal separation the Holy See is willing that they should be decided by the authority of the civil courts.

ART 35. All secondary schools, conducted under ecclesiastical or religious supervision, shall continue to submit themselves to the State examinations, all candidates whether from the above schools or from government institutions being treated on an absolute equality.

ART 36. Italy considers the teaching of Christian doctrine in accordance with Catholic tradition, as both the basis and the crown of public education. It therefore agrees that the religious teaching now given in the public elementary schools shall be extended to the secondary schools, in accordance with a program to be drawn up between the Holy See and the State. Such teaching shall be given by masters and professors, whether priests or religious, approved by ecclesiastical authority, and even by lay masters and professors, who, for this purpose shall be provided with certificates of capacity from the Ordinary of the diocese. The revocation of such a certificate by the Ordinary forthwith deprives the teacher of his right to teach. For such religious instruction in public schools text books may only be used that have been approved by ecclesiastical authority.

ART 37. The directors of the State associations for physical training, for pre-military instruction, for Avanguardisi and for Balilla, in order to allow the youth entrusted to them to take part in religious instruction and services, will arrange their time-tables for Sundays and holidays of obligation in such a way as not to interfere with the performance of religious duties.

In the same way all directors of public schools will make similar arrangements for their pupils on all holidays of obligation.

ART 38. The nomination of the professors of the Catholic University of the Sacred Heart and of the dependent Istituo di Magistero Maria Immacolata, are subject to the *Nihil Obstat* of the Holy See, in order to ensure that there is nothing to take exception to from the point of view of faith or morals.

ART 39. All universities, greater or lesser seminaries, whether diocesan, inter-diocesan or regional, academies, colleges and other Catholic institutions for the formation and education of ecclesiastics will continue to be subject solely to the Holy See, without any interference from the educational authorities of the Kingdom.

ART 40. The degrees in sacred theology conferred by the Faculty approved by the Holy See will be recognized by the Italian State. It will also recognize diplomas conferred by the schools of paleography, of Archives and of diplomatic documents organized in connection with the library and record office of Vatican City.

ART 41. Italy authorizes the use within the Kingdom and in her Colonies of pontifical titles of knighthood after registration of the brevet on production of the original and at the written request of the recipient of the honour.

ART 42. Italy will permit the recognition, by the means of a Royal Decree, of titles of nobility conferred by the Supreme Pontiff even since 1870, and of all those that may be conferred in the future.

In certain cases the authorization in Italy will not be liable to the payment of fees.

ART 43. The Italian State recognizes the organizations forming part of the Italian Catholic Action, in so far as, in accordance with the injunctions of the Holy See, they maintain their activity wholly apart from every political party and under the immediate control of the hierarchy of the Church for the diffusion and practice of Catholic principles. The Holy See takes the opportunity of the drawing up of the present Concordat to renew to all ecclesiastics and religious throughout Italy the prohibition to be members of, or take part in, any political party.

ART 44. If, in the future, any difficulties should arise concerning the interpretation of the present Concordat, the Holy See and Italy will proceed by way of mutual understanding to a friendly solution.

ART 45. The present Concordat will be applied after the exchange of ratifications contemporaneously with the Treaty stipulated between the same High Parties which eliminated the 'Roman Question'.

With the coming into force of the present Concordat all the dispositions of previous Concordats of the former Austrian laws and all laws regulations and decrees of the Italian States shall cease to be applied in Italy. All Austrian laws and all laws, regulations and decrees of the existing Italian State in so far as they are in conflict with the dispositions of the present Concordat are to be considered abrogated as soon as the present Concordat comes into force.

In order to carry out the execution of the present Concordat a Commission shall be set up, immediately after the signing of the same, consisting of persons nominated by both the contracting parties.

Rome, February 11th, 1929.
Signed: *Peter Card. Gasparri*
Benito Mussolini

3. Concordat between the Holy See and the German Reich[1]

His Holiness Pope Pius XI and the President of the German Reich, moved by a common desire to consolidate and enhance friendly relations existing between the Holy See and the German Reich, wish to regulate the relations between the Catholic Church and the State for the whole territory of the German Reich in a permanent manner and on a basis acceptable to both parties. They have decided to conclude a solemn agreement, which will supplement the Concordats already concluded with certain individual German States, and will ensure for the remaining States fundamentally uniform treatment of their respective problems.

For this purpose:

His Holiness Pope Pius XI has appointed as his Plenipotentiary His Eminence the Most Reverend Lord Cardinal Eugenio Pacelli, his Secretary of State.

The President of the German Reich has appointed as Plenipotentiary the Vice-Chancellor of the German Reich, Herr Franz von Papen.

Who, having exchanged their respective credentials and found them to be in due and proper form, have agreed to the following articles:

A R T I. The German Reich guarantees freedom of profession and public practice of the Catholic Religion.

It acknowledges the right of the Catholic Church, within the limit of those laws which are applicable to all, to manage and regulate her own affairs

---

1. *The Persecution of the Catholic Church in the Third Reich: Facts and Documents, translated from the German* (London: Burns and Oates, 1940), 516–22.

independently, and, within the framework of her own competence, to publish laws and articles binding on her members.

ART 2. The Concordats concluded with Bavaria (1924), Prussia (1929) and Baden (1932) remain in force, and the rights and privileges of the Catholic Church recognized therein are secured and unchanged within the territories of the States concerned. For the remaining States the agreements entered into the present Concordat come into force in their entirety. These last are also binding for those States named above in so far as they affect matters not regulated by the regional Concordats or are complementary to the settlement already made.

In future, regional Concordats with States of the German Reich will be concluded only with the agreement of the Reich Government.

ART 3. In order to foster good relations between the Holy See and the German Reich, an Apostolic Nuncio will reside in the capital of the German Reich and an Ambassador of the German Reich at the Holy See, as heretofore.

ART 4. In its relations and correspondence with the bishops, clergy and other members of the Catholic Church in Germany, the Holy See enjoys full freedom. The same applies to the bishops and other diocesan officials in their dealings with the faithful in all matters belonging to their pastoral office.

Instructions, ordinances, Pastoral Letters, official diocesan gazettes and other enactments regarding the spiritual direction of the faithful issued by the ecclesiastical authorities within the framework of their competence (Art 1, Sect. 2) may be published without hinderence and brought to the notice of the faithful in the form hitherto usual.

ART 5. In the exercise of spiritual activities the clergy enjoy the protection of the State in the same way as State officials. The State will take proceedings in accordance with the general provisions of State law against any outrage offered to the clergy personally or directed against their ecclesiastical character, or any interference with the duties of their office, and in case of need will provide official protection.

ART 6. Clerics and Religious are freed from any obligation to undertake official offices and such obligations as, according to the provisions of Canon Law, are incompatible with the clerical or religious state. This applies particularly to the office of magistrate, juryman, member of Taxation Committee or member of the Fiscal Tribunal.

ART 7. The acceptance of an appointment or office in the State, or in any publicly constituted corporation dependant on the State, requires, in the case of the clergy, the *nihil obstat* of the Diocesan Ordinary of the individual concerned, as well as that of the Ordinary of place in which the publicly constituted corporation is situated. The *nihil obstat* may be withdrawn at any time for grave reasons affecting ecclesiastical interests.

ART 8. The official income of the clergy is immune from distraint to the same extent as is the official salary of official of the Reich and State.

ART 9. The clergy may not be required by judicial and other officials to give information concerning matters which have been entrusted to them while exercising the care of souls, and which have therefore come within the obligation of pastoral secrecy.

ART 10. The wearing of clerical dress or of a religious habit on the part of lay folk, or of clerics or religious who have been forbidden to wear them by final and valid injunction made by the competent ecclesiastical authority and officially communicated to the State authority, is liable to the same penalty on the part of the State as the misuse of military uniform.

ART 11. The present organization and demarcation of dioceses of the Catholic Church in the German Reich remains in force. Such rearrangements of a bishopric or of an ecclesiastical province or of other diocesan demarcations as shall seem advisable in the future, so far as they involve changes within the boundaries of a German State, remain subject to the agreement of the Government of the State concerned.

Rearrangements and alterations which extend beyond the boundaries of a German State require the agreement of the Reich Government, to whom it shall be left to secure the consent of the regional Government in question. The same applies to rearrangements or alterations of ecclesiastical Provinces involving several German States. The foregoing conditions do not apply to such ecclesiastical boundaries as are laid down merely in the interests of local pastoral care.

In the case of any territorial reorganization within the German Reich, the Reich Government will communicate with the Holy See with a view to rearrangement of the organization and demarcation of dioceses.

ART 12. Without prejudice to the provisions of Article 11, ecclesiastical offices may be freely constituted and changed, unless the expenditure of State funds is involved. The creation and alteration of parishes shall be carried out according to principles which the diocesan bishops are agreed, and for which the Reich Government will endeavor to secure uniform treatment as far as possible from the State Governments.

ART 13. Catholic parishes, parish and diocesan societies, episcopal sees, bishoprics and chapters, religious Orders and Congregations, as well as institutions, foundations and property which are under the administration of ecclesiastical authority, shall retain or acquire respectively legal competence in the civil domain according to general prescriptions of civil law. They shall remain publicly recognized corporations in so far as they have been such hitherto; similar rights may be granted to the remainder in accordance with those provisions of the law which apply to all.

ART 14. As a matter of principle the Church retains the right to appoint freely to all Church offices and benefices without the co-operation of the State or of civil communities, in so far as other provisions have not been made previous Concordats mentioned in Article 2. The regulation made for the appointment to the Metropolitan See of Freiburg (the Ecclesiastical Province of the Upper Rhine) is to be duly applied to the two suffragan bishoprics of Rottenburg and Mainz, as well as to the bishoprics of Meissen. With regard to Rottenburg and Mainz the same regulation holds for the appointments to the Cathedral Chapter, and for the administration of the right of patronage. Furthermore, there is accord on the following points:

1. Catholic clerics who hold an ecclesiastical office in Germany or who exercise pastoral or educational functions must:

    a. Be German citizens.

    b. Have matriculated from a German secondary school.

    c. Have studied philosophy and theology for at least three years at a German State University, a German ecclesiastical college, or a papal college in Rome.

2. The Bull nominating Archbishops, Coadjutors *cum jure successionis,* or appointing a *Praelatris nullius,* will not be issued until the name of the appointee has been submitted to the representative of the National Government in the territory concerned, and until it has been ascertained that no objections of a general political nature exist.

By agreement between Church and State, Paragraph 1, sections (a) (b) and (c) may be disregarded or set aside.

ART 15. Religious Orders and Congregations are not subject to any special restrictions on the part of the State, either as regards their foundation, the erection of their various establishments, their number, the selection of members (save for special provisions of paragraph 2 in this article), pastoral activity, education, care of the sick and charitable work, or as regards the management of their affairs and the administration of their property.

Religious Superiors whose headquarters are within Germany must be German citizens. Provincials and other Superiors of Orders, whose headquarters be outside Germany, have the right of visitation of those of their establishments which lie within Germany.

The Holy See will endeavor to ensure that the provincial organization of the conventual establishments within the German Reich shall be such that, as far as possible, German establishments do not fall under the jurisdiction of foreign provincials. Agreements may be made with the Reich Government in cases where the small number of houses makes a special German province impracticable, or where special grounds exist for the retention of a provincial organization which is firmly established and has acquired an historic nature.

ART 16. Before bishops take possession of their dioceses they are to take an oath of fealty either to the Reich Representative of the State concerned, or to the President of the Reich, according to the following formula: "Before God and the Holy Gospels I swear and promise, as becomes a bishop, loyalty to the German Reich and the State of ... I swear and promise to honor the legally constituted Government and to cause the clergy of my diocese to honor it. In the performance of my spiritual office and in my solicitude for the welfare and the interests of the German Reich, I will endeavor to avoid all detrimental acts which might endanger it."

ART 17. The property and other rights of public corporations, institutions, foundations and associations of the Catholic Church regarding their vested interests, are guaranteed according to the common law of the land.

No building dedicated to public worship may be destroyed for any reason whatsoever without the previous consent of the ecclesiastical authorities concerned.

ART 18. Should it become necessary to abrogate the performance of obligations undertaken by the State towards the Church, whether based on law, agreement or special charter, the Holy See and the Reich will elaborate in amicable agreement the principles according to which the abrogation is carried out.

Legitimate traditional rights are to be considered as titles in law.

Such abrogation of obligations must be compensated by an equivalent in favor of the claimant.

ART 19. Catholic Theological Faculties in State Universities are to be maintained. Their relation to ecclesiastical authorities will be governed by the respective Concordats and by special Protocols attached to the same, and with due regard to the laws of the Church in their regard. The Reich Government will endeavor to secure for all these Catholic Faculties in Germany a uniformity of practical administration corresponding to the general spirit and tenor of the various agreement concerned.

ART 20. Where other agreements do not exist, the Church has the right to establish theological and philosophical colleges for the training of its clergy, which institutions are to be wholly dependent on the ecclesiastical authorities if no State subsidies are sought.

The establishment, management and administration of theological seminaries and hostels for clerical students, within the limits of the law applicable to all, is exclusively the prerogative of the ecclesiastical authorities.

ART 21. Catholic religious instruction in elementary, senior, secondary and vocational schools constitutes a regular portion of the curriculum and is to be taught in accordance with the principles of the Catholic Church. In religious instruction, special care will be taken to inculcate patriotic, civic and social consciousness and sense of duty in the spirit of the Christian Faith and the moral code, precisely as in the case of other subjects. The syllabus and the selection of textbooks for religious instruction will be arranged by consultative agreement with the ecclesiastical authorities, and these latter have the right to investigate whether pupils are receiving religious instruction in accordance with the teachings and requirements of the Church. Opportunities for such an investigation will be agreed upon with the school authorities.

ART 22. With regard to the appointment of Catholic religious instructors, agreement will be arrived at as a result of mutual consultation on the part of the bishop and the Government of the State concerned. Teachers who have been declared by the bishop unfit for the further exercise of their teaching functions, either on pedagogical grounds or by reason of their moral conduct, may not be employed for religious instruction so long as the obstacle remains.

ART 23. The retention of Catholic denominational schools and the establishment of new ones, is guaranteed. In all parishes in which parents or guardians request it, Catholic elementary schools will be established, provided that the number of pupils available appears sufficient for a school managed and administered in accordance with the standards prescribed by the State, due regard being had to the local conditions of school organisations.

ART 24. In all Catholic elementary schools only such teachers are to be employed as are members of the Catholic Church, and who guarantee to fulfil the special requirements of a Catholic school.

Within the frame-work of the general professional training of teachers, arrangements will be made which will secure the formation and training of Catholic teachers in accordance with the special requirements of Catholic denominational schools.

ART 25. Religious Orders and Congregations are entitled to establish and conduct private schools, subject to the general laws and ordinances governing education. In so far as these schools follow the curriculum prescribed for

State schools, those attending them acquire the same qualifications as are those attending State schools.

The admission of members of religious Orders or Congregations to the teaching office, and their appointment to elementary, secondary or senior schools, are subject to general conditions applicable to all.

ART 26. With certain reservations pending a later comprehensive regulation of the marriage laws, it is understood that, apart from cases of critical illness of one member of an engaged couple which does not permit of a postponement, and in cases of great moral emergency (the presence of which must be confirmed by the proper ecclesiastical authority), the ecclesiastical marriage ceremony should precede the civil ceremony. In such cases the pastor is in duty bound to notify the matter immediately at the Registrar's office.

ART 27. The Church will accord provision to the German army for the spiritual guidance of its Catholic officers, personnel and other officials, as well as for the families of the same.

The administration of such pastoral care for the army is to be vested in the army bishop. The latter's ecclesiastical appointment is to be made by the Holy See after contact has been made with the Reich Government in order to select a suitable candidate who is agreeable to both parties.

The ecclesiastical appointment of military chaplains and other military clergy will be made after previous consultations with the appropriate authorities of the Reich by the army bishop. The army bishop may appoint only such chaplains as receive permission from their diocesan bishop to engage on military pastoral work, together with a certificate of suitability. Military chaplains have the rights of parish priests with regard to the troops and other army personnel assigned to them.

Detailed regulations for the organization of pastoral work by chaplains will be supplied by an Apostolic Brief. Regulations for official aspects of the same will be drawn up by the Reich Government.

ART 28. In hospitals, prisons, and similar public institutions the Church is to retain the right of visitation and of holding divine service, subject to the rules of the said institutions. If regular pastoral care is provided for such institutions, and if pastors be appointed as State or other public officials, such appointments will be made by agreement with the ecclesiastical authorities.

ART 29. Catholic members of a non-German minority living within the Reich, in matters concerning the use of their mother tongue in church services, religious instruction and the conduct of church societies, will be accorded no less favorable treatment than that which is actually and in accordance with law permitted to individuals of German origin and speech living within the boundaries of the corresponding foreign States.

ART 30. On Sundays and Holy days, special prayers, conforming to the Liturgy, will be offered during the principal Mass for the welfare of the German Reich and its people in all episcopal, parish and conventual churches and chapels of the German Reich.

ART 31. Those Catholic organizations and societies which pursue exclusively charitable, cultural or religious ends, and, as such, are placed under the ecclesiastical authorities, will be protected in their institutions and activities.

Those Catholic organizations which to their religious, cultural and charitable pursuits add others, such as social or professional interests, even though they may be brought into national organizations, are to enjoy the protection of Article 31, Section 1, provided they guarantee to develop their activities outside all political parties.

It is reserved to the central Government and the German episcopate, in joint agreement, to determine which organizations and associations come within the scope of this article.

In so far as the Reich and its constituent States take charge of sport and other youth organizations, care will be taken that it shall be possible for the members of the same regularly to practice their religious duties on Sundays and feast days, and that they shall not be required to do anything not in harmony with their religious and moral convictions and obligations.

ART 32. In view of the special situation existing in Germany, and in view of the guarantee provided through this Concordat of legislation directed to safeguard the rights and privileges of the Roman Catholic Church in the Reich and its component States, the Holy See will prescribe regulations for the exclusion of clergy and members of religious Orders from membership of political parties, and from engaging in work on their behalf.

ART 33. All matters relating to clerical persons or ecclesiastical affairs, which have not been treated of in the foregoing articles, will be regulated for the ecclesiastical sphere according to current Canon Law.

Should differences of opinion arise regarding the interpretation or execution of any of the articles of this Concordat, the Holy See and the German Reich will reach a friendly solution by mutual agreement.

ART 34. This Concordat, whose German and Italian texts shall have equal binding force, shall be ratified, and the certificates of ratification shall be exchanged, as soon as possible. It will be in force from the day of such exchange.

In witness hereof, the plenipotentiaries have signed this Concordat. Signed in two original exemplars, in the Vatican City, July 20th, 1933.

Signed: *Eugenio Cardinal Pacelli*
Signed: *Franz von Papen*

The Supplementary Protocol

At the signing of the Concordat concluded today between the Holy See and the German Reich, the undersigned, being regularly thereto empowered, have adjoined the following explanations which form an integral part of the Concordat itself.

In re: Art 3. The Apostolic Nuncio to the German Reich, in accordance with the exchange of notes between the Apostolic Nunciature in Berlin and the Reich Foreign Office on the 11th and the 27th of March respectively, shall be the Doyen of the Diplomatic Corps thereto accredited.

ART 13. It is understood that the Church retains the right to levy Church taxes.

ART 14, PAR 2. It is understood that when objections of a general political nature exist, they shall be presented within the shortest possible time. If after twenty days such representations have not been made, the Holy See may be justified in assuming that no such objections exist to the candidate in question. The names of the persons concerned will be kept confidential until the announcement of the appointment. No right of the State to assert a veto is to be derived from this article.

ART 17. In so far as public buildings or properties are devoted to ecclesiastical purposes, these are to be retained as before subject to existing agreements.

ART 19, PAR 2. This clause is based, at the time of signature of this Concordat, especially on the Apostolic Constitution, *Deus Scientiarum Dominus* on May 24th, 1931, and the Instruction of July 7th, 1932.

ART 20. Hostels which are administered by the Church in connection with certain Universities and secondary schools, will be recognized, from the point of view of taxation, as essentially ecclesiastical institutions in the proper sense of the word, and as integral parts of diocesan organizations.

ART 24. In so far as private institutions are able to meet requirements of the new educational code with regard to the training of teachers, all existing establishments of religious Orders and Congregations will be given due consideration in the accordance of recognition.

ART 26. A severe moral emergency is taken to exist when there are insuperable or disproportionately difficult and costly obstacles impeding the procuring of documents necessary for the marriage at the proper time.

ART 27, PAR 1. Catholic officers, officials and personnel, their families included, do not belong to local parishes and are not to contribute to their maintenance.

PAR. 4. The publication of the Apostolic Brief will take place after consultation with the Reich Government.

ART 28. In cases of urgency entry of the clergy is guaranteed at all times.

ART 29. Since the Reich Government has seen its way to come to an agreement regarding non-German minorities, the Holy See declares—in accordance with the principles it has constantly maintained regarding the right to employ the vernacular in Church services, religious instruction and the conduct of Church societies—that it will bear in mind similar clauses protective of German minorities when establishing Concordats with other countries.

ART 31, PAR 4. The principles laid down in Article 31, Par 4 hold good also for the Labor Service.

ART 32. It is understood that similar provisions regarding activity in Party politics will be introduced by the Reich Government for members of non-Catholic denominations. The conduct, which has been made obligatory for the clergy and members of religious Orders in Germany in virtue of Article 32, does not involve any sort of limitation of official and prescribed preaching and interpretation of the dogmatic and moral teachings and principles of the Church.

At the Vatican City, July 20th, 1933.
Signed: *Eugino Cardinal Pacelli*
Signed: *Franz von Papen*

Bibliography

I. Bibliography on the Concordat with Napoleon's France

Acquaviva, S. S. *The Decline of the Sacred in Industrial Society.* Oxford, 1979.

Bedaria, F., J.-M. Mayeur, J. L. Monneron, and A. Prost. *Histoire du peuple français. Cent ans d'esprit republican.* Paris, 1964.

Bindel, V. *Histoire Religieuse de Napoleon.* 2 vols. Paris, 1940.

Blet, Pierre. *Le Clerge de France et la monarchie.* 2 vols. Rome, 1959.

Boulay de la Meurthe, H. *Documents sur la Negociation du Concordat.* 5 vols. Paris, 1891.

Bredin, Jean-Denis. *The Affair. The Case of Alfred Dreyfus.* New York, 1986.

de Broglie, Abbé A. T. P. *Le Present et l'avenir du catholicisme en France.* Paris, 1892.

Brogan, D. W. *The Development of Modern France, 1800–1939.* New York, 1940.

Brown, Marvin Luther. *Louis Veuillot. French Ultramontane Catholic Journalist and Layman.* Durham, 1977.

Brugerette, J. *Le Prêtre français et la société contemporaine.* 3 vols. Paris, 1933–38.

Burns, Michael. *Rural Society and French Politics. Boulangism and the Dreyfus Affair 1886–1900.* Princeton, 1984.

Byrnes, Robert F. *Antisemitism in Modern France. The Prelude to the Dreyfus Affair.* New Brunswick. 1984.

Carcopino, Claude. *Les Doctrines sociales de Lamennais.* Geneva, 1968.

Caron, Jeanne. *Le Sillon et la démocratie chretienne, 1894–1910.* Paris, 1967.

de Certeau, Michel, and Jean-Marie Domenach. *La Christianism éclate.* Paris, 1974.

Chadwick, Owen. *The Popes and European Revolution.* Oxford, 1981.

Chapman, G. *The Third Republic, 1872–94.* New York, 1962.

Chastenet, J. *Histoire de la Troisième Republique.* 6. v. Paris, 1952–55.

Cholvy, Gerard, Yves-Marie Hilaire, et al. *Histoire religieuse de la France contemporaine.* 3 vols. Toulouse, 1985–88.

Coppa, Frank J. *Pope Pius IX.* Boston, 1979.

Correspondance générale de Félicité de Lamennais. Louis Le Guillou, ed. Paris, 1900.

Coutrot, A., and F. G. Dreyfus. *Les Forces religieuses dans la société francaise.* Paris, 1965.

Dansette, Adrien. *Histoire religieuse de la France contemporaine.* 2 vols. Paris, 1948–51.

Darbon, M. *Le Conflit entre la droite et la gauche dans le Catholicisme français, 1830–1953.* Paris, 1953.

Debidour, A. *L'Église catholique et l'État sous la Troisième Republique, 1870–1906.* 2 vols. Paris, 1960–69.

Delaruelle, E., A. Latreille, J. Palanque, and R. Remond. *Histoire du Catholicisme en France.* 3 vols. Paris, 1962.

Droulers, P. *Action pastorale et problèmes sociaux sous la monarchie de Juillet.* Paris, 1954.

Duroselle, Jean-Baptiste. *Les Debuts du catholicisme sociale en France* (1822–1870). Paris, 1951.

Faguet, Émile. *L'Anticlericalisme.* Paris, 1906.

Fugier, J. *Napoléon et l'Italie.* Paris, 1947.

Gadille, J. *La Pensée et l'action politiques des évêques français au debut la IIIème Republique. 1870–1883*, 2 vols. Paris, 1967.

Gargan, Edward T., ed. *Leo XIII and the Modern World.* New York, 1961.

Goguel, F. *La Politique des partis sous la Troisième Republique.* Paris, 1958.

Gough, Austin. *Paris and Rome. The Gallican Church and the Ultramontane Campaign, 1848–1853.* Oxford, 1986.

Goyau, G. *Histoire religeuse de la France.* Paris, 1922.

Griffiths, Richard. *The Reactionary Revolution. The Catholic Revival in French Literature 1870–1914.* New York, 1965.

Hales, E. E. Y. *Revolution and Papacy 1796–1846.* London, 1960.

———. *Pio Nono.* London, 1954.

Hilaire, Y. M. "La Practique religieuse en France de 1815 a 1878." *Information historique* (Mar.–Apr. 1963): 57–69.

Houtart, François, and Andre Rousseau. *The Church and Revolution.* New York, 1971.

Hufton, Olwen. "The Reconstruction of a Church, 1796–1801." In *Beyond the Terror. Essays in French Regional and Social History, 1794–1815*, edited by G. Lewis and C. Lewis. Cambridge, 1983.

Hutt, M. G. "The Curés and the Third Estate: The Ideas of Reform in the Pamplets of the French Lower Clergy in the Period 1787–1789," *Journal of Ecclesiastical History* 8, no. 1 (April 1957): 74–92.

Isambert, François-André. *Christianisme et classe ouvriere.* Tournai, 1961.

Jedin, H., and J. Dolan, eds. *History of the Church.* New York, 1981.

Kedward, H. R. *The Dreyfus Affair.* London, 1965.

Kselman, Thomas A. *Miracles and Prophecies in Nineteenth-Century France.* New Brunswick, 1983.

Kurtz, L. R. *The Politics of Heresy. The Modernist Crisis in Roman Catholicism.* Berkeley, 1986.

Lamennais, Félicité. *Affaires de Rome.* Paris, 1836–37.

Larkin, Maurice. *Church and State after the Dreyfus Affair. The Separation Issue in France.* London, 1974.

Latreille, André. *L'Église catholique et la Revolution française.* 2 vols. Paris, 1946–50.

———. *Napoleon et la Saint-Siège, 1801–1808.* Paris, 1935.

Latrieille, A., E. Delaruelle, J. R. Palanque, and R. Remond. *Histoire des catholiques en France du XVème siècle a nos jours.* Paris, 1980.

Lebrun, Jean. *Lamennais ou l'inquietude de la liberté.* Paris, 1981.

Lecanuet, E. *L'Église de France sous la Troisième Republique*. 4 vols. Paris, 1907–30.

Leflon, J. *Bernier*. 2 vols. Paris, 1938.

Le Guillou, Louis. *L'Evolution de la pensée religieuse de Félicité Lamennais*. Paris, 1966.

Marcilhacy, Christianne. *Le diocèse d'Orleans sous l'episcopat de Mgr. Dupanloup, 1849–1878*. Paris, 1964.

Martin, Victor. *Le Gallicanisme et la reforme catholique*. Geneva, 1975.

Matagrin, Gabriel. *Politique, Église et foi*. Paris, 1972.

Mathieu, A. *Le Concordat de 1801*. Paris, 1903.

Maurain, J. *La Politique ecclésiastique du Second Empire*. Paris, 1930.

May, Anita Rasi, "Is 'Les Deus France' a Valid Framework for Interpreting the Nineteenth-Century Church? The French Episcopate as a Case Study." *Catholic Historical Review* 73, no. 4 (Oct. 1987), 541–61.

Mayeur, Jean-Marie. "Les Congrès Nationaux de la Démocratie chretienne à Lyon (1896–1897–1898)." *Revue d'histoire moderne et contemporaine* 9 (July–Sept. 1962), 171–206.

————. *La Separation de l'Église et de l'État*. Paris, 1966.

————. *L'Abbé Lemire, 1853–1928. Un Prêtre démocrate*. Tournai, 1968.

————. *Catholicisme social et démocratie chretienne. Principes romains, experiences françaises*. Paris, 1986.

McManners, John. *The French Revolution and the Church*. New York, 1969.

Mehl, Roger. *Le Catholicisme français dans la société actuelle*. Paris, 1977.

Mellor, Alec. *Histoire de l'anticlericalisme français*. Tours, 1966.

Menczer, Bela. *Catholic Political Thought 1789–1848*. Westminster, 1952.

Minier, Marc. *L'Episcopat français du Ralliement à Vatican II*. Padua, 1982.

Montalembert, Charles de. *Les Interets catholiques au XIXe siècle*. Paris, 1852.

Montuclard, Maurice. *Conscience religieuse et democratie. La deuxième démocratie chretienne en France, 1891–1902*. Paris, 1965.

Moody, Joseph N. *The Church as an Enemy. Anticlericalism in Nineteenth-Century French Literature*. Washington, D.C. 1968.

————. *French Education Since Napoleon*. Syracuse, 1978.

————. *Oeuvres completes de F. de la Mennais*. 2 vols. Brussel, 1839.

Osgood, S. *French Royalism under the Third and Fourth Republics*. New York, 1960.

Ozouf, M. *L'École, l'Église, et la Republique, 1871–1914*. Paris, 1963.

Palanque, J. R. *Catholiques Liveraux et Gallicans en France face au Concile du Vatican, 1869–1870*. Paris, 1962.

The Papal Encyclicals 1903–1939, ed. Claudia Carlen. Wilmington, 1981.

Paul, Harry W. *The Second Ralliement. The Rapprochement between Church and State in France in the Twentieth Century*. Washington, D.C., 1967.

Phillips, C. S. *The Church in France, 1789–1907*. 2 vols. New York, 1929–36.

Pierrard. *Le prêtre français*. Paris, 1969.

————. *L'Église et les ouvriers en France (1840–1940)*. Paris, 1984.

Ponteil, F. *Histoire de l'enseignement en France, 1789–1965*. Paris, 1966.

Ravitch, N. "Liberalism, Catholicism, and the Abbé Gregoire," *Church History* 36 (Dec. 1967), 419–39.

Reardon, Bernard. *Liberalism and Tradition. Aspects of Catholic Thought in Nineteenth Century France.* Cambridge, 1985.

Remond, René. *L'anti-clericalisme en France de 1815 a nos jours.* Paris, 1976.

———. *La Droite en France de 1815 a nos jours*, Paris, 1954.

Sedgwick, Alexander. *The Ralliement in French Politics 1890–1898.* Cambridge, 1965.

Sorlin, P. *"La Croix" et les juifs (1880–1899): contribution a l'histoire de l'antisemitisme contemporaine.* Paris, 1967.

———. *Waldeck-Rousseau.* Paris, 1966.

Spencer, Philip. *Politics of Belief in Nineteenth-Century France. Lacordaire, Michon, Veuillot.* London, 1954.

Stearns, Peter N. *Priest and Revolutionary. Lammenais and the Dilemma of French Catholicism.* New York, 1967.

Suarez, F. *Briand, sa vie, son oeuvre.* 5 vols. 1938.

Suffert, Georges. *Les Catholiques et la gauche.* Paris, 1960.

Todd, Emmanuel. *La Nouvelle France.* Paris, 1988.

Vassort-Rousset, Brigitte. *Les Évêques de France en politique.* Paris, 1986.

Vidler, Alec R. *Prophecy and Papacy. A Study of Lamennais, the Church, and Revolution.* New York, 1954.

Vovelle, Michel. *Religion et revolution. La dechristianisation de l'an II.* Paris, 1976.

Weill, G. *Histoire du catholicisme liberal en France, 1828–1908.* Paris, 1909.

Welschinger, H. *Le Pape et L'Empereur, 1804–1815.* Paris, 1905.

Wilson, Stephen. *Ideology and Experience. Antisemitism in France at the Time of the Dreyfus Affair.* Rutherford, N.J., 1982.

Zeldin, Theodore, ed. *Conflicts in French Society. Anticlericalism, Education, and Morals in the Nineteenth Century.* London, 1970.

———. *France, 1848–1945.* 2 vols. Oxford, 1973–77.

II. Bibliography on the Lateran Accords with Mussolini's Italy

ENCYCLICALS, OFFICIAL ACTS, AND OTHER PRINTED DOCUMENTS

Annuario Pontificio per L'anno 1929–1933. Vatican City: Tipografia Poliglotta Vaticana.

Bertone, Domenico, ed. *Discorsi di Pio XI.* Turin: Società Editrice Internazionale, 1960.

Carlen, Claudia, ed. *The Papal Encyclicals, 1903–1939.* Ann Arbor, Michigan: The Pierian Press, 1981.

———. *Papal Pronouncements. A Guide: 1740–1990.* Ann Arbor, Michigan: The Pierian Press, 1992.

Catholic Church. *Five Great Encyclicals: Labor, Education, Marriage, Reconstructing the Social Order, Atheistic Communism.* New York: The Paulist Press, 1939.

Cavalleri, Ottavio, and Germano Gualdo, eds. *L'archivio de monsignore Achille Ratti visitatore apostolico e nunzio a Varsavia (1918–1921).* Vatican City: Archivio Vaticano, 1990.

Freemantle, Anne, ed. *The Papal Encyclicals in Their Historical Context*. New York: G. P. Putnam's Sons, 1956.

Hachey, Thomas E., ed. *Anglo-Vatican Relations 1914–1939: Confidential Reports of the British Minister to the Holy See*. Boston: G. K. Hall, 1972.

Haffner, Paul, ed. *Discourses of the Pope From Pius XI to John Paul II to the Pontifical Academy of Sciences*. Vatican City: Pontificia Academia Scintiarium, 1986.

Handren, Walter J., ed. *No Longer Two: A Commentary on the Encyclical "Casti Connubii" of Pius XI*. Westminster, MD: Newman Press, 1955.

Husselien, Joseph Casper, ed. *The Christian Social Manifesto: An Interpretative Study of the Encyclicals Rerum Novarum and Quadragesimo Anno of Pope Leo XIII and Pope Pius XI*. Milwaukee: The Bruce Publishing Company, 1931.

Husselien, Joseph Casper, ed. *Social Wellsprings: Eighteen Encyclicals of Social Reconstruction by Pope Pius XI*. Milwaukee: Bruce Publishing, 1942.

Koenig, Harry C., ed. *Principles for Peace: Selections from Papal Documents from Leo XIII to Pius XII*. Washington, D.C.: National Catholic Welfare Conference, 1943.

Noel, Gerard, trans. *Records and Documents of the Holy See Relating to the Second World War, The Holy See and the War in Europe*. March 1939–August 1940. Washington, D.C.: Corpus Books, 1963.

Pius XI. "On Catholic Action." *The Catholic Mind* 29 (July 22, 1931), 349–66.

Pius XI. *Sixteen Encyclicals of His Holiness Pope Pius XI, 1926–1937*. Washington D.C: National Catholic Welfare Conference, 1938.

MEMOIRS, DIARIES AND REMINISCENCES

A Papal Chamberlain: The Personal Chronicle of Francis Augustus MacNutt, New York: Longmans, 1936.

Charles-Roux. *Huit ans au Vatican, 1932–1940*. Paris: Flammarion, 1947.

Ciano, Galeazzo. *L'Europa verso la Catasrofe*. Verona: Mondadori, 1948.

De Felice, Renzo. "La Santa Sede e il conflitto Italo-Ethipio Nel Diario di Bernardino Nogara," *Storia Contemporanea* 8 (1977), 823–34.

Maffi, Pietro. *Lettere, omelie e discorsi*. Turin: Società Editrice Internazionale, 1931.

Martini, Angelo. ed. *Studi sulla questione romana e la conciliazione*. Rome: Cinque Lune, 1963.

Morgan, Thomas B. *The Listening Post, Eighteen Years on Vatican Hill*. New York, Putnam, 1944.

———. *A Reporter at the Papal Court: A Narrative of the Reign of Pope Pius XI*. New York: Longmans, Green and Co., 1937.

Pacelli, Francesco. *Diaria della Conciliazione*. Vatican City: Libreria Editrice Vaticana, 1959.

Pius XI [Achille Ratti]. *Essays in History*. (Later Pius XI). Freeport, NY: Books for Libraries, 1967.

LATERAN ACCORDS INCLUDING 1929 CONCORDAT WITH FASCIST ITALY

Biggini, Alberto. *Storia inedita della conciliazione.* Milan: Garzanti, 1942.

Broglio, Francesco Margiotto. *Italia e Santa Sede dalla grande guerra alla conciliazione.* Bari: Laterza, 1966.

Carrillo, Elisa A. "Alcide De Gaspari and the Lateran Pacts," *Catholic Historical Review.* XLIX, no. 4. (January 1964), 532–39.

Carlton, J. H. "Italy and the Vatican Agree: II—The Settlement," *The Commonweal,* 3 April 1929, 261.

Castelli, L. *Quel tanto di territorio: Ricordi di lavori ed opere eseguite nel Vaticano durante il pontificato di Pio XI.* (1922–39). Rome, 1940.

Cavagna, A. M. *Pio XI e L'azione Cattolica.* 1929.

Chiesa e Stato: Studi storici e giuridici per il decennale della conciliazione tra la S. Sede e L'Italia. 2 vols. Milan: Univ. del S. Cuore di Milano, 1939.

Cicchetti, Arnaldo Suriani. "L'Opposizione italiana (1929–1931) al Patti Lateranensi." *Nuova Antologia* July 1952.

De Franciscis, Maria Elisabeta. *Italy and the Vatican: The 1984 Concordat between Church and State, Studies in Modern European History,* ed. Frank J. Coppa. New York: Peter Lang, 1989.

De Rosa, Gabriele. *I conservatori nazionali.* Brescia: Marcelliana, 1962.

———. *L'Osservatore Romano,* 27 February 1926.

Dissard, François. "Les concordats de Pie XI," *Revue des sciences politiques* 58 (1935), 554–76.

Drake, Richard. "Julius Evola, Radical Fascism, and the Lateran Accords," *Catholic Historical Review* 74 (1988), 403–19.

Ellery, Eloise. "Vatican's Censure of the *Fascisti*," *Current History*, February 1927, 740–741.

Gessi, Leone. *La Città del Vaticano.* Vatican City, 1937.

Giannini, Amedeo. *Il cammino della Conciliazione,* Milan: Vita e pensiero, 1946.

Giannini, A. *I concordati postbellici.* 2 vols. Milan, 1926–36.

Kent, Peter C. *The Pope and the Duce.* New York: St. Martin's Press, 1981.

———. "La Conciliazione fra lo Stato Italiano e la Chiesa." *Civiltà Cattolica,* 2 March 1929.

Maritini, Angelo. ed. *Studi sulla questione romana e la conciliazione.* Rome: Cinque Lune, 1963.

Muchray, Robert. "The Vatican's Present Position in Europe," *Current History* June (1926): 359–64.

Pacelli, Francesco. *Diario della Conciliazione.* Vatican City: Libreria Editrice Vaticana, 1959.

Pollard, John F. *The Vatican and Italian Fascism, 1929–1932: A Study in Conflict.* Cambridge: Cambridge University Press, 1985.

Rossi, Ernesto. *Il Managnello e l'aspersorio.* Florence: Parenti, 1959.

Ryan, Edwin. "Papal Concordats in Modern Times." *Catholic Historical Review* 16, 302–310 (October 1930).

Scaglia, Giovanni Battista. "Igino Righetti, President of FUCI and Founder of the Laureate Movement of Catholic Action." *Studium* 81, no. 1 (1985): 11–44.

Spadolini, Giovanni, ed. *Il Cardinale Gasparri e la Questione Romana*. Florence: Le Monnier, 1973.

Tagliacozzo, Enzo. "Il Concordato va abolito." *Ulisse*, Winter 1958.

"The Vatican's Diplomatic Position." *Literary Digest*, August 3, 1929: 23–24.

Tripodi, Nino. *I Patti lateranese e il fascismo*. Bologna: Capelli, 1960.

POPE PIUS XI

Anderson, Robin. *Between Two Wars: The Story of Pope Pius XI*. Chicago: Franciscan Herald Press, 1977.

Aradi, Zsolt. *Pius XI: The Pope and the Man*. Garden City, N.Y.: Hanover House, 1958.

Ardali, Paolo. *Mussolini e Pio XI*. Mantore, 1926.

Bruehl, Charles Paul. *The Pope's Plan for Social Reconstruction: A Commentary on the Social Encyclicals of Pius XI*. New York: Devin Adair, 1939.

Cecchetti, I. "Pius XI nella luce di una grande idea," *Bullettino Ceciliano* 34 (1939): 3–92.

Clonmore, Sir William. *Pope Pius XI and World Peace*. New York: E. P. Dutton & Co., Inc., 1938.

Confalonieri, C. "Nella luce di Pio XI." *La scuola cattolica*, 1944.

———. "Pio XI nel decennio del beato transito," *L'Osservatore Romano*, 10 February 1949.

Confalonieri, C. *Pio XI visto da vicino*. Turin: Edizioni S.A.I.E., 1957.

Cuddihy, Robert, and Shuster, George N. *Pope Pius XI and the American Public Opinion*. New York: Funk and Wagnalls, 1939.

D'Orazi, Lucio. *Protagonisti*. Rome: Edizioni Logos, 1989.

Fontenelle, R. *His Holiness Pope Pius XI*. Trans. M. E. Fowler. London: The Catholic Book Club, 1939.

Fouilloux, Etienne. "The Vatican Between Hitler and Stalin." *Histoire* 70 (1984): 34–42.

Galbiati, G. *Papa P. XI*. Editrice Ancora: Milano: 1939.

Gasquet, Francis Aidan. *His Holiness Pius XI: A Pen Portrait*. London: D. O'Connor, 1922.

Gemelli, Agostino. "La grandezza Storica di Pio XI," in *Annuario del Universita Cattolica del Sacro Cuore*. Milan, 1939.

Gwinn, Dennis-Rolleston. *Pius XI*. London: Holmes Press, 1932.

Hughes, Philip. *Pope Pius XI*. New York: Sheed & Ward, 1937.

Kent, Peter C. "A Tale of Two Popes: Pius XI, Pius XII and the Rome-Berlin Axis." *Journal of Contemporary History* 23, no. 4 (1988): 589–608.

Kent, Peter C. *The Pope and the Duce*. New York: St. Martin's Press, 1981.

Marongiu Buonaiuti, Cesare. "The Holy See and The Republic of Spain After the Constitution, 9 December 1931 to 19 November 1933." *Storia e Politica* 23, no. 4 (1984): 600–644.

Olf, Lilian. *Pius XI: Apostle of Peace*. New York: Macmillan, 1938.

————. *Their Name is Pius*. Milwaukee: Bruce, 1941.

Pellegrinetti, E. *Pius XI: L'uomo nel papa i el Papa nell'uomo*. Rome: 1940.

Regnier, Jerome. "Diffusion and Interpretation of Quadragesimo Anno." *Revue de Nord*, 73, nos. 290–291 (1991): 357–363.

Teeling, William. *Pope Pius XI and World Affairs*. New York: Frederick A. Stokes Co., 1937.

Townsend, Walter. *The Biography of His Holiness Pope Pius XI*. London: A. E. Marriott, 1930.

Walsh, Edmund Aloysius. *Why Pope Pius XI Asked Prayers for Russia on March 19, 1930: A Review of the Facts in the Case Together with Proofs of the International Program of the Soviet Government*. New York: Catholic Near East Welfare Association, 1930.

Williams, Michael. "Pope Pius XI," *Catholic World* 15 (1922): 1–9.

CATHOLIC CHURCH AND FASCIST ITALY

Alfieri, Dino. *Dictators Face to Face*. Translated by D. Moore. Westport, Conn.: Greenwood Press, 1978.

Alvarez, David. "The Vatican and the War in the Far East, 1941–1943." *Historian* 40 (1978): 508–23.

Anderson, Robin. *Between Two Wars: The Story of Pope Pius XI*. Chicago: Franciscan Herald Press, 1977.

Ascoli, Max. "The Roman Catholic Church and Political Action," *Foreign Affairs* 13 (April 1935): 447–48.

————. "The Vatican's Diplomatic Position." *Literary Digest*, (August 3, 1929).

Binchy, D. A. *Church and State in Fascist Italy*. New York: Oxford University Press, 1941.

Brezzi, Paolo. *Il Papato*. Rome: Editrice Studium, 1951.

Calisse, Carlo. "Il Cardinale Pietro Gasparri." *Nuova Antologia* 68, no. 366 (1933): 225–236.

Cianfarra, Camille M. *The War and the Vatican*. London: Burns, Oates and Washbourne, 1945.

Ciano, Galeazzo. *L'Europa verso La Catastrofe*. Verona: Arnaldo Mondadori, 1948.

Charles-Roux, Francois. *Huit ans au Vatican*. Paris: Flammarion, 1947.

Dalla Torre, G. *Azione Cattolica e Fascismo: Il Conflitto del 1931*. Rome: 1945.

De Begnac, Ivon. *Palazzo Venezia—Storia di un regime*. Rome: La Rocca, 1950.

De Felice, Renzo. *Mussolini, Il Duce, Gli anni del consenso, 1929–1936*. Turin: Einaudi, 1974.

Delzell, Charles F., ed. *The Papacy and Totalitarianism Between the Two World Wars* New York: John Wiley and Sons, 1974.

De Rosa, Gabriele. *I conservatori nazionali*. Brescia: Marchelliana, 1962.

Ellery, Eloise. "The Vatican's Censure of the Fascisti." *Current History* (February 1927): 740.

Falconi, Carlo. *The Silence of Pius XII*, translated by Bernard Wall. Boston: Little, Brown and Co., 1970.

Ferrari, Liliana. *Una storia dell'Azione Cattolica. Gli Ordimamenti Statutari da Pio IX a Pio XII*. Genoa: Marietti, 1989.

Germino, Dante. *The Italian Fascist Party in Power: A Study in Totalitarian Rule.* Minneapolis: University of Minnesota Press, 1959.

Giuntella, Maria Cristina. "Cicoli Cattolici e organizzazioni Giovanili fasciste in Umbria." In *Cattolici e Fascisti in Umbria (1922–1945)*, ed. Albertino Monticone. Bologna: Il Mulino, 1978.

Hearley, John. *Pope or Mussolini.* New York: Macaulay Co., 1929.

Jemolo, Arturo Carlo. *Chiesa e stato in Italia negli ultimi cento anni.* Turin: Einaudi, 1948.

Kent, Peter C. "Between Rome and London: Pius XI, the Catholic Church, and The Abyssinian Crisis of 1935–1936," *International History Review* 11, no. 2 (1989): 252–271.

Kent, Peter C. *The Pope and the Duce.* New York: St. Martin's, 1981.

La Piana, George. "The Political Heritage of Pius XII," *Foreign Affairs* 18 (1940): 486–506.

Lapide, Pinchas. *Three Popes and the Jews.* New York: Hawthorn Books, Inc., 1967.

Luisa, Maria, and Paronetto Valier. "A Fierce Dispute Over Nothing: The 1933 Crisis in the Roman Circle of the Federazione Universitaria Cattolica Italiana." *Studium* 77, no. 1 (1981): 25–44.

Lukacs, John. "The Diplomac of the Holy See Before the End of World War II in Europe." *Catholic Historical Review* 69 (July 1983): 416.

Martina, Giacomo. "Ecclesiologia prevalente nel pontificato di Pio XI." In *Cattolici e Fascisti in Umbria (1922–1945)*, edited by Alberto Monticone. Bologna: Il Mulino, 1978.

"Melanges de l'Ecole Française de Rome." *Moyen Age–Temps Modernes* 98, no. 2 (1986): 863–888.

Miccoli, Goivanni. "Santa Sede e Chiesa Italiana di fronte alle leggi antiebraiche del 1938," *Studi Storici* 29 (1988): 821–902.

Morley, John F. *Vatican Diplomacy and the Jews During the Holocaust 1939–1943.* New York: KTAV Publishing House, 1980.

O'Brien, Albert. "Italian Youth in Conflict: Catholic Action and Fascist Italy, 1929–1931." *Catholic Historical Review* 68, no.4 (1982): 625.

O'Carroll, Michael. *Pius XII, Greatness Dishonoured: A Documented Study.* Chicago: Franciscan Herald Press, 1980.

Papeleux, L. "La diplomatie vaticane et L'Italie après Stalingrad." *Revue d'Histoire de la Deuxième Guerre Mondiale* 27 (1977): 19–36.

Pellicani, Antonio. *Il Papa di tutti, La Chiesa Cattolica, il fascismo, e il razzismo, 1929–1945.* Milan: Sugar Editore, 1964.

Pollard, John F. *The Vatican and Italian Fascism, 1929–1932: A Study in Conflict.* Cambridge: Cambridge University Press, 1985.

Rhodes, Anthony. *The Vatican in the Age of Dictators, 1922–1945.* New York: Holt, Rinehart and Winston, 1973.

Rossi, Ernesto. *Il Managnello e l'aspersorio.* Florence: Parenti, 1958.

Rossini, Giuseppe. *Il fascismo e la resistenza.* Rome: Cinque Lune, 1955.

Sigmund, Paul E. "The Catholic Tradition and Modern Democracy." *Review of Politics* 49, no. 4 (1987): 530–548.

Scoppola, Pietro. "Chiesa e Fascismo nella Realta' Locale," *Cattolici e fascisiti in Umbria (1922–1945)*, edited by Alberto Monticone, 17–27 Bologna: Il Mulino, 1978.

Scoppola, Pietro, and Francesco Traniello, eds. *I Cattolici tra fascsmo e democrazia.* Bologna: Il Mulino, 1975.

Seldes, George. "The Vatican and Nationalism." *The Commonweal*, 1 March 1 1935, 504–06.

Spadolini, Giovanni. "115 Years of Relations Between The Two Sides of the Tiber," *Rassegna Storica Toscana* 30 no. 1 (1984): 3–20.

Sturzo, Luigi. *L'Italia e l'ordine internazionale.* Turin: Einaudi, 1946.

Tannenbaum, Edward R. *The Fascist Experience: Italian Society and Culture, 1922–1945.* New York: Basic Books, Inc., 1972.

Webster, Richard A. *The Cross and the Fasces.* Stanford: Stanford University Press, 1960.

Webster, Richard A. *Christian Democracy in Italy, 1860–1960.* London: Hollis and Carter, 1961.

Wolff, Richard J. "The Federazione universitaria cattlica Italiana." *Risorgimento,* (1982), 1/2, 61–62.

———. "Italy: Catholics, the Clergy, and the Church—Complex Reactions to Fascism." 137–57 in R. Wolff and J. Hoensch, eds., *Catholics, the State and the European Radical Right, 1919–1945.* New York: Columbia University Press, 1987.

———. "A Re-Examination of the Relationship between Catholicism and Fascism." *Italian Quarterly* (Summer 1982): 70.

———. "The University under Mussolini: The Fascist-Catholic Struggle for Italian Youth, 1922–1943." *History of Higher Education Annual* (1981): 132–147.

———. "Battista Montini and Italian Politics, 1897–1933: The Early Life of Pope Paul VI." *Catholic Historical Review* 81, no. 2 (April 1985): 245.

———. "Catholicism, Fascism and Italian Education from the Riforma Gentile to the Carta della Scuola 1922–1939." *History of Education Quarterly* (Spring 1980):

———. "Between Pope and Duce: Catholic Students in Fascist Italy." In *Studies in Modern European History.* Vol. 1. Edited by Frank J. Coppa. New York: Peter Lang, 1990.

Wood, L.J.S. "Mussolini and the Roman Question." *Catholic World* (1924): 64–75.

Zunino, Pier Giorgio. *La questione cattolica nella sinistra italiana 1919–1939.* Bologna: Il Mulino, 1975.

PAPACY AND CATHOLIC CHURCH IN
THE TWENTIETH CENTURY

von Aretin, Karl Otmar. *The Papacy and the Modern World.* Translated by Roland Hill. New York: 1970.

Ascoli, Max. "The Roman Church and Political Action." *Foreign Affairs* (1935): 441–452.

Aubert, Roger. *The Church in a Secularized Society.* Vol. 5 of *The Christian Centuries.* New York: Paulist Press, 1978.

Daim, Wilfrid. *The Vatican and Eastern Europe.* Translated by Alexander Gode. New York: F. Ungar, 1970.

Giovanetti, Alberto. *El Vaticano y la Guerra, 1939–1940.* Madrid: Espapa, 1961.

Gurian, Waldemar. Introduction to *The Catholic Church in World Affairs.* Notre Dame: University of Notre Dame Press, 1954.

Hales, E.E.Y. *The Catholic Church in the Modern World.* Garden City, NY: Hanover House, 1958.

Holmes, Derek. *The Papacy in the Modern World, 1914–1978.* New York: Crossroad Publishers, 1981.

Koenig, Harry. "The Popes and Peace in the Twentieth Century." In *The Catholic Church in World Affairs,* ed. W. Gurian, 48–68. Notre Dame, 1954.

Lukacs, John. "The Diplomacy of the Holy See During World War II." *The Catholic Historical Review* 60 (July 1974): 275.

McKnight, John P. *The Papacy: A New Appraisal.* London: McGraw-Hill, 1953.

Purdy, W. A. *The Church On the Move: The Character and Policies of Pius XII and John XXIII.* New York: John Day, 1966.

Poulat, Émile. *Une Eglise Ébranlée. Changement, conflict et continuité de Pie XII à Jean-Paul II.* Paris: Casterman, 1980.

Stehle, Hanjakob. *Eastern Politics of the Vatican.* Translated by Sandra Smith. Athens, Ohio: Ohio University Press, 1981.

Wolff, Richard J. "The Catholic Church and the Dictatorships in Slovakia and Croatia, 1939–1945." *Records of the American Catholic Historical Society,* (1978): 3.

III. Bibliography on the Concordat with Hitler's Germany

Adolph, Walter. *Geheime Aufzeichnungen aus dem nationalsozialistischen Kirchenkampf 1935–1943.* Edited by Ulrich von Hehl. Mainz: Matthias-Grünewald-Verlag, 1979. Recently uncovered notes and records of the Vicar General and assistant to Cardinal Preysing of Berlin. The previously unpublished notes were discovered after the author's death in 1975 and have been edited by Ulrich von Hehl with the assistance of other leading scholars of the Church struggle such as Klaus Gotto, Rudolf Lill, Konrad Repgen and Ludwig Volk. Most of the documents are from 1937 and 1938 and provide insight into Cardinal Preysing's actions in the aftermath of *Mit brennender Sorge.*

————. *Hirtenamt und Hitler-Diktatur.* 2nd ed. Berlin: Morus-Verlag, 1965. A memoir of the author's observations as an assistant to Cardinal Preysing of Berlin. There are short chapters on various aspects of the Church Struggle, biographical sketches of Cardinals Bertram and von Preysing, and a selection of correspondence between them. Provides essential perspectives on two of the Catholic Church's most important leaders during the Third Reich.

————. *Kardinal Preysing und zwei Diktaturen. Sein Widerstand gegen die totalitäre Macht.* Berlin: Morus-Verlag, 1971. An overview of Cardinal Preysing's opposition to both the Nazi and Communist dictatorships, written by his assistant. The volume contains some previously published material and some that is new. Not intended to be a biography, it is primarily concerned with the years 1935–1945 and contains correspondence between Preysing and the government on the subjects of euthanasia and the persecution of the Jews; also correspondence with the Vatican.

Albrecht, Dieter. "Der Heilige Stuhl und das Dritte Reich." In *Die Katholiken und das Dritte Reich*, edited by Klaus Gotto and Konrad Repgen. Mainz: Matthias-Grünewald-Verlag, 1980. An overview of Vatican relations with the Third Reich by a leading German historian of the Church Struggle. Also published in this paperback collection are articles on various issues by other leading scholars.

———, ed. *Der Notenwechsel zwischen dem Heiligen Stuhl und der Deutschen Reichsregierung.* 3 vols. Mainz: Matthias-Grünewald-Verlag, 1965. An unprecedented and authoritative collection of the correspondence between the Holy See and the German government from 1933 to 1943. It was sponsored by the Commission for Contemporary History of the Catholic Academy in Bavaria. The collection documents the complaints by the Vatican of the violations of the Concordat and the events of the Church Struggle. Volume I contains the text of the Concordat and *Mit brennender Sorge.*

———, ed. *Katholische Kirche im Dritten Reich. Eine Aufsatzsammlung.* Mainz: Matthias-Grünewald-Verlag, 1976. An early paperback collection for popular consumption of articles by leading scholars that summarize various aspects of the Church Struggle.

Baumgärtner, Raimund. *Weltanschauungskampf im Dritten Reich.* Mainz: Matthias-Grünewald-Verlag, 1977. A scholarly work analyzing the role of the ideas of Alfred Rosenberg and *The Myth of the Twentieth Century.* The ideological and philosophical background of the views of the churches versus Rosenberg and their opposition is examined.

Biesinger, Joseph A. "The Presidential Elections in Bavaria in 1925 and 1932 in Relation to the Reich." Ph.D. diss., Rutgers-The State University of New Jersey, 1972. A comparative analysis of the presidential elections in Bavaria and the Reich. Its main focus is on the political forces in Bavaria and their influence on both elections of Hindenburg. Also emphasized is the BVP opposition to the Nazis in 1932.

Bleistein, Roman. "Die Jesuiten in der Erzdiözese München und Freising." In *Das Erzbistum München und Freising in der Zeit der nationalsozialistischen Herrschaft.* Vol. 2. Edited by Georg Schwaiger. München: Schnell and Steiner, 1984. An overview of the Jesuits during the Third Reich describes how they were hated and persecuted by the Nazis. Bleistein first considers their general history as they were affected during the morality trials, school and cloister closings, trials and incarcerations, and involvement in the Kreisau Circle. The fate of their famous journal, *Stimmen der Zeit,* is described, those of individual Jesuits like P. Augustin Rösch and P. Lother König are profiled, and Jesuits punished in Dachau are remembered.

Broszat, Martin, and Elke Frölich, eds. *Bayern in der NS-Zeit.* Vol. 2, *Herrschaft und Gesellschaft in Konflikt.* München: R. Oldenbourg Verlag, 1979. One of a series of six volumes of research on the Nazi period in Bavaria, sponsored by the Institute for Contemporary History in Munich and the research project Resistance and Persecution in Bavaria. This volume focuses on anti-Semitism, the concentration camps of Dachau and Flossenbürg, the press, theater, industry, and Catholic youth.

Brüning, Heinrich. *Memoiren, 1918–1934*. Stuttgart: Deutsche Verlags-Anstalt, 1970. These recollections provide Brüning's perspectives on his life in politics. He justifies his policies while Chancellor and is critical of Ludwig Kaas's role in the Enabling Act and the Concordat.

Chadwick, Owen. *Britain and the Vatican during the Second World War*. Cambridge: Cambridge University Press, 1986. An excellent and balanced study of Vatican policy during WWII from British diplomatic sources. Covers the reign of Pius XI after 1935 and Pius XII through 1945. Especially important for information on the Pope and the Jews in 1942 and all the intricacies of the war. Emphasizes Pius XII's goal of negotiations to end the war rather than condemning German and Italian aggression.

Conway, J. S. *The Nazi Persecution of the Churches 1933–45*. New York: Basic Books, 1968. Still a good introduction to the persecution and resistance of both Protestant and Catholic churches to National Socialism. At the time it was written it was the first comprehensive study in English, and responded to the issues raised by the criticisms during the 1960s of Pope Pius XII by Hans Müller, E.W. Böckenförde, Kurt Sontheimer, Gordon Zahn and Guenter Lewy. Generalizes too much about the Church leadership and fails to analyze the roles and policies of individual churchmen. A recurring theme is why the Catholic Church failed to lead resistance against the regime.

Dietrich, Donald J. *Catholic Citizens in the Third Reich: Psycho-Social Principles and Moral Reasoning*. New Brunswick, N.J.: Transaction Press, 1988. An examination of the motivations of German Catholics from Weimar through the end of the war. Dietrich employs the results of social science research to explain individual and group responses to Nazi ideals, propaganda, institutions, and policies, sometimes adapting, sometimes resisting. Dietrich concludes that German Catholics adhered to their nationalistic ideals and failed to defend the norms of Christian brotherhood.

Documents on British Foreign Policy. Series 2, vol. 5. London: H.M. Stationery Office, 1956. A collection of documents covering 1919–1939. Based on reports from all over Europe, this volume includes negotiations following the Four Power Pact of 1933, the Disarmament Conference, Germany's withdrawal from the League, and rearmament.

Documents of German Foreign Policy, 1918–1945. Series C, vols. 1 and 4 of *1933–1937, The Third Reich: First Phase. January 30–October 14, 1933*. Washington, D.C.: U.S. Department of State, 1957. A joint publication by Great Britain, the U.S., and France of captured archives of the German Foreign Ministry and the Reich Chancellery. The British edition covers the events between January 30, 1933 and December 1941. Volume 1 contains correspondence between the Vatican and the Third Reich concerning negotiations over the Concordat. An English translation of the Concordat is included.

Dokumente der deutschen Politik und Geschichte von 1848 bis zur Gegenwart. Hohlfeld, Johannes, ed. Band 4 der Die Zeit der nationalsozialistischen Diktatur, 1933–1945. Aufbau und Entwicklung, 1933–1938. Berlin: Herbert Wendler & Co, 1954. This volume is a collection of documents covering 1933–1938 previously published in the

Reichgesetzblatt and daily journals. Contains speeches, ordinances, treaties and correspondence.

Domarus, Max. *Hitler, Speeches and Proclamations, 1932–1945.* 4 vols. Translated by Fran Gilbert. Wauconda, IL: Bolchazy-Carducci, 1990. The most comprehensive collection in English of Hitler's speeches and proclamations, placed in historical context.

Evans, Ellen Lovell. *The German Center Party, 1870–1933.* Carbondale, Ill.: Southern Illinois University Press, 1981. A study of the history of the Center Party from its origins to its demise in 1933. The author interprets the existence of a Catholic denominational party as a natural expression of the ideological principles of Catholicism in the context of German religious and socio-economic divisions. Especially emphasized is the role of the clergy in the party, the relation of the Center to other parties, and the problems and compromises that arose due to the diversity of constituencies. Although the Concordat made the dissolution of the Center acceptable, Evans does not link the Enabling Act with the Treaty.

Gallin, Mary Alice, O.S.U. *German Resistance To Hitler. Ethical and Religious Factors.* Washington, D.C.: The Catholic University of America Press, 1961. An early study of the principles and issues involved in resistance to the Nazi totalitarian regime. Its author consulted many of the resources available at the time, but the study predates the important research of Ludwig Volk and others. She contradicts the commonly held view that the Concordat weakened the Church in its battle against Nazism. Rather, the hierarchy used the Concordat as a legal instrument to challenge the state's violation of the rights of the Church.

———. "The Cardinal and the State: Faulhaber and the Third Reich." *Journal of Church and State* 12 (1970): 385–404. A reassessment of the role of Cardinal Faulhaber vis-à-vis the Nazi regime, based on the new insights provided by the research of Ludwig Volk and Burkhard Schneider, yet without the benefit of all of Faulhaber's correspondence, which had not yet been published. The author is critical of Faulhaber's position that support for the regime as the legal authority was God's will.

Goebbels, Joseph. *Die Tagebücher von Joseph Goebbels. Sämtliche Fragmente.* Teil I. Bd. 3, 1937–1939. Edited by Elke Frölich. München: K.G. Saur, 1987. These volumes contain Goebbels's diaries from 1924 until his death. He discusses his daily activities providing insights into his and Hitler's policies and attitudes. Volume three covers the response to *Mit brennender Sorge.*

Gotto, Klaus, and Konrad Repgen, eds. *Die Katholiken und das Dritte Reich.* Mainz: Matthias-Grünewald-Verlag, 1990. A recent collection of articles addressing many of the central questions on the Church Struggle by some of Germany's leading church historians. This volume brings up to date the scholarship of the earlier editions of these popular paperback publications.

Gotto, Klaus, Hans Günter Hockerts, and Konrad Repgen. "Nationalsozislistische Herausforderung und kirchliche Antwort. Eine Bilanz." In *Die Katholiken und das Dritte Reich,* edited by Klaus Gotto and Konrad Repgen. Mainz: Matthias-Grünewald-Verlag, 1990. An evaluation of the concept of resistance as it applied to the Church and the regime. The concept is placed in the context of the totalitarian state and the levels of possible opposition that could have been manifested. Interprets the Church's resistance as basically defensive, even though the Nazis considered it to be offensive.

Gritschneder, Otto. "Pater Rupert Mayer vor dem Sondergericht." In *Dokumente der Verhandlung vor dem Sondergericht zu München am 22 und 23 Juli, 1937.* München-Salzburg: Verlag Anton Pustet, 1965. The most famous of Bavaria's clerical protesters, Rupert Mayer, S.J., is here remembered by way of the records of his 1937 trial before a special court for crimes against the state. The official transcript is enriched by Gritschneder's commentary.

Harrigan, William M. "Nazi Germany and the Holy See, 1933–1936." *Catholic Historical Review* 47 (1961): 164–198. An early overview of the development of the Church Struggle from the Concordat to the Encyclical that focuses on the decline of the hoped-for 'modus vivendi' that some Catholics thought possible. Despite the willingness of the bishops to be cooperative, the government persisted in its persecution leading to the Encyclical and the end of cooperation. Based on the sources available during the 1950s.

———. "Pius XII's Efforts to Effect a Détente in German-Vatican Relations, 1939–1940." *Catholic Historical Review* 49 (1963): 173–191. Another example of the Church's attempt to secure a 'modus vivendi' with the Third Reich involved the new pope, Pius XII, at the beginning of WWII. Harrigan concludes that Pius XII engaged in a policy of conciliation with the Third Reich in order to act as a mediator in the coming war. Pius had both a concern for the restoration of peace and for the freedom of German Catholics to practice their faith. This attempt at détente ended by June 1942.

Hausberger, Karl. "Das Konzentrationslager Dachau." In vol. 1 of *Das Erzbistum München-Freising in der Zeit der nationalsozialistischen Herrschaft,* edited by Georg Schwaiger. München: Verlag Schnell & Steiner, 1984. The first of the concentration camps is here described as the germ cell of the whole system of camps in the SS state. Covers the founding in 1933–34 and provides an excellent overview including medical experiments and statistical charts. Four times as many Polish as German priests died here. Excellent notes and sources.

Hehl, Ulrich von. *Katholische Kirche und Nationalsozialismus im Erzbistum Köln, 1933–1945.* Mainz: Matthias-Grünewald-Verlag, 1977. Based on his dissertation at Bonn as a student of Konrad Repgen, Ulrich von Hehl has established himself as one of the leading scholars on the Church Struggle in Nazi Germany. Beginning with an explanation of how the Church resisted the rise of National Socialism, the topics generally follow the same pattern of events as occurred throughout the Reich, including provocations in 1934–35, the morality trials, the break over the Encyclical, euthanasia, and the war years. Excellent notes and bibliography.

———. "Kirche und Nationalsozialismus: Ein Forschungsbericht." In *Kirche im Nationalsozialismus,* edited by the Geschichtsverein der Diözese Rottenburg-Stuttgart. Sigmaringen: Thorbecke Verlag, 1984. Historiographical survey providing an overview of the debate concerning the Church Struggle. Hehl explains the controversial issues and the posiition of the principal historians beginning with the end of

WWII. Many of the other articles in this collection provide information on the church in the diocese of Rottenburg-Stuttgart.

——————. *Priester unter Hitlers Terror: Eine Biographische und Statistische Erhebung.* Mainz: Matthias-Grünewald-Verlag, 1984. An unprecedented and comprehensive biographical and statistical research project concerning the clergy who were charged with crimes. One-third of the secular clergy and one-fifth of the clergy of religious orders were accused. The biographical data is divided by diocese. Which acts were illegal is explained and the violations are statistically categorized. The study demonstrates the extent of clerical disobedience and protest against Nazi policies, and also the extent to which this professional group was threatened.

Helmreich, Ernst C., *The German Churches under Hitler.* Detroit: Wayne State University Press, 1979. Since its publication, this broad study of both the Protestant and Catholic churches has been the standard source in English. Beginning with an explanation of the historical complexity of German religious history, he analyzes the situation during Weimar. Most of the chapters are devoted to the complex history of the Protestant churches, while the more uniform experience among Catholics is nonetheless adequately explained. Most extensively researched, this is a balanced interpretation with a massive bibliography.

Hitler, Adolf. *Mein Kampf.* New York: Reynal and Hitchcock, 1941. This edition of Hitler's classic is quite helpful because of the scholarly commentary provided by Professor Baynes. Extensive explanations are provided of the historical context and the meaning of the text.

Hockerts, Hans Günter. "Die Nationalsozialistische Kirchen politik im Neuen Licht der Goebbels-Tagebucher." *Aus Politik und Zeitgeschichte, Beilage zur Wochenzeitung: Das Parlament.* B, no. 30 (1983): 23–38. Goebbels was forbidden by Hitler to leave the Church for tactical reasons even though he had long hated the Church and its clergy. The Goebbels diaries provide such insights and are here evaluated as a source for Nazi policy toward the Church, especially in the volume covering the aftermath of the Encyclical.

——————. *Die Sittlichkeitsprozesse gegen katholische Ordensangehörige und Priester, 1936/1937.* Mainz: Matthias-Grünewald-Verlag, 1971. A study of the morality trials used by the state as a principal weapon against the clergy and to smear the Church's reputation with the public. The basic general study of the subject. Excellent notes and bibliography.

Holmes, J. Derek. *The Papacy in the Modern World, 1914–1978.* New York: Crossroad Publishing Co., 1981. A general history of the papacy during the twentieth century by a respected church historian. With an introduction by John Tracy Ellis, this brief survey displays a favorable attitude toward the Church, yet not without an accounting of problems in and errors of the Church. Holmes appears to rely heavily on secondary sources, and does not cite primary sources, yet with undoubted scholarly credentials writes an interesting survey of pontificates from Benedict XV to Pope John Paul I.

Horn, Daniel. "The Struggle for Catholic Youth in Hitler's Germany: An Assessment." *The Catholic Historical Review* 65, no.4 (1979): 561–582. Horn critiques the shortcomings of the historians of the sixties concerning the effectiveness of the

Hitler Youth against Catholic Youth organizations. Demonstrating the need to sift the details found in the sources, he points out that as of 1936 the enrollment in the Hitler Youth had become compulsory, because only 53% of eligible youth had been so far enrolled on a voluntary basis. Pointing to alternative Catholic groups that challenged the HJ dominance, he maintains that the Church generally maintained the allegiance of much of its youth.

Hughes, John Jay. "The Pope's Pact With Hitler." *Journal of Church and State* 17 (1975): 63–80. The thesis here argued is that the leaders of the Church could not have refused to sign a concordat in 1933. Without the Concordat Hitler would have been able to persecute the Church without restrictions. With the Concordat the Vatican was able to involve itself in Germany's domestic religious affairs. Hughes asserts that the Church's failure was to inform and mobilize Catholics to defend the Church while it continued to rely on diplomatic protests. The initiative of the Concordat is judged to have come from the Reich government in April, 1933 and not through any machinations of Monsignor Kaas or Cardinal Pacelli. With the scholarship of Kupper and Volk available, Hughes made a valuable contribution to the literature of the time. Very similar to the 1974 article.

———. "The Reich Concordat 1933: Capitulation or Compromise?" *Australian Journal of Politics and History* 20 (1974): 164–175. The earlier publication of the rewritten article above. The basis of his defense of the Church's conclusion of the Concordat is the research of Alfons Kupper and Ludwig Volk. Hughes maintains that the Vatican did not betray the Center Party and that the Church was more realistic than were others in negotiating the Treaty as a wall of defense.

Hürten, Heinz. *Deutsche Katholiken, 1918–1945*. Paderborn: Ferdinand Schöningh, 1992. A recent in depth survey of German Catholicism from the end of the Kaiserreich to 1945 by one of Germany's leading church historians. Hürten analyzes the place and role of the Catholic minority in the tensions of national and social integration, and its attempts to preserve its identity and its tradition. The controversial moral and political issues that Catholics faced under the Nazi regime are examined in chapters with the usual themes; also included are discussions of the Jews, German guilt, and the resistance. Thoroughly researched with an extensive bibliography. A new standard.

———. "Selbstbehauptung und Widerstand der katholischen Kirche." In *Der Widerstand gegen den Nationalsozialismus*, edited by Jürgen Schmädeke and Peter Steinbach, 240–253. München: Piper Verlag, 1985. A short article concerning the Catholic Church in an extensive collection by leading German scholars concerned with the various expressions of resistance against the Nazi regime. Hürten provides a summary of the various considerations necessary to understand the nature of Catholic resistance.

———. *Verfolgung, Widerstand und Zeugnis: Kirche im Nationalsozialismus; Fragen einer Historikers.* Mainz: Matthias-Grünewald-Verlag, 1987. In this short study Hürten examines the multi-faceted aspects of the meaning of resistance among Catholics. Different definitions and perspectives are evaluated in the context of the realities of what it meant to live under Nazi totalitarianism.

Kent, George O. "Pope Pius XII and Germany: Some Aspects of German-Vatican Relations, 1933–1943." *American Historical Review* 70 (1964): 59–78. Based on documents made available between 1953–1962, this is an early attempt by a coeditor of the *Documents on German Foreign Policy, 1918–1945* to explain the relations between Pius XII and Nazi Germany. The actions and reticence of the Pope are here seen as the result of the dilemma facing him: the choice between Bolshevism and National Socialism, yet being desirous of peace and hopeful of a role as mediator between the warring parties.

Kent, Peter C., and John F. Pollard. *Papal Diplomacy in the Modern Age.* Westport, Conn: Praeger, 1994. This is an excellent collection of essays dealing with different issues and periods of papal diplomacy. Pertinent to Nazi Germany, World War II and the Holocaust is John S. Conway's "The Vatican, Germany and the Holocaust." It is an excellent analysis of the main issues concerning the role of the Vatican and the Holocaust. Conway relies on eleven volumes of recently released documents from the Vatican archives, which give a clearer picture of what the papacy did to help the Jews. It became clear that the Pope was concerned with the fate of Jewish victims. The article also explains the problems confronting Pius XII which inspired the Pope's silence. Conway judges that a strong papal protest would not have succeeded in changing the anti-Semitism that facilitated the Holocaust. The horrors of the Holocaust did not, however, influence a theological reorientation toward the Jews during the war and for twenty years afterward. Two other articles in the volume are of interest for the period of the Second World War which are "Pope Pius XII, Italy and the Second World War," by Italo Garzia, and "Italy, the Holy See and the United States, 1939–1945," by Elisa A. Carrillo.

Kershaw, Ian. *Popular Opinion and Political Dissent in the Third Reich: Bavaria, 1933–1945.* Oxford: Clarendon Press, 1983. A revision of an earlier work in German, this is more extensively researched including Sopade, Sicherheitsdienst (SD), and Gestapo reports from areas outside Bavaria. The work received much support from the German historical community. The book focuses on the propaganda image-building process making Hitler the symbol of the German nation, and explains why so many Germans including Church leaders failed to blame Hitler for their oppression rather than other Nazi leaders. Explains how a radical solution to the Jewish question was made possible.

———. *The 'Hitler Myth': Image and Reality in the Third Reich.* Oxford: Oxford University Press, 1990. An excellent study on the limits of propaganda and emphasizes that Germans were not completely united behind Hitler. Though primarily based on Bavarian sources, Kershaw considers his conclusions to have been true throughout the Reich. The understandable difficulty of reconstructing popular opinion under a totalitarian dictatorship was not insurmountable. The responses of different social classes to the 'national community', to the assault on traditional Christian social values, and to racial anti-Semitism are examined. The lower clergy were found to be ambivalent toward anti-Semitism and did little to foster anti-racist attitudes.

Kleinöder, Eva Maria. "Der Kampf um die katholische Schule in Bayern in der NS-Zeit." In vol. 1 of *Das Erzbistum München und Freising in der Zeit der nationalsozial-*

istischen Herrschaft. Edited by Georg Schwaiger. München: Schnell and Steiner, 1984. A survey of the conflict with Nazis over the Catholic schools in Bavaria. The essay explains how the struggle over the schools violated both the Bavarian and Reich concordats. Themes examined include the destruction of the confessional schools between 1935–1938, the dismissal of nuns from and the measures against religious instruction in public schools.

————. "Verfolgung und Widerstand der katholischen Jugendvereine. Eine Fallstudie über Eichstätt." In *Bayern in der NS-Zeit, II. Herrschaft und Gesellschaft in Konflikt*. Edited by Martin Broszat and Elke Frölich. München: R. Oldenbourg Verlag, 1979. A case study in the repression and resistance of Catholic Youth organizations in Eichstätt, Bavaria. Before 1933 the Church and its organizations were dominant in this small episcopal center. The study provides an excellent microanalysis of the Church Struggle. The article was published in a six-volume collection of studies on various aspects of resistance in Bavaria.

Koenig, Harry C., ed. *Principles for Peace. Selections from Papal Documents from Leo XIII to Pius XII*. Washington, DC.: National Catholic Welfare Conference, 1943. A wartime collection of papal documents issued by the popes concerning peace up to Pius XII's Christmas message of 1942. Produced during WWII, all the documents were translated in abbreviated form only from sources available in the United States. The editor emphasized the importance of the world following these principles to lay the foundation for a lasting peace. The failure of the world powers to include Benedict XV in the peacemaking after WWI and the refusal to make peace on just Christian principles are asserted to have caused WWII.

Koerbling, Anton, S.J. *Father Rupert Mayer*. München: Schnell and Steiner, 1956. Beatified by the Catholic Church in 1987, the Jesuit Rupert Mayer, became a famous protester against the Nazis who needed to be silenced. He was imprisoned three times in camps including Sachsenhausen for disobedience against Nazi prohibitions, and was finally removed to Ettal, a Benedictine monastery, until the end of the war. This early biography by a fellow Jesuit is justifiably laudatory and was published in English, yet is not a scholarly one. Along with Paul Riesterer, S.J., Koerbling published in 1975 an expanded biography.

Küng, Hans. *Judaism: Betweeen Yesterday and Tomorrow*. Translated by John Bowden. New York: Continuum Publishing Co., 1996. A monumental study of Judaism in its historical, political and social context by an outstanding non-Jewish scholar. Hans Küng is the Director of the Institute for Ecumenical Research in Tübingen. His study includes an analysis of the Holocaust and Christianity, theological disputes between Christians and Jews, and the relation between Jews and Muslims in the state of Israel.

Kupper, Alfons. *Staatliche Akten über die Reichskondordats-verhandlungen, 1933*. Mainz: Matthias-Grünewald-Verlag, 1969. A publication, second in the famous series of the Kommission für Zeitgeschichte by the Catholic Academy in Bavaria, is a definitive edition of all the extant German documents released from 2 April to 2 November 1933 concerning the negotiations of the Concordat. Before the 1960s the church documents published here were not available for the discussion of how the

Concordat came into being. This collection also contains records from the Foreign Ministry and the papers of Rudolf Buttmann. This collection supports the thesis that the initiative for the Concordat came from the Reich government.

Lapomarda, Vincent A. *The Jesuits and the Third Reich*. Lewiston, N.Y.: The Edwin Mellen Press, 1989. This study focuses on what the Jesuits did in opposing the Nazis throughout some sixteen European nations. The author discusses the ideas and roles of Jesuits both individually and collectively and their relation to episcopal hierarchies. Although based on extensive research, the author's primary source collection was the Edmund A. Walsh papers on the activities of the Jesuits during the Third Reich and the documentary sources published by the Institute for Contemporary History of the Catholic Academy of Bavaria. A special emphasis of the author is that the Church was not silent in its response to the Holocaust.

Lenz, Johann Maria. *Christus in Dachau*. Wien: Buchversand "Libri Catholici", 1957. A memoir of this priest's five years in Dachau. Father Lenz recounts experiences very vividly and communicates his spiritual motivation and fortitude.

Lewy, Guenter. *The Catholic Church and Nazi Germany*. New York: McGraw-Hill, 1964. One of a group of controversial revisionist studies from the 1960s that were critical of the Catholic Church's role in Nazi Germany. Lewy alleges that the Church collaborated with the Nazis, supported their nationalist ambitions, and failed to resist the annihilation of the Jews. Lewy researched primarily, although selectively, in diocesan archives. His work is broadly focused on the institutional relationship of the Church to the Nazi state. He views the lack of resistance by the bishops not only as a failure to protect the liberty of the Church, but to have made impossible any successful resistance. The Concordat is seen to fail in its purpose of protecting Catholic organizations. His work has been critiqued by the defenders of the Church, Ludwig Volk and Konrad Repgen.

Lill, Rudolf. "Katholische Kirche und Nationalsozialismus." In *Machtverfall und Machtergreifung*. Edited by Rudolf Lill and Heinrich Oberreuter. München: Bayerische Landeszentrale Für Politische Bildungsarbeit, 1983. This essay along with the others in this collection derived from lectures of the faculty of Political Science and Contemporary History at the University of Passau. Lill provides an excellent outline of the history, issues, controversies, and phases of the Church Struggle.

Lukacs, John. "The Diplomacy of the Holy See during World War II." *The Catholic Historical Review* 60 (July 1974): 271–278. A review of the recently published volumes 6 and 7 of the *Actes et Documents du Saint Siège relatifs à la Seconde Guerre Mondiale* edited by Robert A. Graham and others. These volumes concern the efforts or lack thereof of the Holy See during the war on behalf of the Jews and others. Volume 6 is seen as less significant, while volume 7 supports the thesis that the Pope regarded Communism as a greater threat than Nazism. The article finds the faults of papal policy in 1943 to have been mainly of omission, and suggests that the renowned prudence of the Pope might have been grounded in a lack of confidence.

May, Georg. *Ludwig Kaas; der Priester, der Politiker und der Gelehrte aus der Schule von Ulrich Stutz*. 3 vols. Amsterdam: Verlag B. R. Grüner, 1981–1982. In this three-volume study, Monsignor Ludwig Kaas receives the detailed attention that his career deserves. The biography is a wide-ranging work by the monsignor in charge of the diocesan archives in Regensburg. Lacking personal records from Kaas, Dr. May exhausted all others, both primary and secondary.

McCarthy, Timothy G. *The Catholic Tradition: Before and After Vatican II, 1878–1993.* Chicago: Loyola University Press, 1994. A thematic history of the Catholic Church in the modern Church which explores profound changes in the institutional, intellectual, and devotional life of the Church. The study explains why Vatican II made changes in ecumenism, identity, mission, liturgy and religious freedom.

Morley, John F. *Vatican Diplomacy and the Jews during the Holocaust, 1939–1943.* New York: KTAV, 1980. An ambitious goal of Father Morley is the evaluation of how the prelates of the Catholic Church responded to the Holocaust. Since most Jews were not saved through Vatican efforts, the study focused on the protests against the treatment of the Jews and expressions of solidarity. Vatican diplomacy is surveyed for many of the countries of Europe. Vatican and Jewish sources have been consulted, although references to documents and records of German historians are limited and unsatisfactory. Morley's conclusions include that the Vatican diplomats intervened with the authorities on behalf of Jews both baptized and not. However, they failed to exercise the pressure of which their office was capable. As for Pius XII who preferred not to offend Germany, the author criticizes his lack of utilization of the important diplomatic system of the Vatican to help the Jews.

Müller, Hans. *Katholische Kirche und Nationalsozialismus. Dokumente, 1930–1935.* Munich: Nymphenburger Verlagshandlung, 1963. An older short collection of documents of the Church Struggle, this book is an expression of the 1960s scholarship so critical of the Church under Nazism. Müller was criticized by other German scholars as being too selective in his choice of documents, which resulted in distorted views.

Noakes, Jeremy. "The Oldenburg Crucifix Struggle of November, 1936: A Case Study of Opposition in the Third Reich." In *The Shaping of the Nazi State,* edited by Peter Stachura. New York: Barnes and Noble, 1978. A study of one of the lesser-known examples of protest during the Third Reich. A socio-political analysis provides a context for understanding the Catholic minority of this area in the Münster diocese of Bishop Galen. The article covers the Nazi impact on Catholic education and the attempt to remove the crucifixes form the denominational schools in 1936. The dramatic victory of the Catholic population in stopping the regime reflects, Noakes believes, their exceptional homogeneity and determination to preserve their traditions. In the end, unfortunately, this determination was insufficient to prevail against the Nazis, because in 1938 all the denominational schools were abolished.

Phayer, Michael. "The Catholic Resistance Circle in Berlin and the German Catholic Bishops during the Holocaust." *Holocaust and Genocide Studies* 7 (1993): 216–229.

———. "German Catholic Bishops, the Vatican and the Holocaust in the Postwar Era." In *The Netherlands and Nazi Genocide: Papers of the 21st Annual Scholars' Conference.* Edited by G. Jan Colijn and Marcia S. Littell. New York: The Edwin Mellen Press, 1992.

———. "The German Catholic Church after the Holocaust." *Holocaust and Genocide Studies* 10 (1996): 151–167.

———, and Frank M. Buscher. "German Catholic Bishops and the Holocaust, 1940–1952." *German Studies Review* 11 (1988): 463–485. All of these articles by Phayer have the common theme of the role of the German Catholic bishops during and after the Holocaust. The first studies the Catholic resistance circle in Berlin and its effectiveness, evaluating why the bishops did not explicitly protest the Holocaust. The latter three articles examine the history of the Church's self-judgment of its accomodation and resistance to the Nazi regime and its guilt relative to Holocaust. The second and third include the period of the Second Vatican Council whereas the last examines the debate and relation of the German bishops to the occupation regime and denazification.

Portman, Heinrich. *Bischof Graf von Galen spricht! Ein apostolischer kampf und sein Widerhall.* Freiburg im Breisgau: Herder, 1946). An early collection of the anti-Nazi sermons of Bishop von Galen, the Lion of Münster.

———. *Cardinal von Galen.* Translated and adapted by R.L. Sedgwick. London: Jarrolds, 1957. An abridged version of Portman's biography, first published in 1953. The editor, R.L. Sedgwick, was personally acquainted with Galen. The biography extends from his early life through the Nazi period until his death.

Raem, Heinz-Albert. *Pius XI und der Nationalsozialismus. Die Enzyklika 'Mit brennender Sorge' vom 14 März 1937.* Paderborn: Ferdinand Schöningh, 1979. Evaluated in the context of the Concordat, this is a comprehensive study of the background, content, publication and consequences of the Encyclical. The Encyclical is evaluated in the context of the papal teaching on totalitarianism. The historical debate surrounding the Encyclical is reviewed.

Repgen, Konrad. "Das Ende der Zentrumspartei und die Entstehung des Reichskonkordats." *Militärselsorge,* 2 (1970): 83–122, and later reissued in *Historische Klopfsignale für die Gegenwart.* Münster: Verlag Aschendorff, 1974. With the publication of the two volumes of sources in 1969 by Alfons Kupper and Ludwig Volk on the subject of concordat negotiations, Repgen here says that the accurate historical interpretation of the negotiations in 1933 can begin. He discusses the documents that are missing and points out that judgments as to the motivations of Hitler and others are not beyond doubt. Presenting an instructive evaluation of documents and the historiography of the Concordat, Repgen especially critiques K.D. Bracher's accusation that there was a connection between the dissolution of the Center Party and the Concordat. Repgen's conclusions include that the Center Party was not traded by the Vatican for a concordat, nor did the Vatican consider the Lateran concordat as a model for a German concordat. Kaas is defended against the accusation by Josef Joos that he was the "Ephialtes der Zentrumspartei."

———. "Dokumentation: Zur Vatikanischen Strategie Beim Reichskonkordat." *Vierteljahrshefte für Zeitgeschichte* 31 (1983): 506–535. An analysis of a report and commentary written by Robert Lieber, S.J., the secretary to Cardinal Pacelli. It was dated from July 1933 and the subject was the intentions of the Holy See toward the issue of clerical participation in politics. Repgen interprets the report as an explanation of Vatican strategy in the concordat negotiations which supports the thesis that clerical participation in politics was not bargained away as a means of obtaining the Concordat, as was argued by Klaus Scholder. Rather, the prohibition was conceded late in June 1933 after the dissolution of political parties had occurred. Lieber's document does not conclusively support Repgen's conclusions.

———. "Hitlers Machtergreifung und der deutsche Katholizismus. Versuch einer Bilanz." In *Katholische Kirche im Dritte Reich*, edited by Dieter Albrecht. Mainz: Matthias-Grünewald-Verlag, 1976. Part of the first paperback collection of articles by leading German historians on the Church Struggle. Repgen reviews the events from Hitler's appointment as Chancellor to the conclusion of the Concordat. In his discussion of the historiography of the sixties that was so critical of the Church, Repgen suggests a "balanced" interpretation. He sees the Catholic opposition to the increasing totalitarian power of the Nazis as a hopeless effort and the Concordat as a legal defense. Kaas and the Vatican are absolved of their critics' accusations of initiating the negotiations and making a deal to vote for the Enabling Act.

———. "Über die Entstehung der Reichskondordats Offerte im Frühjahr 1933 und die Bedeutung des Reichskonkordats." *Vierteljahrshefte für Zeitgeschichte* 25 (1978): 499–534. A principal thesis of the liberal Protestant, Klaus Scholder, in his two-volume *Die Kirchen und das Dritte Reich* was that Hitler's initiation of concordat negotiations influenced Ludwig Kaas and the Center Party's vote for the Enabling Act. Here Repgen provides a detailed critique of that thesis, denying any connection between the two. Kaas is also defended against Scholder's circumstantial case. As a defender of the Church, Repgen praises the Concordat as a legal protection against the Nazi regime and evidence of the Church's resistance to coordination.

———. "Ungedruckte Nachkriegsquellen zum Reichskonkordat. Eine Dokumentation." *Historisches Jahrbuch.* 89 (1979): 375–413. An historiographical analysis of the debate over the Concordat since 1945. Many of Repgen's prior theses are repeated, such as the relation of the Concordat to the Enabling Act. The reader is informed of the connection between historical interpretations and political debates in West German politics. New sources are published and critiqued by Repgen.

Repgen, Konrad, ed. *Die Katholiken und das Dritte Reich.* Mainz: Matthias-Grünewald-Verlag, 1990. The latest collection of essays on the Church struggle in a paperback edition. Contributing in their areas of specialization are Rudolf Morsey, Dieter Albrecht, Ludwig Volk, Ulrich von Hehl, Jürgen Aretz, Rudolf Lill, Burkhard van Schewick, Klaus Gotto, Hans Günter Hockerts, and Heinz Hürten.

Rhodes, Anthony. *The Vatican in the Age of the Dictators, 1922–1945.* New York: Holt, Rinehart and Winston, 1973. This interestingly written general study responds to the issues raised during the sixties by the historians who criticized the Church for its support of fascist dictators, the lack of Vatican condemnation of the invasion of neutral countries in 1940, and the silence of the Pope concerning the genocide of the Jews. This book, Rhodes' first on church history, is directed toward a broader audience, yet is widely researched and is replete with appropriate quotations. Though balanced in his interpretations, he is critical of Vatican mistakes. One conclusion is that the Church's basic concern was its pastoral mission, and that it saw fascism and Nazism as lesser evils in comparison to communism. The attitude of Pius XII toward the Jews is extensively analyzed, rebutting the sensational accusations of Hochhuth's play, *The Deputy*. Sometimes his judgments are disputable and his sources are not always reliable.

Sandfuchs, Wilhelm. "Für die Rechte der Kirche und die Freiheit. Pater Rupert Mayer, S.J.—unerschrockener Bekenner und Glaubenszeuge im Kirchenkampf." In vol. 2, *Das Erzbistum München und Freising in der Zeit der nationsozialistischen Herschaft*, edited by Georg Schwaiger. München: Verlag Schnell & Steiner, 1984. A scholarly biographical portrait in this collection of articles on the Munich archdiocese during the Nazi period.

Schneider, Burkhart, ed. *Die Briefe Pius XII. An die Deutschen Bischöfe, 1939–1944*. Mainz: Matthias-Grünewald-Verlag, 1966. The fourth volume in the list sponsored by the Commission for Contemporary History of the Catholic Academy in Bavaria. A comprehensive collection of the correspondence of Pius XII with the German bishops. The correspondence is in the original Italian with German translations. The Pope's pastoral concerns are evident, the problems in Germany are discussed, the Pope's concern to remain neutral and his efforts to end the war are manifest. The documents are placed in historical context in an introduction by Konrad Repgen.

Scholder, Klaus. "Altes und Neues zur Vorgeschichte des Reichskonkordat." *Vierteljahrshefte für Zeitgeschichte* 25 (1978): 535–570. In this response to Konrad Repgen's article in the same journal, Klaus Scholder argues his position utilizing Heinrich Brüning's *Memoirs* and other documents. He argues that Kaas and the Vatican were interested in a concordat and therefore influenced the Center Party to vote for the Enabling Act.

———. *A Requiem for Hitler and other new perspectives on the German church struggle.* Translated by John Bowden. Philadelphia: Trinity Press International, 1989. A collection of Klaus Scholder's articles reprinted after his death. The perspectives that appeared in his major history of the churches and the Nazis are evident. The essays are on such themes as the Nuremberg trials, modern German protestant theology, the Church Struggle, the issue of political resistance, the Catholic Episcopate, and Judaism and Christianity. Scholder's perspectives neither accuse nor condemn. He belonged to the school of historicism, was a convinced liberal, and a student of Karl Barth's dialectical theology. On the subject of the Church Struggle he took a multi-denominational approach because he thought the experiences of the churches were interdependent.

———. *The Churches and the Third Reich.* 2 vols. Translated by John Bowden from *Die Kirchen und das Dritte Reich*. Philadelphia: Fortress Press, 1988. Written by one of Germany's leading liberal protestant church historians. A popular professor at Tübingen he gathered a following of students. His masterful analysis began with the 1920s and sought to portray the interdependence of both Protestant and Catholic churches in the struggle with the Third Reich. In his prehistory of the Reich Concordat he asserts that Hitler exchanged a promise to conclude a concordat for Rome's promise to abandon the Center Party, which aroused a historical de-

bate with Konrad Repgen. Scholder's account does not spare criticism of either de-
nomination for their opportunism, stupidity, lies, and arrogance. The treatment of
the Protestant churches is more extensive because of the chaos and confusion in the
twenty-eight Landeskirchen whereas the Catholic Church could be treated more as
a unit.

Schönhoven, Klaus. "Zwischen Anpassung und Ausschaltung. Die Bayerische Volkspartei in der Endphase der Weimarer Republik, 1932/33." *Historische Zeitschrift* 224
(1977): 340–378. A history of the Center's right-wing sister party in Bavaria during
the crucial final phase of its existence. Schönhoven is the historian of the BVP to
consult for an understanding of the party's participation in parliamentary politics
and its relation to the Center.

Schwaiger, Georg, ed. *Das Erzbistum München und Freising in der Zeit der national-
sozislistischen Herrschaft.* 2 vols. München: Verlag Schnell & Steiner, 1984. Edited by
one of the leading historians of the Bavarian church, this two-volume collection of
articles extensively and intensively documents life under the Third Reich in the
archdiocese of Munich-Freising. The subjects include general essays on church life
and the Nazis, but also on Cardinal Faulhaber, Dachau, the prosecution of the
clergy, conflict over the Catholic schools, Catholic Youth, the "White Rose," and
the numerous religious orders.

Schwalbach, Bruno. *Erzbischof Conrad Gröber und die nationalsozialistische Diktatur:
Eine Studie zum Episkopat des Metropoliten des Oberrheinischen Kirchenprovinz
während des Dritten Reiches.* Karlsruhe: Badenia, 1985. The biography is based on
Schwalbach's dissertation from the University Fridericiana in Karlsruhe. It is comprehensive and deals with the many controversial issues surrounding Gröber: his
encouragement of cooperation with the Nazis, his role in the negotiations for the
Concordat, his membership in the SS, his opposition to euthanasia, and relation to
the Jews. The best biography available.

Seward, Desmond. *Napoleon and Hitler.* New York: Simon and Schuster, 1988. A chal-
lenging comparative biography of the two dictators inspired by the famous historian of Napoleon, Pieter Geyl. Although Hitler was incomparably more evil than
Napoleon, they both were contemptuous of human life, outsiders struggling for acceptance, megalomaniacs who achieved military domination of Europe, and ended
their dictatorships with disastrous invasions of Russia.

Stasiewski, Bernhard. *Akten Deutsche Bischöfe über die Lage der Kirche 1933–1945.* 3 vols.
Mainz: Matthias-Grünewald-Verlag, 1968–1985. A collection of archival documents
of the correspondence, proclamations, etc. of the German bishops during the Nazi
period. It is part of a series to make available basic documentary sources to reveal
the truth about the Church in Nazi Germany. These volumes have extensive notes,
an index of persons and places. The correspondence in Volume 1 contains extensive
discussions concerning the articles and issues of the Concordat.

Stehle, Hansjakob. *Eastern Politics of the Vatican.* Translated by Sandra Smith. Athens,
Ohio: Ohio State University Press, 1981. This study of Vatican Ostpolitik was written by one of the journalists who accompanied Pope John Paul on his historic trips
to Poland and elsewhere. The study focuses on Vatican policy in Eastern Europe

and provides insights into the motives behind Church policy and negotiations from Benedict XV to John Paul II. The popes, Stehle says, were all neither "reactionaries" nor "progressives." Two chapters are concerned with the Vatican's false hopes for Hitler's anti–communism and the crusade that failed to materialize. Well researched, analytical, comparative and admirably translated.

Stehle, Hansjakob. "Motive des Reichskonkordats." *Aussenpolitik* 7 (1956): 556–573. An early answer to the question why a concordat was concluded within four months after Hitler became chancellor. Based on the records of the German Foreign Office (Akten des Auswärtigen Amtes). Stehle attributes the initiation of the negotiations to Hitler and von Papen. The Vatican's motivation to negotiate was a fulfillment of the concordat policy of Pius XI.

Stehlin, Stewart A. *Weimar and the Vatican, 1919–1933. German-Vatican Relations in the Interwar Years.* Princeton: Princeton University Press, 1983. Revealing the intricacies and problems of international relations between the Weimar Republic and the Vatican, Stewart Stehlin has written a major contribution to the subject. He demonstrates how Berlin was supported by the Vatican on the reparations issue and the Ruhr occupation. The Vatican sought to limit French power and restrain the spread of Bolshevism. The concordats with Bavaria, Prussia, and Baden are discussed in detail as well as the insurmountable problems of a concordat with the Reich. The Concordat with Hitler is clearly explained. Stehlin's research in the primary sources and varied archives makes for an unquestionably authoritative work.

Tinnemann, Sister Ethel Mary. "The German Catholic Bishops and the Jewish Question: Explanation and Judgment." *Holocaust Studies Annual: The Churches' Response to the Holocaust.* Edited by Jack Fischel and Sanford Pinsker. Greenwood, Fla: Penkevill, 1986. Using the primary documentary collections, this essay is an excellent analysis of the positions of the episcopal leadership on the Jewish question. The author studies the role of the six bishops who played the major role in church-state relations. The dynamics of the church-state struggle, anti-Semitism, and the cultural and religious orientation of the bishops are used to explain their positions on the Holocaust.

Volk, Ludwig. "Adolf Bertram (1859–1945)." In *Zeitgeschichte in Lebensbildern.* Edited by Rudolf Morsey. Mainz: Matthias-Grünewald-Verlag, 1973. A short biography of Cardinal Bertram of Breslau is contained in this collection by Rudolf Morsey, which includes biographies of cardinals Faulhaber and Galen, Franz von Papen, and Ludwig Kaas.

———. *Akten Deutscher Bischöfe über die Lage der Kirche, 1936–1939.* Mainz: Matthias-Grünewald-Verlag, 1981. A collection of primary documents concerning the activities of the German bishops during the crucial phase of the Church Struggle from the eve of the Encyclical to the beginning of World War II.

———. *Akten Kardinal Michael von Faulhaber, 1917–1945.* Vol. 1, 1917–1934; vol. 2, 1935–1945. Mainz: Matthias-Grünewald-Verlag, 1975. The papers of the influential cardinal of Munich from 1917–1945. Included are the correspondence between the German bishops and Faulhaber, but also official documents such as protocols and memoranda, as well as correspondence with the government and the Vatican. A fundamental resource.

———. *Das Reichskonkordat vom 20 Juli 1933.* Mainz: Matthias-Grünewald-Verlag, 1972. Since its publication this study has been recognized as the most scholarly study of the subject based on Volk's access to extensive Church sources. It is the foundation of a balanced view of the concordat countering the revisionists of the sixties.

———. *Der bayerische Episkopat und der Nationalsozialismus, 1930–1934.* Mainz: Matthias-Grünewald-Verlag, 1965. Along with the *Akten Faulhabers* this shorter but detailed study of the Bavarian episcopate placed Ludwig Volk in the forefront of scholarship on the Church Struggle. The earlier resistance of the Church to Nazism is well documented here as is the role of Faulhaber and the Bavarian church at the time of the Concordat.

———. "Die Enzyklika *Mit brennender Sorge.*" In *Katholische Kirche und Nationalsozislismus: ausgewälte Aufsätze.* Edited by Dieter Albrecht, et al. Mainz: Matthias-Grünewald-Verlag, 1987. Researched and written to commemorate the centenary of Cardinal Faulhaber on March 5, 1969, Volk provides an overview of events leading up to the Encyclical, its publication and aftermath.

———. "Die Fuldaer Bischofskonferenz von Hitlers Machtergreifung bis zur Enzyklika 'Mit brennender Sorge'." In *Katholische Kirche und Nationalsozislismus: ausgewälte Aufsätze.* Edited by Dieter Albrecht, et al., 11–33. Mainz: Matthias-Grünewald-Verlag, 1987. Published earlier and here reissued in the memorial collection of his articles, Volk surveys events leading up to the Concordat, the negotiations, conclusion and beginning of the struggle against the regime's violations of the Concordat until 1937.

———. "Die Fuldaer Bischofskonferenz von der Enzyklika *Mit brennender Sorge* bis zum Ende der NS-Herrschaft." In *Katholische Kirche und Nationalsozislismus: ausgewälte Aufsätze.* Edited by Dieter Albrecht et al., 56–82. Mainz: Matthias-Grünewald-Verlag, 1987. The second part of his survey of the Church Struggle covering from 1937 to the end of the war. Especially helpful analysis of Cardinal Bertram's policy of petitioning the government (Eingaben Politik) rather an adopting a more aggressive opposition.

———. "Kardinal Faulhabers Stellung zur Weimarer Republik und zum NS-Staat." *Simmmen der Zeit,* 177 (1966–1967): 173–195. An early overview concerning Cardinal Faulhaber's role in both the Weimar Republic and Third Reich. Volk wrote this shortly after his research and publication of the Cardinal's papers.

———. *Katholische Kirche und Nationalsozialismus: ausgewälte Aufsätze.* Edited by Dieter Albrecht. Mainz: Matthias Grünewald Verlag, 1987. A memorial collection (Volk died on 4 December, 1984) of his numerous articles on the historical theme to which he has contributed more than any other German historian. After his ordination in 1956 he taught and wrote, but in 1968 he was given the freedom by the Jesuit order to follow full-time research. Besides the many articles on the Church Struggle, the collection contains entries on Faulhaber, Bertram, Preysing and Bishop Johannes Sproll of Rottenburg. Most helpful historiographically are his cri-

tiques of the memoirs of Heinrich Brüning, the works of Rolf Hochhuth, Guenter
Lewy, J.S. Conway and Klaus Scholder. Also included is a complete bibliography of
Volk's publications.

————. *Kirchliche Akten über die Reichskonkordatsverhandlungen, 1933.* Mainz: Matthias-
Grünewald-Verlag, 1969. A collection of primary documents concerning the Concordat negotiations and aftermath from March to October, 1933. Documents were
collected from diocesan archives and the Vatican. Correspondence between the par-
ticipants and Pacelli are included. A fundamental source.

————. "Nationalsozialistischer Kirchenkampf und deutscher Episkopat." In *Die
Katholiken und das Dritte Reich,* edited by Klaus Gotto and Konrad Repgen, 49–91.
Mainz: Matthias-Grünewald-Verlag, 1990. An overview of the basic issues of the
Church Struggle and the role of the bishops from 1933–1945. Published before his
death in 1984, it has been reissued with other articles by leading scholars in this latest paperback collection. Herein Volk discusses Bertram's "petition politics," opposition to euthanasia, the Final Solution and the meaning of resistance.

————. "Päpstliche Laudatio auf Hitler?" *Stimmen der Zeit* 173 (1963): 221–229. One of
Volk's earlier publication on the events leading up to the Concordat. Here he eval-
uates Cardinal Faulhaber's witness to what he thought was praise of Hitler by Pope
Pius XI during a consistory in the Vatican held on March 13, 1933.

————. "Zur Kundgebung des deutschen Episkopats vom 28. März 1933," *Stimmen der
Zeit* 173 (1963–1964): 431–456. An early examination of the German bishop's change
of position from oppostion to toleration of National Socialism, how it came about,
the role of Bertram and other bishops, and its impact.

————. "Zwischen Geschichtsschreibung und Hochhuthprosa. Kritisches und
Grundsätzliches zu einer Neuerscheinung über Kirche und Nationalsozialismus."
Stimmen der Zeit 176 (1965): 29–41, and in *Katholische Kirche im Dritten Reich. Eine
Aufsatzsammlung.* Edited by Dieter Albrecht, et al. Mainz: Matthias-Grünewald-
Verlag, 1976. A historiographical analysis and critique of sources and method of
Guenter Lewy, one of the leading critics of the Church in the sixties.

Walker, Lawrence D. *Hitler Youth and Catholic Youth, 1933–1936: A Study in Totalitarian
Conquest.* Washington, D.C.: The Catholic University of America Press, 1970. A
study of the struggle between the Hitler Youth and the largest of Catholic Youth
organizations, the Catholic Young Men's Association. The pressures of Nazi are examined during the crucial years up to 1936. The struggle culminated in 1935–36 as
groups were restricted, banned, or individuals were discriminated against in employment or universities. Based on primary documents at the Hoover Institution
and the Bundesarchiv, Koblenz.

————. "Young Priests as Opponents: Factors Associated with Clerical Opposition to
the Nazis in Bavaria, 1933." *The Catholic Historical Review* 65 (July 1979): 402–413. A
brief evaluation of the question as to whether it was primarily the younger clergy
which protested against the regime. Through a limited sample of 118 clergy, Walker
found that the mean age of offenders was 45.

Witetschek, Helmut, ed. *Die Kirchliche Lage in Bayern nach den Regierungspräsidentenberichten, 1933–1943. Regierungsbezirk, Ober- und Mittelfranken.* Mainz: Matthias-

Grünewald-Verlag, 1967. Volume two in the document series on the situation reports of the District Presidents concerning the conditions of the churches in Bavaria. The reports are especially informative on sermons and arrests. The introduction to the reports provides an overview of the Church Struggle in that district. Also included are a chronology, and a register of persons, towns and topics.

Zeender, John. "The Genesis of the German Concordat of 1933." *Studies in Catholic History*. Edited by N.H. Minnich, Robert B. Enno, S.S. & Robert F. Trisco. Wilmington, Delaware: Michael Glazier, 1985. An excellent historiographical analysis of the controversial scholarship concerning the origin of the Concordat. Zeender takes a position that is best described as a modification of Klaus Scholder's. The role of Ludwig Kaas is interpreted as being of significant importance in the Center Party's historic decision to vote for the Enabling Act. Circumstantial evidence, he concludes, indicates that a causal connection existed between that vote and the beginning of concordat negotiations.

———. "Germany: The Catholic Church and the Nazi Regime 1933–1945." *Catholics, the State and the European Radical Right, 1919–1945*. Edited by Richard J. Wolff and Jörg K. Hoensch. New York: Columbia University Press, 1987. An excellent overview of the German Catholic Church and the Third Reich. John Zeender's familiarity with the literature and his insights into the Church's problems and the complexities of the Church struggle, World War II and the Holocaust make this a valuable short essay.

Zumholz, Maria Anna. "Clemens August Graf von Galen und der deutsche Episkopat, 1933–1945." In *Clemens August Graf von Galen: Neue Forschungen zum Leben und Wirken des Bischofs von Münster*, edited by Joachim Kuropka. Münster: Verlag Regensberg, 1992. One of a collection of articles of recent research into the life and influence of Cardinal von Galen, a central figure in the protest and resistance against the Nazi regime. Zumholz's research shows how Galen changed from being an admonisher to the leader in pressing for an offensive strategy against the regime which the research previously had attributed to Cardinal Preysing. Galen also wanted the bishops to fundamentally condemn National Socialism because of its violation of basic human rights, a proposal to which the bishops never gave their support. Afterwards, he concentrated on forming a broad opposition to the totalitarian foundations of Nazi ideology.

Index

Controversial Concordats: The Vatican's Relations with Napoleon, Mussolini, and Hitler
was composed in Adobe Caslon by Running Feet Books, Durham, North Carolina;
printed on 60-pound Glatfelter Natural Smooth and bound by Braun-Brumfield, Inc.,
Ann Arbor, Michigan; and designed by Kachergis Book Design, Pittsboro,
North Carolina.